# BUREAUCRATIC CULTURE AND ESCALATING WORLD PROBLEMS

# Advancing the Sociological Imagination
## A Series from Paradigm Publishers

**Edited by Bernard Phillips and J. David Knottnerus**

*Goffman Unbound! A New Paradigm for Social Science*
By Thomas J. Scheff (2006)

*The Invisible Crisis of Contemporary Society: Reconstructing Sociology's Fundamental Assumptions*
By Bernard Phillips and Louis C. Johnston (2007)

*Understanding Terrorism: Building on the Sociological Imagination*
Edited by Bernard Phillips (2007)

*Armageddon or Evolution? The Scientific Method and Escalating World Problems*
By Bernard Phillips (2008)

*Postmodern Cowboy: C. Wright Mills and a New 21st-Century Sociology*
By Keith Kerr (2008)

*Struggles before* Brown: *Early Civil Rights Protests and Their Significance Today*
By Jean Van Delinder (2008)

*The Treadmill of Production: Injustice and Unsustainability in the Global Economy*
By Kenneth A. Gould, David N. Pellow, and Allan Schnaiberg (2008)

*Bureaucratic Culture and Escalating World Problems: Advancing the Sociological Imagination*
Edited by J. David Knottnerus and Bernard Phillips (2009)

## Forthcoming

*Ritual as a Missing Link within Sociology: Structural Ritualization Theory and Research*
By J. David Knottnerus (2009)

# Bureaucratic Culture and Escalating World Problems

## Advancing the Sociological Imagination

*edited by J. David Knottnerus and Bernard Phillips*

**Paradigm Publishers**
Boulder • London

Copyright © 2009 Paradigm Publishers

Published in the United States by Paradigm Publishers,
3360 Mitchell Lane, Suite E, Boulder, CO 80301 USA.

Paradigm Publishers is the trade name of Birkenkamp & Company, LLC,
Dean Birkenkamp, President and Publisher.

Library of Congress Cataloging-in-Publication Data
Bureaucratic culture and escalating world problems : advancing the sociological
imagination / edited by J. David Knottnerus and Bernard Phillips.
    p. cm.
  Includes bibliographical references and index.
  ISBN 978-1-59451-653-5 (hardcover : alk. paper)
1. Bureaucracy.  2. Organizational sociology.  I. Knottnerus, J. David.
II. Phillips, Bernard S.
  HM806.B89 2009
  302.3'5--dc22

                                                                    2008044769

Printed and bound in the United States of America on acid-free paper that meets the standards of the American National Standard for Permanence of Paper for Printed Library Materials.

Designed and Typeset by Straight Creek Bookmakers.

13  12  11  10  09    1  2  3  4  5

# Contents

# Preface

*Bureaucratic Culture and Escalating World Problems* makes its appearance on the 50th anniversary of the publication of C. Wright Mills's *The Sociological Imagination* (1959),[1] voted by the members of the International Sociological Association as the second most influential book for sociologists that was published throughout the entire 20th century (with first honors going to Weber's *Economy and Society*). Where are we today with respect to the problems in society that Mills wrote about in 1959? And where has the discipline of sociology come after all of these years? Mills is being honored this year by the publication of a special issue of *Teaching Sociology* celebrating this anniversary by examining the book's significance, one of a great many honors that his work has achieved over the years. Yet have we sociologists succeeded in carrying forward his insights into the alienation that pervades contemporary society with our sense of feeling "trapped" by threatening forces that we neither understand nor can control? Have we carried forward his insights into our bureaucratic society with its threats to the Enlightenment dream of freedom and reason? Have Mills's insights in his *The Causes of World War III* been carried forward? And have we carried his insights into our approach to the current wide range of threatening yet unsolved problems?

In his penultimate chapter, "On Reason and Freedom," Mills took a hard look at his colleagues in the social sciences, ending with these words:

> I do not know the answer to the question of political irresponsibility in our time or to the cultural and political question of The Cheerful Robot [alienated man]. But is it not clear that no answers will be found unless these problems are at least confronted? Is it not obvious, that the ones to confront them above all others, are the social scientists of

the rich societies? That many of them do not now do so is surely the greatest human default being committed by privileged men in our times. (1959: 176)

It was bureaucratic social scientists along with their "bureaucratic social science" whom Mills was castigating for their "political irresponsibility" in the face of the mammoth problems of the day, including a Cold War that might morph into a hot war and take civilization along with it. Have we contemporary social scientists succeeded in learning the lesson that Mills was trying to teach, the lesson of taking on our shoulders the incredible responsibility of confronting our own mammoth problems, which appear to us to be even more threatening than the Cold War? Or have we, instead—while continuing to heap praise on Mills—proceeded even further in what Mills called "the greatest human default being committed by privileged men in our times"? In Mills's time there were relatively few specialized areas of sociology with limited communication among them; in our own day we have no less than forty-six—and counting—sections of the American Sociological Association but still with limited communication among them. Not only does bureaucratic social science continue to live in our own day, but it has continued to prosper. We give Mills lip service, but we simultaneously continue to trash his ideals—they are also the ideals of contemporary society—of reason and freedom.

The junior editor of this volume was a student of Mills at Columbia University, and both of us editors were deeply influenced by him. Following his optimism about sociology's possibilities, we are proud of not having given in to pessimism at this time in history despite the feelings of gloom and doom that pervade the social sciences. We look back at Mills not to worship him but rather to build on his understanding, his commitment, and his achievements. The bureaucratic social science that he fought against emerged to a substantial extent as a result of the impact of four volumes based on social research on the armed forces during World War II: *The American Soldier: Adjustment During Army Life*, *The American Soldier: Combat and Its Aftermath*, *Experiments in Mass Communication*, and *Measurement and Prediction*. Those books—coupled with ideas of philosophers who saw physical-science procedures as the epitome of the scientific method—have continued to influence social scientists to focus on mathematics and quantitative techniques to the exclusion of the broad approach that Mills championed. Yet the poverty of these narrow sociological and philosophical approaches is becoming ever more apparent. Further, escalating problems are becoming ever more obvious in contemporary societies.

The concept of culture, central to the discipline of anthropology, generally is treated as a stepchild by sociologists, given their love affair with patterns of social organization like social stratification and bureaucracy.

As a result, Mills's idea of the "bureaucratic ethos"—the heading of one of his chapters—must appear to many to be outside of the mainstream of sociological thought. Yet culture is a structure—that is, it involves repeated patterns of ideas or beliefs and interests or values—no less than social stratification, granting that it is less tangible than patterns of social organization. Mills recognized its importance, and so do a growing body of contemporary sociologists. A focus of this volume is on "bureaucratic culture," which is quite distinct from patterns of social organization like bureaucracy and social stratification. Yet this is no easy task, for our bureaucratic culture has gone underground in the face of the rising tides of democratic cultural values that have accompanied the Enlightenment ideals of reason and freedom. Just as Mills raised bureaucratic social science up to the surface, so can we also raise the more general idea of bureaucratic culture—which is presently quite invisible—up to the surface. For such patterns of beliefs and commitments—like racism, sexism, ethnocentrism, ageism, classism, and nationalism—are alive and well in contemporary society, granting the existence of opposing and highly visible democratic ideals. By making our bureaucratic culture more visible, we can learn how to negate it and move toward those democratic values, just as we can learn to do the same in the case of bureaucratic social science and the ideals Mills expressed in *The Sociological Imagination*.

Just as those four volumes of social research on the armed forces worked to shift sociologists toward bureaucratic social science, we hope that the five books that we and our colleagues in the Sociological Imagination Group have published in this new century—and the present book as well—will help to turn the tide of social science research in the direction that Mills was traveling. That direction by no means rejected quantitative sociology and the use of mathematics. Yet it was broad enough to include in addition a variety of other procedures, many of which go by the name of qualitative analysis. And just as the philosophy of science of an earlier day helped to convince social scientists to travel a narrow road leading toward social science research—paralleling the road taken by the physical sciences—we believe that the contemporary philosophy of science can help to open up for us an alternative path. And we have also come to believe in the urgent necessity of shifting away from a bureaucratic way of life, given our escalating problems.

Yet that alternative path can accomplish little unless it succeeds in attracting more and more of the traffic on the well-traveled road of bureaucratic social science. What we believe is needed at this time in history is a growing movement throughout the social sciences along that alternative path. What we believe is required now are individuals as deeply committed as Mills was to "the promise of sociology." What we believe is wanted now are individuals who do not see themselves as wedded to communicating only within a narrow specialized area but who are interested in the full range of social science knowledge and who follow Mills's lead by communicating outside of the academic world. What we believe is called for at the present time are growing numbers of social scientists who are able to rekindle the embers of their earlier optimism as to the possibility of fulfilling the Enlightenment dream of societies based on the Enlightenment dream. And what we believe is absolutely essential is a vast and growing movement of social scientists who test the alternative path that we are charting, or, at the very least, who work toward developing their own alternative path. To fail to do so is, in our view, "surely the greatest human default being committed by privileged men in our times."

We believe that this volume together with our earlier books will provide the basis for the deep commitment that is now required—at this time in history—of privileged social scientists throughout the world to join us in our efforts to fulfill the promise of sociology. It is we social scientists who bear the full responsibility of showing the way for others, just as Gouldner (1972) claimed in his comments on *The Coming Crisis of Western Sociology:*

> At decisive points the ordinary language and conventional understandings fail and must be transcended. It is essentially the task of the social sciences, more generally, to create new and "extraordinary" languages, to help men learn to speak them, and to mediate between the deficient understandings of ordinary language and the different and liberating perspectives of the extraordinary languages of social theory.

We would like to acknowledge the essential contributions of Harold Kincaid and Thomas J. Scheff to the emergence of the Sociological Imagination Group and to our approach to the scientific method, and we thank them for their commitment and all of their efforts. Harold brought forward his broad background within the philosophy of social science and shaped the history of our group. His new volume written with ten other philosophers of science, *Value-Free Science? Ideals and Illusions,* effectively argues that value-neutrality—an idea that supports bureaucratic social science—is neither possible nor desirable for the progress of science. Tom's Part/Whole approach, developed within three monographs during the 1990s, became the basis for enlarging the scope of our methodological orientation. We shifted from "the web approach" to "the Web and Part/Whole Approach," learning to move very far down language's "ladder" of abstraction to the concrete emotional dynamics within any given scene. We want to also single out Paradigm's publisher, Dean Birkenkamp, for our feelings of gratitude as a result of his continuing encouragement. We believe that he is in a class by himself among all publishers in the depth of his understanding of sociology and in his commitment to working toward fulfilling "the promise of sociology." We also owe a large debt of gratitude to J. I. Hans Bakker, Frank W. Elwell, Douglas Hartmann, Debbie V. S. Kasper, Louis Kontos, Vince Montes, Thomas J. Scheff, Arlene Stein, and Jason S. Ulsperger for their commitment to this project despite the uncertainty of achieving publication for any volume that collects conference papers, and for their willingness to rewrite their original papers several times.

Finally, all of these efforts would have gone for naught if the history of sociology had not yielded the elements of knowledge that we and the authors in this volume have attempted to tie together. Our approach to the scientific method has been strengthened by the contributions to our understanding of how language works and what its potentials are that were developed within our previous emphasis on the Web and Part/Whole Approach. As a result, our present understanding of the scientific method departs from traditional research procedures in that it opens up to the full range of phenomena involved in the complexity of human behavior. It is sufficiently broad so that it can find useful ideas from almost any book or article that has ever been written. Our problem is not how to find ideas from the past, but rather how to select the most important ideas from the past for a given problem. The classical founders of sociology—Marx, Durkheim, Weber, and Simmel—loom large in all of our publications. And the contributions of Mills and Gouldner have also proved to be fundamental. Many other sociologists—as indicated in our references—provided key elements for this volume, and we thank all of them. But we would prove to be narrow in our orientation if we did not mention the significance of philosophers such as Nietzsche, Peirce, and Kaplan, of educators such as Dewey, Freire, and Illich, of novelists such as Orwell, Hesse, and Van Vogt, and of others such as Gandhi, Horney, and Chua.

*J. David Knottnerus and Bernard Phillips*

## Notes

1. Citations in the preface are listed in the references at the end of chapter 1.

# PART I

# Introduction

THIS BOOK APPEARS on the 50th anniversary of the publication of C. Wright Mills's *The Sociological Imagination* (1959).[1] Yet far more important than the book's appearance on this anniversary is its appearance at a time in history when the entire future of the human race is beginning to hang in the balance. As suggested by this book's title, problems are increasing throughout the world, and it is entirely possible that we may not be able to solve them before they take matters into their own hands. Mills wrote *The Causes of World War III* (1958) in an era when the Cold War was threatening to become a hot war, a highly problematic situation that we somehow managed to escape from by, what Thornton Wilder called in his play, *The Skin of Our Teeth* (1942/1957). Those of us who lived through that era are well aware of how close we came to Armageddon. Yet the threats today to the existence of humanity appear to be far worse.

Anyone who keeps up with current events can easily list a host of growing problems: the production and increasing spread of ever more powerful weapons of mass destruction, the proliferation and increasing effectiveness of groups like Al Qaeda bent on worldwide terrorism, global warming, the increasing gap between the rich and the poor, growing pessimism and hopelessness about the future, the failures of political leaders to solve any of the fundamental problems of contemporary society, and the helplessness of leaders in other institutions—economic, educational, scientific, family, and religious—in coping with developing problems within their own areas of society.

Yet there are also relatively invisible and escalating problems that add to this most threatening mix, problems that fail to make it into the

1

mass media. For example, Sir Martin Rees—England's Astronomer Royal and Royal Society Professor at Cambridge University—has forecasted that the odds are no better than fifty-fifty that we humans will survive to the end of this century (2003). He cites increasing threats from accelerating technologies that would be more dangerous than nuclear devastation, such as threats from lethal engineered airborne viruses that could be produced by a single individual. Following the work of the Sociological Imagination Group, there is also the threat of a growing gap between expectations and their fulfillment over a wide range of cultural values, a relatively invisible danger that nevertheless works to tear each of us apart (Phillips and Johnston, 2007).

Yet we are not prophets of doom and gloom; there is already more than enough of that throughout the world. We believe it is essential that we be steeped in realism, but it is equally essential that we open up to human possibilities. Our very ability to raise up to the surface the above threats—versus ostrich-like behavior—suggests the possibility that we can learn to confront them effectively. Indeed, this is the way the scientific method itself has worked over the past five centuries, where the definition of and commitment to a problem became the first and most important step of a method for solving that problem. And this has resulted in enormous optimism about the power of the scientific method for helping us humans to solve any problem whatsoever.

But it is essential that we distinguish here between biophysical science and social science, for the complexity of human behavior far exceeds that of biophysical phenomena. Granting that biophysical science along with its technologies has succeeded in shaping our entire way of life over the past five centuries, that shaping has been for ill as well as for good, as we can see from current and increasing threats from those technologies. We have learned to produce AK-47s and hydrogen bombs, but we have not learned how to prevent their production, distribution, or potential use. In Alexander Pope's poem—"An Essay on Criticism"—published in 1711, he wrote: "A little learning is a dangerous thing." He was writing about the individual who becomes intoxicated by the heights in science and art that he has scaled after an initial success. Yet we can apply that same proverb to biophysical scientists as a whole who have become so intoxicated with their knowledge that they feel they can ignore knowledge of human behavior. This is not just a question of there being nothing in the book by England's Astronomer Royal—referred to in the preface— suggesting that science consists of anything but biophysical science, letting social science go hang. Also, it is not just a question of NOVA—our award-winning PBS documentary science series—seeing science in much the same way (Phillips, 2001: 101–102). And it is not just a question of the emptiness of *The 9/11 Commission Report* (Kean and Hamilton, n.d.) of any suspicion that there is such a thing as social science. Rather, it is a question of all of these things combined, and a great deal more evidence, indicating that social science is an ignored and undernourished stepchild of the powers that be.

George A. Lundberg, a professor of sociology at the University of Washington, published these words two years after Mills's book appeared:

> A leader, however admirable in ability and intentions, attempting to administer centrally a large society today is somewhat in the position of a pilot trying to fly the modern stratoliner without an instrument board or charts.... Only as a result of the development of the basic physical sciences can a large modern airplane either be built or flown. Only through a comparable development of the social sciences can a workable world order be either constructed or administered. The appalling thing is the flimsy and inadequate information on the basis of which even a conscientious executive of a large state is today obliged to act. It comes down, then, to this: Shall we put our faith in science or in something else?
>
> ... If it is answered in the affirmative, then social research institutions will make their appearance, which will rank with Massachusetts and California Institutes of Technology, Mellon Institute, the research laboratories of Bell Telephone, General Electric and General Motors, not to mention several thousand others.... Finally, a word should be said to those who find the methods of science too slow. They want to know what we shall do while we wait for the social sciences to develop. Well, we shall doubtless continue to suffer.... We shall probably become much sicker before we consent to take the only medicine which can help us. (1947/1961: 142–143)

In our view we have indeed become much sicker—indeed so sick that we seem to be heading for extinction—since Lundberg wrote those words. But we also have what we see as very good news to report. We referred in the preface to six books of the Sociological Imagination Group, including this one, stating that perhaps they "will help to turn the tide of social science research in the direction that Mills was traveling." It is our deep belief that they provide the basis for an understanding of the scientific method with the potential to speed up enormously the progress of social science. Yet our optimism about this potential is not simply based on our own efforts since we formed our group at the beginning of this century. It is based more generally on what we see as the capacities of the human race, capacities based on our biological structure, the potential that language gives us, and the potential of the scientific method. But what we mean by "the scientific method" is neither what physicists make use of, what philosophers of science have written, what Mills wrote in

*The Sociological Imagination,* what social scientists generally employ, or even what we have written in our previous five books, granting that all of these ideas have contributed to our present understanding. In the following introductory chapter to this volume, "The Scientific Method," we shall spell out what we mean. What we have in mind is not simply a method that can be applied to human behavior, but rather a method that can be applied to all phenomena and all problems, and a method that can be applied by all people and not just scientists. Just as in the case of any method, it is to be judged by its fruitfulness: its ability to help us understand the world and ourselves, and to address effectively what Mills called "personal troubles" and "public issues."

## Notes

1. References for citations in this introduction are included in the reference list at the end of chapter 1.

CHAPTER 1

# The Scientific Method

*Bernard Phillips and J. David Knottnerus*

IN THIS FIRST CHAPTER, introducing the volume as a whole, we shall proceed to (1) provide a sketch of the scientific method, (2) introduce the material in part II of the book, "Social Problems," and (3) introduce part III of the book, "Conclusions."

When the Sociological Imagination Group held its first conference in 2000—which became the basis for its first volume (Phillips, Kincaid, and Scheff, eds., 2002)—our focus was on what we called the "web approach" to the scientific method. That approach was based largely on the manuscript for our soon-to-be-published first book (Phillips, 2001). During the period between these publications and our next two publications (Phillips and Johnston, 2007; Phillips, ed., 2007), we expanded our understanding of the web approach, calling it the Web and Part/Whole Approach. This was due to the influence of Thomas J. Scheff, whose three monographs published in the 1990s (1990, 1994, 1997) had developed what he called the "part/whole" approach to social research. Whereas the web approach had been illustrated largely with the aid of abstract or general sociological concepts, the part/whole approach emphasized the concrete dynamics of the momentary situation. By combining the two procedures into a single one, we were following Mills's advice in his *The Sociological Imagination* "to shuttle between levels of abstraction." In all of this work we were guided by the philosophical understanding of our resident

5

philosopher, Harold Kincaid, who emphasized the enormous complexity of human behavior as well as the necessity of attending to the "web" of interrelated forces that shape any given instance of human behavior along with the metaphysical assumptions shaping those very forces.

Since the publication of those books in 2007—largely as a result of a new book (Phillips, 2009), of an unpublished manuscript commemorating the 50th anniversary of Mills's book (Phillips, 2008), and of the publication of a book by Harold Kincaid and his fellow philosophers of science (Kincaid, Dupre, and Wylie, eds., 2007)—we believe that we have developed further understanding of how to move toward the ideals of the scientific method with the aid of the Web and Part/Whole Approach. For example, we understand more clearly that the doctrine of value neutrality is neither possible nor desirable for the progress of science. Also, we have come to believe that our efforts need no longer be seen as a poor stepchild of the research methods used throughout the biophysical sciences. We have certainly learned a great deal about the nature of the scientific method from the history of the biophysical sciences over the past five centuries. Yet we have also learned about the limitations of the methods used by those scientists. For example, their exclusion of investigating human phenomena in a scientific way has drastically limited any ability on their part to learn about the repercussions of their efforts on society, such as the impact of their production of weapons of mass destruction. They have succeeded in influencing society over these centuries for ill as well as for good. This exclusion of human phenomena departs radically from the ideals of the scientific method, which call for opening up to the full range of forces linked to a given investigation. Such exclusion has also affected their own scientific progress, as illustrated by the work of Thomas Kuhn (1962), who documented problems of conformity and traditionalism that have held back possibilities for scientific revolutions.

By contrast, our own use of the scientific method opens up to physical and biological phenomena no less than to human phenomena. Thus, we believe that biophysical scientists have a good deal to learn from our own usage of this method. Yet we recognize that such learning—along with the recognition by society of the overriding importance of the social sciences at this time in history—will not occur unless we social scientists learn to fulfill more of our potential for understanding and making progress on problems, granting their extreme complexity. Just as we stated in the preface, we believe that this calls for "a vast and growing movement of social scientists who proceed to test the alternative path that we are charting, or, at the very least, who work toward developing their own alternative path." We see this as a most urgent and mammoth responsibility that should weigh on the shoulders of every single social scientist at the present time. For no other group has the potential that we have to address the enormous complexity of escalating problems throughout society, to learn to understand those problems, and to discover ways to make progress toward solving them. That is the promise of sociology, a promise that we believe social scientists are now in a position to fulfill. Following Gouldner's comments on his *The Coming Crisis of Western Sociology* (1972), as quoted in the preface, it is we social scientists who carry on our shoulders the full responsibility "to create new and 'extraordinary' languages, to help men learn to speak them, and to mediate between the deficient understandings of ordinary language and the different and liberating perspectives of the extraordinary languages of social theory" (1972: 16). We now proceed with the first section of this chapter: sketching the scientific method.

## Sketch of the Scientific Method

We define the scientific method as procedures for achieving increasing understanding of problems that (1) build on prior recorded knowledge that is relevant, (2) develop ideas or hypotheses bearing on the range of phenomena involved, and (3) are tested by evidence in a demonstrable way. With this definition, our efforts to understand the problems we face in everyday life become scientific only to the degree that we open up to all three of these criteria. Thus, generally our everyday procedures use the scientific method only to a limited degree. And the same is the case for all of the efforts of human beings to understand problems throughout our history up to, say, the 16th century, For it was the invention and use of the printing press in the late 15th century that made it increasingly possible to read what had been discovered previously. And it was subsequent procedures in physics—by such figures as Kepler, Galileo, and Newton—that illustrate early efforts to build on prior relevant knowledge and develop demonstrable evidence bearing on the range of phenomena involved in a given problem. Further, the scientific method is continuing to develop as we learn ever more about (1) what prior knowledge is relevant, (2) what range of phenomena is relevant to a given problem, and (3) how to achieve demonstrable evidence. This is not to deny the importance of earlier efforts to understand problems along with the successes that were achieved prior to the 16th century. Nor is it to deny the importance of our everyday efforts to understand problems together with our everyday successes. Yet by distinguishing those efforts from the scientific method we open up a direction for improving those efforts to an ever-increasing extent.

Given the centrality of the scientific method for social science research in general and for this volume in particular, it is most useful to elaborate on its nature. This will also help us to understand more fully the role of the Web and Part/Whole Approach as procedures that strengthen the scientific method. We might differentiate among six components of the scientific method: (1) definition of a problem and commitment to increasing our understanding of it; (2) building on prior recorded and informal knowledge that is relevant to the problem; (3) developing ideas or hypotheses for making progress on the problem that address the range of phenomena involved; (4) testing these ideas against evidence deriving from demonstrable procedures such as observation, experimentation, and the use of available information; (5) changing or strengthening those initial ideas or hypotheses based on this evidence; and (6) repeating this entire process as is needed, with no limit to the possibility of continuing progress on the problem. This also suggests the possibility of continuing nonbiological evolution of the individual and society, given that present-day civilization is largely based on the scientific knowledge developed since the 16th century. Yet, following our understanding of the philosophy of science, there is no certainty to the understanding that this method achieves. Nevertheless, on the basis of past experience the scientific method is the best procedure that we have for increasing our understanding of problems.

Let us note that this definition centers on "procedures for achieving increasing *understanding* of problems" rather than procedures for *solving* problems. Yet these same procedures for understanding problems have proved to be equally effective for learning how to actually solve problems. For one thing, understanding a problem is generally enormously helpful for learning how to solve it. And for another thing, the "problem" posed need not be simply to understand it but actually how to solve it. It is technologists like engineers and physicians who focus on solutions rather than understanding, granting that their work often yields increased understanding. In addition, we have a variety of "social technologists" who attempt to solve problems that focus on human behavior, like governmental officials, businesspeople, attorneys, teachers, the clergy, and social workers. Although they frequently attempt to use the scientific method to solve their problems, the failure of social scientists to integrate their knowledge to a substantial degree drastically limits the ability of social technologists to do so. For they remain unable to follow (2) by building on the range of prior knowledge, to follow (3) by addressing the range of phenomena involved in the problem, or to follow (4) by developing demonstrable evidence bearing on their problems. From our own perspective, however, social technologists can indeed learn to use the scientific method to make progress on their problems by working with social scientists. At the same time, social scientists can learn to make their work more relevant to solving problems by working with social technologists. This was recommended by the junior editor of this book in the edited volume, *Understanding Terrorism: Building on the Sociological Imagination* (Phillips, ed., 2007: 207–208).

Metaphorically or figuratively, we might conceive of the scientific method as a pendulum that swings back and forth from the definition of and commitment to a problem on the left-hand side to the development of understanding of that problem on the right-hand side. If all goes well, the pendulum swings in widening arcs, where movement further to the right yields increased momentum for movement further to the left, and so on. Literally, increasing understanding of a problem can improve the definition of and commitment to the problem, and that can in turn provide the basis for improved understanding of the problem, and so on. Mills made good use of metaphors in his publications. Appropriate metaphors can be most important for an effective scientific method, given the focus of that method on achieving understanding of problems. For metaphors can help both investigators and their audiences to gain such understanding. Unfortunately, scientists generally see metaphorical language as taking away from the systematic nature and precision of the language they use to communicate their ideas. Yet this need not be the case, since metaphorical language can be used to embrace—rather than substitute for—literal language that is systematic and precise. We might see Mills's *The Sociological Imagination* as illustrating the kind of writing that has achieved its influence largely because of its integration of metaphorical and literal language.

Granting that social scientists generally fail to use much of language's metaphorical potential, it is also true that they generally fail to make much use of language's gradation potential, that is, its ability to convey matters of degree. That potential is also most important for the effectiveness of the scientific method. If we return to the six elements of that method, all of them invoke language's gradational potential. As for (1), the investigator's commitment is a matter of degree; there is also a degree to which one can build, in (2), on the vast arrays of knowledge preceding any investigation; with respect to (3), that same matter of degree applies to the investigator's ability to address the full range of phenomena linked to a problem; with respect to (4), one can always proceed to collect more evidence using demonstrable procedures; as for (5), one can continue indefinitely to improve one's understanding of the problem with the aid of better hypotheses; and with reference to (6), this entire process can continue to yield much the same: ever better understanding of the problem. Overall, we might even see the scientific method as pointing toward the continuing nonbiological evolution of the individual and society.

In addition to language's metaphorical and gradational potentials, there is a third potential of language that is central to the scientific method: language's dichotomous or either-or potential. Every word in every language divides the world into two parts: whatever the word refers to, on the one hand, and everything else, on the other hand. It is, then, dichotomous language that is by far the major way in which we think and communicate with others. Written language, especially as communicated with the aid of the printing press, has been fundamental to the development of the scientific method from the 16th century onward. Each of these three potentials of language has been emphasized by a different part of the academic world. Metaphors or figures of speech are emphasized within the humanities; gradational thought, as illustrated by the use of mathematics, generally is the focus of the biophysical sciences; and it is throughout the social sciences—along with our everyday thought and speech—that we find an emphasis on dichotomous language. Yet by opening up to all three of these potentials of language, the social scientist—and everyone else—can learn to reach out to the breadth of understanding that Mills so eloquently illustrated.

We are now in a position to understand how our previous focus on the Web and Part/Whole Approach fits into our present broad approach to the scientific method. Here is the earliest statement of the web approach, later supplemented by the emphasis of the part/whole approach on step (3):

> (1) We should not shirk from addressing absolutely fundamental problems within society. (2) We should move far up language's ladder of abstraction so as to utilize very abstract concepts. (3) We should come far down that ladder so as to examine the concrete evidence that bears on our ideas. (4) We should work to integrate our knowledge so that our approach is broad enough to enable us ... to shift from one perspective to another. (5) We should develop ... a.... reflexive analysis and interactive worldview. (Phillips, 2001: 4, 35)

Our focus in these five steps of the scientific method is on addressing the enormous complexity of human behavior by making full use of the way language works: by moving up and down a "ladder" of linguistic abstraction in steps (2) and (3), and thus achieving the integration of knowledge referred to in step (4). Our sketch of the scientific method in this chapter with its description of six elements of that method was oriented toward the achievement of ever greater understanding, yet it did not include these linguistic procedures—shuttling between levels of abstraction—which can in fact yield such increasing understanding. It is this shuttling that can enable the investigator to link one problem with others and thus arrive at what (1) above calls for: "addressing absolutely fundamental problems within society." And it is also this shuttling which enables the investigator to reach so high as to address—using a "reflexive analysis"—his or her own metaphysical assumptions or "worldview" and move toward an alternative "interactive worldview" that encourages rather than opposes the scientific method, as suggested by (5) above. Thus, the Web and Part/Whole Approach brings to our understanding of the scientific method the importance of making full use of the potentials of language. Here, we can add the importance of its metaphorical, gradational, and dichotomous potentials, for they apply to human behavior as well as to biophysical phenomena. And by so doing we open up to the wide range of knowledge throughout the humanities, the biophysical sciences, and the social sciences that must be taken into account in order to build on prior knowledge and to invoke the range of phenomena relevant to a given problem. Thus, by invoking the human being's two most powerful tools—language and the scientific method—the investigator can learn to address ever more effectively the full complexity of any problem, whether of human behavior or of biophysical phenomena

To illustrate the role of language for social science, there are the relatively concrete concepts of "racism," "sexism," "ageism," "ethnocentrism," "classism," and "nationalism." And there is also the relatively abstract concept of "social stratification." Sociologists generally fail to move up language's ladder of abstraction from the former concepts to the latter one so as to take seriously the general phenomenon of social stratification. If they did so, then they would be able to come down that ladder to other concrete examples of social stratification, given their narrow commitment to only one of those concrete concepts. This approach is nothing less than the way language works in general, as detailed by Alfred Korzybski (1933) and Samuel I. Hayakawa (1949) in their development of the field of general semantics. It is a field that continues to live in the journal *ETC* and in the Institute of General Semantics. We move up from the relatively concrete concept of "rose" or "daffodil" or "tulip" to the more abstract concept of "flower," and then we move down again. And in this way we learn to understand the nature of all of these flowers and not just one of them, just as we learn about racism *and* sexism *and* ageism, and not just about *either* racism *or* sexism *or* ageism. Thus, we learn to move into ever deeper understanding of the complexity of the phenomena around us—whether we are social scientists who focus on understanding human behavior, or are individuals outside of academia—in our everyday lives from one moment to the next. And we also learn that the saying, "Jack of all trades, master of none," has no validity.

It is this understanding of the way the scientific method can and should work that suggests our effort to build on Mills's work in a systematic way. His concept of "the sociological imagination" still inspires us, just as it inspires so many others:

The sociological imagination . . . is the capacity to shift from one perspective to another—from the political to the psychological; from examination of a single family to comparative assessment of the national budgets of the world; from the theological school to the military establishment; from considerations of an oil industry to studies of contemporary poetry.

It is the capacity to range from the most impersonal and remote trans-
formations to the most intimate features of the human self—and to see
the relations between the two. (1959: 7)

This all-too-brief sketch of the scientific method illustrates the enormous complexity of human behavior and the importance of fulfilling the
infinite potentials of language in order to penetrate that complexity and
move toward fulfilling what Mills called "the promise of sociology." Little
or no attention is generally paid to those potentials of language, which are
stressed by the Web and Part/Whole Approach, and which are important
for biophysical science no less than social science. Let us now proceed
to the second section of this chapter where we preview part II, Social
Problems, which includes those problems inside of as well as outside of
the academic world. It is the scientific method coupled with language's
infinite potentials that can succeed in penetrating the complexity of
those problems and yield an ever-deeper understanding of them. And that
deepening understanding, in turn, can yield increasing abilities to solve
them. Those solutions cannot be limited to the work of academic social
scientists. They must include the problems that all of us face—including
academic social scientists—as we proceed with our everyday lives.

## Social Problems

Each of the authors in part II, Social Problems, starts out from a unique
set of experiences encountered while working within the discipline of
sociology. This has yielded interest in diverse problems, diverse concepts,
and diverse research procedures. Nevertheless, they all share key elements of the approach to the scientific method discussed above. There
is a common commitment to address fundamental problems in social science or society, a basic element of the scientific method. These authors
also share optimism about the potential of the scientific method to help
them achieve increasing understanding of these problems. In addition,
they see themselves as part of a community of social scientists who can
and should build on one another's work. And they also utilize—to varying
degrees—language's potential for fostering the scientific method. Thus,
they parallel Mills's own commitment to gaining understanding of the
fundamental problems in society, and they parallel Mills's optimism as
to the possibilities of achieving that understanding. However, they differ
from Mills in that they see themselves not as loners but rather as part of
a developing movement throughout the social sciences aimed at fulfilling
what Mills called "the promise of sociology."

In chapter 2, "Reclaiming the Sociological Imagination: A Brief Overview and Framework," Douglas Hartmann reexamines Mills's book. This is

an effort to go back to Mills's broad vision of the sociological imagination in order to oppose "an increasingly fragmented academic climate," as is well illustrated by the limited communication among the specialized and subspecialized fields throughout the social sciences. He emphasizes the importance of Mills's "contextualizing vision," which extends over the breadth of human experience so as to include the full range of "social conditions and historical forces" that affect all of us in our daily lives. Yet Mills also had a "critical vision" that was no less important, centering on "how things in the world might be different, how they might be made better." For Hartmann, Mills points us toward "putting context and critique together" in a dialectical way. And to accomplish this ongoing process or dialogue, we must learn to cultivate the sociological imagination, just as Mills gives us advice on how to accomplish this in his appendix.

Apparently the discipline of sociology—in common with the other social sciences—has moved in the narrow direction of bureaucratic social science since Mills's time, although sociologists still cling to the term "sociological imagination" as a slogan that they aspire to. Hartmann's chapter alerts us to the gap between Mills's combination of a contextual and a critical vision, on the one hand, and current practices in the social sciences, on the other. Here, then, is Mills's broad understanding of the nature of the scientific method as including both a deep sense of problem as well as opening up to the full range of phenomena that social scientists must address to make progress on a problem. To take Mills's vision seriously, then, we must also take culture seriously no less than patterns of social organization and history, for they all shape the contexts that affect our lives. Equally, we must look to understanding the fundamental problems that this context alerts us to, and we must move to confront those problems effectively, thus opposing the widespread commitment of social scientists to the doctrine of value neutrality.

Chapter 3, Debbie V. S. Kasper's "Putting It All Together: Toward Increasing Sociology's Relevance to Ecological Research," is critical of the general failure of sociology to analyze "the environmental repercussions of what we do," as illustrated by social problems such as "Global climate change. Species extinction. Desertification. Water scarcity." Yet "process sociology"—illustrated by the theories of Norbert Elias, Pierre Bourdieu, and Anthony Giddens—can help sociologists to open up to the breadth of perspective that they require for such research. And "environmental sociology"—using the concepts of "human exemptionalism" and "ecological habitus"—can point social scientists in a crucial direction. Kasper believes that "process sociology" and environmental sociology are aligned with the "overarching goal of effecting a paradigm shift." The alternative to increasing understanding and action on environmental problems is environmental unsustainability that threatens the future of the human race. Kasper ends optimistically: "Strategies that encourage seeing the fuller complexity of human social life are essential steps toward a social science that is more widely deemed socially relevant."

Kasper puts forward a broad approach to the scientific method that contrasts with bureaucratic social science and resonates with the approach of C. Wright Mills, thus pointing toward the integration of what social scientists have learned. It is an orientation that differs from the present-day general exclusion by sociologists of the importance of human interaction with the environment and their resulting failure to address fundamental problems like global climate change. The "process sociology" that she recommends is broad enough to open up to the range of culture, to environmental interaction, and to much more, thus getting at the enormous complexity of human behavior. Yet all of this requires a paradigm shift in the fundamental assumptions that govern the narrow approach to the scientific method of social scientists. It is a shift that would also point to fundamental changes in culture, social organization, and the individual. And it would require social scientists to move away from their doctrine of value neutrality so as to address our fundamental ecological problems.

Chapter 4, J. I. (Hans) Bakker's "C. Wright Mills and Education" centers on the implications of Mills's *The Sociological Imagination* for an education broad enough to include mind, body, and spirit. Bakker assesses Mills's weaknesses no less than his strengths, helping us to move away from worshipping Mills's own understanding of the "sociological imagination" due to the limitations of his polemical side. Bakker's own very broad perspective builds on his background in Eastern thought, leaving us with a broad direction for how we might continue to develop "the true sociological imagination," and how we might use that imagination to guide us in reconstructing our educational institutions. For example, there is hatha yoga's orientation to the human body and the importance of the combination of body, mind, and spirit. If we are indeed to move further toward developing a sociological imagination, then it is the entire individual—and not just the individual's imagination—that must become involved in that journey.

Just as Kasper emphasizes the importance of physical structures like the physical environment, so does Bakker emphasize biological structures like the human body. And also in common with Kasper, Bakker's orientation to the scientific method is extremely broad, even carrying further Mills's own incredible breadth in his vision of the sociological imagination. That breadth must take culture most seriously, as illustrated by Bakker's emphasis on Eastern thought with its orientation to the entire individual. Here we have a sharp contrast with the present approach of sociologists, where the individual generally is seen as the province of psychology and not sociology. To follow Bakker's approach it would be essential to point toward an educational institution that would be different from our present one in fundamental ways, an education that would require nothing less than a basic change in Western culture so as to include substantial elements of Eastern culture. And that would also yield a direction for fundamental changes in the individual.

Chapter 5, J. David Knottnerus's "Structural Ritualization Theory: Application and Change," begins by describing a theory that—building on the work of Emile Durkheim, Erving Goffman, W. Lloyd Warner, and Randall Collins—has guided a long series of investigations by him and his associates over the past decade. His focus is "on everyday life and the central role rituals play in human behavior," by contrast with the focus on macro phenomena throughout the social sciences. That role is so central because such repetitive behavior is both meaningful and expressive, thus reaching out broadly to key elements of our behavior. Knottnerus presents illustrations from a number of studies that flesh out the nature of structural ritualization theory. Given this extremely broad approach to ritual coupled with diverse examples, he proceeds to explore the implications of these analyses for understanding change and addressing social and personal problems that are experienced in people's everyday lives. It is this broad methodological and theoretical approach that is the basis for his joint work with Jason S. Ulsperger on elder abuse, as discussed in chapter 9.

By contrast with the bureaucratic approach to the scientific method adopted in sociology and the other social sciences, Knottnerus's investigations and those of his coworkers provide a model for a scientific method broad enough to penetrate the enormous complexity of human behavior and, thus, follow our scientific ideals. For example, ritual is a key element of human behavior, as illustrated by such figures as Durkheim, Goffman, Warner, and Collins, yet sociologists have succeeded in paying little attention to what may well be seen as nothing less than a missing link in human behavior. What Knottnerus sees as crucial for a broad approach to the scientific method is that ritual be seen as including both meaningful and expressive elements, thus bringing in culture no less than social organization, and also pointing toward a deep understanding of change. It is in this way that he succeeds in linking tiny micro phenomena with the broadest macro aspects of society, as illustrated by his study of concentration camps with its contrast between rituals oriented toward life versus rituals oriented toward death.

Chapter 6, Frank W. Elwell's "Harry Braverman and the Working Class," extends Braverman's 1900–1970 analysis—in his well-known *Labor and Monopoly Capitalism*—and analyzes the impact of capitalism on work in the 20th century in the United States through to 2001. To what extent is Braverman's "biting critique of the growing degradation of work in America" that "centered on the 'deskilling' of jobs . . . in a systematic effort . . . to maximize profit" valid for 1970–2001? Elwell's chapter follows the spirit of Mills and his broad methodological approach. He sees Braverman as moving up and down language's ladder of abstraction, using evidence from a variety of sources, and being reflexive in including an autobiographical sketch. Elwell's own approach is similar, yielding a direction for penetrating the complexity of the forces that are continuing in our own times to produce "the degradation of work and workers ... and rising tides of alienation and anomie." If anyone illustrates Mills's "critical vision," it is Karl Marx, assisted in this chapter by Braverman and Elwell.

Just as Kasper is committed to confronting our enormous environmental problems in chapter 3, so are Marx, Braverman, and Elwell committed to the enormous problems faced by the labor force within our capitalistic economy at this time in history, as illustrated by "the degradation of work" and "rising tides of alienation and anomie." The doctrine of value neutrality that works to guide bureaucratic social science is nowhere to be seen in this chapter. Granting the tremendous importance of examining patterns of social organization for understanding capitalism—as emphasized by Marx and Braverman—Elwell also succeeds in bringing in the phenomenon of culture, and by no means in a minor way. For example, he refers to the importance of "the sociocultural web of population, technological and environmental relationships, bureaucratization, nationalism, consumerism, advance of science, and rationalization." More generally, Elwell's approach to the scientific method follows the breadth of Mills's own vision, and he succeeds in being quite systematic.

Chapter 7, Vince Montes's "The Web Approach to State Strategy in Puerto Rico" centers on—by contrast with a simplistic focus on state repression—"a vast array of strategies that states utilize to maintain their authority." By so doing, he avoids "the fragmentation that has ... produced limited concepts that prevent far-reaching levels of abstraction." Behind his study is the assumption—which applies to all social problems—of the enormous complexity of human behavior, following the broad approach to human behavior championed by Mills in *The Sociological Imagination.* For example, state control is achieved in part by procedures of "facilitation" that "target the general public with social aid provisions and employment." These state strategies, following Montes's conclusion, "are more pervasive and hegemonic than any analysis of state repression would be able to uncover."

If we think of social stratification as a most powerful force that is to be found everywhere and is intrinsic to our stratified or bureaucratic worldview, then Montes's analysis of the relationships between the United States and Puerto Rico carries our understanding of that force further, moving our pendulum to the right. We have here a detailed case study not just of the political process of repression but of many facilitative ways—such as the use of the U.S. Military as a vehicle for social integration as well as the provision of employment and social aid—in which the economic institution can be brought to bear so as to bolster repression by giving it a humanistic face. Montes's analysis thus requires serious attention to the range of phenomena to be found within a given culture, attention that is omitted by a focus on state repression. His recognition of the enormous complexity of the United States–Puerto Rico relationship suggests a key rationale for building on Mills's broad approach to the scientific method. Otherwise, we shall continue to remain largely ignorant of the forces that are creating our escalating problems.

Chapter 8, Thomas J. Scheff's "Macho/Madonna Link? Hypermasculine Violence as a Social System" focuses on how "both men and women contribute to ... systems of violence." His effort to understand these systems follows his very broad approach to the scientific method, as illustrated by his earlier works. He claims that "it may be necessary to study emotional/relational configurations of men and women, in addition to the usual studies of power and domination," an approach that is generally lacking throughout the social sciences. Scheff hypothesizes that "hypermasculine aggression is generated by the suppression of the vulnerable emotions (shame, fear, and grief)," and that "hyper-feminine women encourage ... this behavior because they suppress anger and act out fear." He concludes that "It is particularly necessary to remove the taboo on shame, so that the basic processes in the emotional/relational world become visible," and that the testing of these ideas requires that they be "translated into testable propositions based on clearly defined concepts."

As a cofounder of the Sociological Imagination Group, Scheff has already shaped the direction of this group to emphasize the importance of moving far down language's ladder of abstraction so as to include the dynamics of emotional behavior within any given momentary scene. His focus here on violence is most timely, given the wide range of such threats throughout the world and given the emphasis on visible and large-scale phenomena rather than the world of emotions and intimate or close relationships. This new emphasis on how sex roles can work to structure emotions in men as well as in women moves into the nature of our contemporary culture as a whole, and he combines that approach with his previous focus on emotions within small-scale situations. It is a further example of his part/whole methodological approach, with the whole being the nature of culture. His chapter points us in both directions of the pendulum. His broad analysis that includes key elements of culture and emotions moves us in the direction of developing solutions to the mammoth problems of contemporary society. Failing any systematic attention to the problems within our emotional lives, there is little hope of solving such problems as violence, whether in the small group or in international affairs.

Chapter 9, Jason S. Ulsperger's and J. David Knottnerus's "Institutionalized Elder Abuse: The Bureaucratic Ritualization and Transformation of Physical Neglect in Nursing Homes," applies structural ritualization theory to a study of elder abuse in nursing homes. Their focus is on the bureaucratization of U.S. nursing homes as they proceed to examine forty autobiographies, biographies, and research monographs. And they find substantial evidence that bureaucratic themes "contribute to the unintended maltreatment of residents," as illustrated by staff separation from residents and staff treatment of residents in hierarchical ways. They conclude by considering "alternative patterns of interaction that have the ability to counter bureaucracy and lower resident neglect," and they make a series of policy recommendations that point away from bureaucratic relationships and toward "alternative ritualized practices that would foster the physical, emotional, and mental health of nursing home residents."

By so doing, they carry further the orientation to application and change of Knottnerus's presentation in chapter 5. If bureaucratic culture is indeed operative throughout contemporary society, then a focus on bureaucratic organizations—provided that it follows a broad and systematic approach to the scientific method—also can help us to understand more fully the nature of bureaucratic culture. The authors' focus on rituals is so elemental that it facilitates their analysis of the many autobiographies, biographies, and research monographs that they analyzed. They are certainly not alone in the social science literature on the negative impact of bureaucracy, yet their analysis uniquely builds on the concept of ritual that illustrates the breadth of their methodological approach. It includes a detailed historical analysis together with a series of quotations getting at concrete situations and illustrating their key points. Their eight policy recommendations include not only general ideas (such as downplaying the bureaucratic structure) but also quite specific ones (such as designing more appropriate clothing). The result is a clear demonstration of the poverty of a value-neutral orientation, given the sociologist's potential for confronting mammoth social problems in a way that is based on a range of knowledge that practitioners almost invariably ignore.

Chapter 10 presents Arlene Stein's "Discipline and Publish: Public Sociology in an Age of Professionalization." She gives the reader a historical view of the efforts of American sociologists to communicate to publics outside of their own discipline—or to become "public intellectuals"—just as Mills, Riesman, and Lynd did. Have sociologists indeed experienced the rise and fall of popular sociology? The question is not easily answered, given the complexity of the forces involved. What are the prospects for reinvigorating the tradition of a "public sociology"? The ideals of democracy require a public that is sufficiently educated so that it can make effective decisions in confronting world, national, and local problems. Stein concludes: "Helping sociologists understand their work in a holistic way could go a long way toward empowering them to be credible public analysts of the complex public issues that shape the world.... [S]uch efforts could renew and reinvigorate the discipline, and deepen public intellectual engagement in general."

Stein documents, chapter and verse, just how far we have come from an age when Riesman, Mills, and Lynd managed to communicate to a wide public outside of sociology, thus presenting our appalling failure to communicate to nonsociologists. This change has been accompanied by—and driven by—the narrow specialization, with limited communication across specialized fields, that is fostered by bureaucracy and a bureaucratic culture. Yet Stein devotes much of her chapter to discussing what would be involved in changing this trend and moving "toward a more public sociology." Here she follows not only the ideals of Mills but also contemporary sociologists like Gans, Gitlin, Patterson, and Buroway. Such a direction need not water down communication outside of the discipline: "Rather than sacrificing rigor for range, the public sociologist makes use of analytic clarity to speak to both academic and nonacademic audiences, addressing and enlarging the democratic public sphere." For this task, "sociologists must enlarge our sociological imagination and go beyond the current vision of a bureaucratic science ... that analyzes discrete problems having little connection to one another." Given what appear to be escalating social problems throughout the world, the failure of sociologists to enter the mass media may well be what Mills called "the greatest human default being committed by privileged men in our times."

Kontos's chapter 11—which is also the basis for the "deep dialogue" to be presented in chapter 12 of part III—presents "Public Opinion and Social Movements: A Sociological Analysis." Social movement organizations normally try to influence public opinion and to convert passive public support into active participation. This involves framing issues as "problems" within compelling narratives—that is, narratives that embody a sense of urgency or crises and that provide pragmatic solutions. We should understand that such narratives are invariably ideological in nature, in that they draw on collective concepts, themes, imagery, and myths that represent the commonsense of any given culture, and that inform generalized expectations and judgments. In which case the question arises as to how any movement can change the cultural framework within which it operates, given that it makes good use of that cultural framework in its efforts to achieve the changes that it advocates. The question is relevant to any sociology that posits the need for social change and that understands itself as having a stake in the outcome of progressive movements, as in the case of this volume.

Kontos thus raises a question that we editors should address, and we will attempt to do so—and also to interact with Kontos's other ideas—within the dialogue in chapter 12. How are we to succeed in advocating changes in bureaucratic culture when we make use of elements of bureaucratic culture as we proceed with our arguments? We can look back at Mills's own failure to achieve the changes that he fought for to illustrate Kontos's argument. Granted that Mills envisioned the importance of a broad sociological imagination by contrast with what he called "bureaucratic social science," did that lone wolf in fact illustrate the hierarchical orientation to be found in bureaucracy by castigating fellow sociologists instead of learning to work with them to develop a sociology that fulfilled its promise? Is it indeed possible for those following the spirit of the Sociological Imagination Group to avoid proclaiming their own superiority over other social scientists? Can they instead learn to communicate with other social scientists on an equal plane? Is there indeed the possibility that all of us—including social scientists—can learn to engage in the kind of dialogue that illustrates such communication?

## Conclusions

Each of the chapters in part II raises questions that require thorough examination as well as further research, if answers are to be reached. These questions along with others raised by the authors in part II are only answered partially within the covers of this book. Yet raising such questions can become the first and perhaps the most important step of a scientific method that requires commitment to a problem to motivate efforts to gain understanding of that problem. Yet all of those specific questions also imply a more general question: How can social scientists learn to follow the ideals of the scientific method, given the bureaucratic culture that pervades contemporary society and invokes bureaucratic social science? More specifically, how can social scientists—including all of the authors in this volume—learn to make ever fuller use of the infinite potentials that language opens up to all of us? And still more specifically, how can social scientists proceed to integrate their knowledge of human behavior so as to provide—more and more—a solid basis for social technologists to solve escalating problems, preferably with the aid of social scientists?

One partial answer to these general questions derives from Thomas Kuhn's *The Structure of Scientific Revolutions* (1962). It requires movement far up language's ladder of abstraction to the metaphysical assumptions that shape our bureaucratic culture or, in Mills's terms, our "bureaucratic ethos." And by so doing we can locate the contradictions between those assumptions and our democratic ideals. And we can also learn to develop alternative assumptions—and the vision of an alternative way of life—that promise to resolve those contradictions and help us to fulfill those ideals. It is those alternative assumptions and that vision that are the basis for the two chapters in part III: "Deep Dialogue and Deep

Democracy" by Bernard Phillips and Louis Kontos, and "The East-West Strategy" by the editors of this volume. Both are examples of efforts to learn how to use the scientific method in everyday life. While the former focuses on our everyday conversations and institutional relationships, the latter encompasses the full range of our behavior. Those chapters provide a direction for social scientists to follow the biblical injunction, "Physician, heal thyself." It is also a direction for the rest of us. If we social scientists wish to change bureaucratic social science and the bureaucratic ethos, then we must first look to our own deep involvement in our bureaucratic way of life and begin to change it.

# References

Gouldner, Alvin W. 1972. "The Politics of the Mind: Reflections on Flack's Review of *The Coming Crisis of Western Sociology,*" *Social Policy* 5 (March/April), 13–21, 54–58.

Hayakawa, Samuel I. 1949. *Language in Thought and Action.* New York: Harcourt, Brace & World.

Kean, Thomas H., and Lee H. Hamilton. n.d. *The 9/11 Commission Report.* New York: W. W. Norton.

Kincaid, Harold, John Dupre, and Alison Wylie, eds. 2007. *Value-Free Science: Ideal or Illusion?* Cambridge, UK: Cambridge Univ. Press.

Korzybski, Alfred. 1933. *Science and Sanity.* Garden City, New York: Country Life.

Kuhn, Thomas S. 1962. *The Structure of Scientific Revolutions.* Chicago: Univ. of Chicago Press.

Lundberg, George A. 1947/1961. *Can Science Save Us?* New York: David McKay.

Mills, C. Wright. 1958. *The Causes of World War Three.* New York: Simon and Schuster.

———. 1959. *The Sociological Imagination.* New York: Oxford Univ. Press

Phillips, Bernard. 2001. *Beyond Sociology's Tower of Babel: Reconstructing the Scientific Method.* New York: Aldine de Gruyter.

———, ed. 2007. *Understanding Terrorism: Building on the Sociological Imagination.* Boulder, Colo.: Paradigm Publishers.

———. 2008. "The Bureaucratic Ethos and the Promise of Sociology," unpublished manuscript.

———. 2009. *Armageddon or Evolution? The Scientific Method and Escalating World Problems.* Boulder, Colo.: Paradigm Publishers.

Phillips, Bernard, and Louis C. Johnston. 2007. *The Invisible Crisis of Contemporary Society: Reconstructing Sociology's Fundamental Assumptions.* Boulder, Colo.: Paradigm Publishers.

Phillips, Bernard, Harold Kincaid, and Thomas J. Scheff, eds. 2002. *Toward a Sociological Imagination: Bridging Specialized Fields.* Lanham, Md.: University Press of America.

Rees, Martin. 2003. *Our Final Hour: A Scientist's Warning: How Terror, Error, and Environmental Disaster Threaten Humankind's Future in This Century—On Earth and Beyond*. New York: Basic Books.

Scheff, Thomas J. 1990. *Microsociology: Discourse, Emotion, and Social Structure*. Chicago: Univ. of Chicago Press.

———. 1994. *Bloody Revenge: Emotions, Nationalism, and War*. Boulder, Colo.: Westview.

———. 1997. *Emotions, the Social Bond, and Human Reality: Part/Whole Analysis*. Cambridge, UK: Cambridge University Press.

Wilder, Thornton. [1942]1957. *Three Plays: Our Town, The Skin of Our Teeth, The Matchmaker*. New York: Avon Books, Harper & Row, 65–137.

# PART II

# The Sociological Imagination and Social Problems

THE TEN CHAPTERS IN PART II range widely so as to include a reexamination of Mills's concept of the sociological imagination, treatment of the relevance of ecological research, a look at Mills's implications for education, a focus on a theory of ritualization, an extension of Harry Braverman's analysis of the working class, an analysis of the complex political relations between the U.S. government and Puerto Rico, an exploration of the linkage between sex roles and violence, research on how bureaucracy yields physical neglect in nursing homes, and a discussion of the forces that have stood in the way of the development of public sociology. These diverse topics reflect the diversity of sociology itself. Yet what on earth could possibly justify joining such diverse studies within the covers of a single book?

However, these chapters are held together by a common commitment to a new and broad approach to the scientific method that had been given the label, "the Web and Part/Whole Approach." As we noted in chapter 1, that approach emphasized the importance of integrating the problem-solving potentials of language to the scientific method. Thus, we might do well to think of the Web and Part/Whole Approach more simply as a very broad approach to the scientific method. It is a system of procedures

23

that aims to fulfill what C. Wright Mills called "the promise of sociology." These procedures also point us toward opening up to the full range of phenomena that are relevant to a given defined research problem. We believe that sociology and the other social sciences have, up to this point, very largely failed contemporary society in following this scientific ideal, given the narrow specialization and subspecialization—with very limited communication across specialized areas—that is the name of the game throughout these disciplines. And we believe that this failure is genuinely life threatening for contemporary societies, given what we see as escalating and fundamental social problems throughout the world.

Nevertheless, we are most optimistic—even at this very late date—about the possibility of fulfilling "the promise of sociology." Each one of the chapters to follow was written by a sociologist who has somehow managed to hold on to the optimism that Mills displayed about sociology's possibilities. And these authors have managed to accomplish this despite the prevailing pessimism and cynicism throughout the discipline of sociology, and despite the nightmarish nature of contemporary world events. It was one thing for Mills to be optimistic about sociology's possibilities in the 1950s, when the discipline was still riding a crest of enthusiasm and support from society prior to its fall from grace in the 1970s and on to present times. But it is quite another thing to recapture that sense of possibility at a time when films about the end of the human race have invaded our psyche.

We hope that readers will take heart from these chapters and reach deep down into the place where they have buried their earlier ideas about sociology's possibilities. For we know that those ideas have never been completely lost, given the widespread commitment throughout the discipline to the slogan of "the sociological imagination." We hope that each of you will once again raise the ideal of "the promise of sociology" to the surface as you proceed to read the following chapters. And we hope that you will come to see the possibilities of following in the footsteps of these authors by considering how you might apply the broad approach to the scientific method that they used in this volume to your own research and teaching. For the scientific method need no longer be the narrow quantitative or qualitative approach—divorced from broad theory or fundamental social problems—that, very largely, it is today. Rather, it can be an effort that builds on Mills's vision of "the sociological imagination."

CHAPTER 2

# Reclaiming the Sociological Imagination

## A Brief Overview and Guide

*Douglas Hartmann*

> "You can't depend upon your eyes when your imagination is out of focus."
>
> —*Mark Twain*

IN GRADUATE SCHOOL THERE WAS A PROFESSOR in my department who loved to talk about the need for each generation of sociologists to "claim its theoretical inheritance anew." What this instructor meant by this phrase went beyond just knowing the classic authors and texts and concepts. His intention was more oriented toward the task of cultivating and continually reinvigorating the diverse but ultimately interlinked ways of thinking that distinguish the sociological enterprise in the modern world and the contemporary academy, the mindset and approach that mark sociology as what Karl Mannheim might have called a distinctive "style of thought" or what Kenneth Burke would have termed "the rhetoric of sociology." In an academic universe of perpetual ferment (interdisciplinarity, budget crises, specialization, and the like), I believe that the project of reclaiming core sociological thought and practice may be more necessary and difficult than ever.

There are many different ways to go about this reclamation project. For some, it can involve rereading and rethinking classic texts like Weber's *Protestant Ethic* or Durkheim's *Elementary Forms.* For others, it may take shape in formulating new concepts and theoretical treatments—Pierre Bourdieu's ideas about habitus, field, and practice come to mind for example, or Anthony Giddens's notions of structuration. For still others the task of revitalization may entail carrying out creative, critical analyses of new social forces or phenomena. This chapter takes a somewhat different tack. It attempts to make a contribution to the cultivation of sociological thought by reexamining one of its most powerful and evocative phrases: the "sociological imagination." It is a project that I believe not only provides a general, conceptual foundation for the insights and methodological innovations that are at the core of this volume, but it also outlines some basic, practical steps that might guide and inspire all sociologists in their pursuit of the craft and science that is sociology.

## C. Wright Mills and Beyond

In 1959 at the end of one of the most productive and stimulating decades of work in the history of American sociology, C. Wright Mills released a slim volume that bore the title *The Sociological Imagination.* I don't know if Mills was the first to use the phrase, and I'm also not sure whether the book, brilliant as it was, really changed a whole lot in the field. Many of the problems Mills identified—the tendency toward either abstracted empiricism on the one hand or grand theory on the other, not to mention substantive overspecialization and narrowness—appear as entrenched now as when Mills was writing over a half century ago; indeed, they are precisely what bring the contributors to this volume, and the Web and Part/Whole Approach more generally, into common cause (cf. Phillips, 2001; Phillips, Kincaid, and Scheff, 2002; Phillips and Johnston, 2007). Nevertheless, I do believe that the phrase "the sociological imagination" has shaped the thinking of almost every sociologist who has come in Mills's wake. It is, in my view, one of those rare phrases that motivates, inspires, and informs sociologists of all subfields and methodological inclinations, appealing as much to first-year undergraduates as to luminaries in the field. "The sociological imagination" is a phrase, in short, that unites us.

Yet I fear that the phrase "the sociological imagination" may roll off the tongue too easily—at the cost of papering over key tensions and debates in the field, debates about the practice of sociology that keep all of us intellectually vibrant, engaged, and engaging. Indeed, it seems the phrase is now so ubiquitous and watered down that much of its original ambition and intent would seem to have worn off. The challenge for the discipline, therefore, is to recapture and enrich—rather than eliminate— the contentious mix of ideas, insights, and approaches inspired by Mills's wonderful phrase, book, and lifelong project.

Revitalizing the concept of the sociological imagination is not, however, just a matter of going back to the formulations of the master. A good deal of the challenge has to do with Mills's own relatively cavalier definitions and surprisingly sparse use of the term. Despite the book's title, Mills does not say a lot about the sociological imagination in its pages. Only two references appear in the book's main chapters. They are both in the first chapter of the book, and neither is particularly well-developed. "The sociological imagination," Mills writes in its first appearance, "enables its possessor to understand the larger historical scene in terms of its meaning for the inner life and external career of a variety of individuals" (1959: 5). He then offers the definition that is perhaps most famous and widely quoted: "The sociological imagination enables us to grasp history and biography and the relations between the two within society. That is its task and its promise" (6).

In his second reference, Mills describes the sociological imagination as "the quality of mind that seems most dramatically to promise an understanding of the intimate realities of ourselves in connection with larger social realities" (15), and speculates halfheartedly about the probability of it eventually displacing physical and biological science as "the common denominator of serious reflection and popular metaphysics in Western societies" (14). A footnote on his preference for the phrase "social studies" over "the social sciences" (18-19) provides a bit of context for these formulations, but only in an appendix entitled "On Intellectual Craftsmanship" (212-217) does Mills return to the term explicitly. (The book is essentially a critique of approaches that, in Mills's view, fall short of the full glory of the sociological imagination, and a series of chapters on his ideas about the proper practice and values of social science.)

Of course, the generality and imprecision are part of the charm, and in many ways key to Mills's rhetorical genius. Not unlike powerful symbols and social rituals, the theoretical constructs that motivate and inspire large numbers of students and scholars tend to be relatively abstract and multivalent. For all of the uses of ambiguity (Levine, 1988), however, there is also a time for precision and clarity. That is what this essay is all about.

In the pages that follow I will offer some reflections on the two interpretations of Mills's sociological imagination that I believe are most dominant and familiar in the discipline today. The first is the impulse to situate social phenomena in broad structural and historical contexts. The second is the commitment to cultivating critical-theoretical perspectives in, through, and against which to deepen and expand our understandings of things as they are (not to mention how they might be made different). In homage to Mills's own dialectical inclinations, I will sketch the core assumptions and insights of these alternative visions, highlight their respective strengths and weaknesses, and argue that the two are actually deeply intertwined and both essential to the ongoing project of imagining the world sociologically. By way of connecting this essentially theoretical reconstruction with the issues of sociological practice and method that are the focus of this volume, I will then conclude by returning to Mills's neglected appendix "On Intellectual Craftsmanship." Based upon Mills's advice and example, I will sketch out some basic steps that both practicing and aspiring sociologists can take in cultivating their own sociological imaginations and contributing to the ongoing reclamation project we call sociology.

## Two Variations on the Theme

The most basic and, I believe, most widely accepted interpretation of the sociological imagination in contemporary disciplinary parlance is the notion that any phenomenon of the human realm must be situated in its broader social and historical context if it is to be understood properly. This is what I think of as sociology's *contextualizing impulse.* Perhaps the most fundamental motivation and contribution of the sociological impulse to "put things in context" is to call attention to the social conditions and historical forces that limit and constrain human agency and choice. But the concern with context—or structure, as it is often called—is more complicated and multifaceted than just this. In the sociological imagination, context also serves to frame, focus, and organize an otherwise disorderly social world, thus empowering human beings to take action and give meaning to their lives. This is the famous Durkheimian notion of "enabling constraints." Furthermore, the project of situating people in their social worlds is intimately bound up with, and almost inevitably gives rise to, holistic ways of thinking about communities and societies and the component parts and sets of social relationships that make them up. Seeing "the forest for the trees," in the words of one notable introduction (Johnson, 1997), allows sociologists to understand how complex social systems operate, the conflicts and inequalities they generate, and why they are often resisted and sometimes break down.

What makes this holistic, contextualizing vision of the sociological imagination so unique and powerful is that most human beings—especially Americans with their rationalist and individualist worldviews (Cf. Gusfield, 1990; Wrong, 1990)—are almost tragically unaware of the social structures and historical forces that shape and constrain their lives. The sociological imagination in this contextualizing mode thus involves bringing to light structures and social forces that are typically not seen or simply taken for granted. The oft-used example of the fish and the water is illustrative: The fish probably doesn't even know what water is until you take the creature out of it—and at that point, its reality and substance suddenly become obvious. The project for the contextualizing sociologist is to make manifest "the water" that constitutes the social world.

The project of convincing unseeing, doubting others of the power of context, history, and social structure is far from an act of faith for sociologists. On the contrary, it tends to be a thoroughly empirical enterprise. Sociologists do case studies or analyze survey data to demonstrate (as well as analyze) the reality and impact of structuring forces ranging from bureaucratic rationality and globalization, to racial prejudice, peer pressure, or cultural norms and values. More often than not, what makes claims about context compelling and convincing is empirical, material evidence of social forces that human actors are otherwise not aware of. Sociology's engagement with the empirical realities of the world is one of its great strengths, one of the operational characteristics that distinguish it from other humanistic inquiries such as cultural studies, philosophy, or literature.

C. Wright Mills, it is worth noting, was in complete accord with this empiricist emphasis and contribution. "The purpose of empirical inquiry is to settle disagreement and doubts about facts, and thus to make arguments more fruitful by basing all sides more substantively" (1959: 205). Yet Mills also had an acute appreciation for the challenges and ultimate limitations of purely empirical work. As evidenced in his broadside attack on "abstracted empiricism" in the third chapter of *The Sociological Imagination,* Mills was convinced that empirical facts never speak for themselves, no matter how sophisticated the methods from which they were derived. Indeed, some of the "facts" that he considered most dangerous were precisely those that were most commonly and uncritically accepted by so-called experts or the masses in society. Social facts always, as the Mark Twain quote at the head of this chapter suggests, require interpretation and theoretical synthesis.

Perhaps the biggest danger of the standard sociological emphasis on context, structure, and conditions—at least insofar as a vibrant, creative analysis of society is concerned—is that it can easily deteriorate into an empiricist or even positivist exercise wherein "context" is posited as singular and absolute, yet detectable only by sociological methods that are authoritative and beyond dispute. Conceived and constructed in this way, the imaginative aspect of the enterprise disappears, or is severely circumscribed. Put even more provocatively: In the empiricist contextualizing mode, the sociological imagination can become less an act of creative, interpretive engagement with the social world than a valorized, ritualistic documentation of forces that are presumed to be both self-evident and impervious to change.

Which brings us to the second common interpretation of the sociological imagination, which I describe as sociology's *critical orientation* to the social world. Sociologists, of course, are notorious critics—of individualism, of inequality, of social control (or the lack thereof), of conflict and change (or the lack thereof). There are sociological marxists, feminists, critical race scholars, institutionalists, and others. We need not concern ourselves with any of the specific substantive criticisms sociologists may have here. What is important is that these criticisms have their roots in a vision of how things in the world might be different, how they might be made better. And these various critical perspectives afford sociologists analytic standpoints and standards that they can use to conceptualize and evaluate the social world as it exists in current, everyday practice. The key insight for critical sociologists is that the analysis and understanding of the social world requires a certain conceptual distance and detachment, comparative standards or perspectives in and through which to situate one's self and one's conception of society in relation to the social world itself. Suffice it to say that this aspect of the sociological imagination takes the concept of imagination very literally: to understand and/or explain how things in the empirical world are, one must have some imaginative conception of what they are not.

I obviously cannot offer a full explanation of all of the reasons why sociology's critical, theoretical orientation is so vital and important to the discipline and to society (the first few chapters of Craig Calhoun's 1995 book on critical theory provides a useful start; see also Phillips, 2008). But however convinced I am of its significance, I also have to point out one potential downfall of sociological critique: the way in which analysts can get so enamored with their own imagined, critical perspectives that they lose sight of the empirical realities of the world as it is.

When critical perspectives overtake reality itself, the sociological imagination becomes an unthinking perspective—a knee-jerk, Pavlovian response to everything including the empirical foundations and validity of sociological claims. In Mills's terms, this is the seduction of "grand theory," abstract theoretical formulations that are so intricate or held so obsessively by their authors that they lose touch with the world that is actually lived and experienced by real human beings. Today, this tendency expresses itself, not in the grand, abstract formulations of a Talcott Parsons, but in the rigid adherence to theoretical paradigms. For example, we race, class, and gender scholars have a tendency to see race, class, and gender everywhere, structuring and determining everything, even when our theories may not be the most useful and meaningful categories for analyzing real world social actors and phenomena.

## Putting Context and Critique Together

When I was an undergraduate at the University of Chicago, we were of-ten given essay topics that asked us to take a stand on arguments, texts, terms, or theories that were positioned in diametrical opposition to one another: Nature versus nurture. Individual rights or social responsibilities? Is history made by great individuals or determined by impersonal social forces? Is human life meaningful—or meaningless? Having been schooled in the competitive rigors of high school debate, I eagerly and all-too-easily embraced the combative terms suggested in the either/or formulation of these paper topics. After several less-than-successful attempts to pick a side and carry the day, I came to realize that students who got better grades and (presumably) wrote better papers tended to advocate for some kind of conceptual synthesis of the two ostensibly competing positions or perspectives. Basically, they argued "both/and," rather than "either/or." This reframing of the problem allowed my classmates to generate subtler, more nuanced arguments, analyses that incorporated the insights and contributions of two seemingly opposed alternatives while avoiding their shortcomings or blind spots. That is pretty much the approach I think we need to take in trying to reconcile these two distinctive visions of the sociological imagination: not to choose one over the other, but to recognize that both are useful and indeed necessary. (For a similar style of thought in the tradition of the Web and Part/Whole approach, see Kincaid [1996]).

The both/and synthesis of sociology's contextualizing and critical impulses is made easier because the two conceptions mirror each other so clearly. Where the penchant for contextualizing has the tendency to devolve into rote description of how things are, the critical orientation requires the sociologist to imagine things as they are not and, almost in-evitably, leads us to think about if and how we might bring about change. On the other hand, if critical perspectives sometimes lose touch with the realities and constraints of concrete human existence, sociological contextualizers are quick to bring these ideas back down to the ground and remind us that much of social life is structured and determined by forces we can only vaguely comprehend, and can never fully control or completely reshape. The strengths of the one reflect the weaknesses of the other; contextualizing and criticizing are not only equally necessary to the sociological imagination, they are profoundly complementary.

The challenge, of course, is to figure out how the two fit together. And the solution—yes, I am already to the solution—is to realize that the project of integrating sociology's contextualizing and criticizing dimen-sions cannot and should not ever be solved completely. The proper bal-ance between contextualizing and critique is not something that can be fixed or formalized; rather, these two, seemingly alternative approaches need to be held in deep and constant tension with one another. We must cultivate and operationalize both in everything we do—in our thinking, our research, and our writing.

Elusive as it can be, the argument for the synthesis and ongoing, reciprocal interaction of the two different aspects of the sociological imagination that I have just posited is not particularly new or unique. It can be found in the work of classic founding sociologists ranging from Emile Durkheim, Max Weber, and Georg Simmel to Karl Marx and W.E.B. DuBois. It is what I think motivates the editors of this volume in their quest for a meaningful, systematic approach to the parts and pieces that make up the whole web of modern, 21st-century social life. And it is a lot like an argument that former ASA President Michael Burawoy (1998) offered about how to reconcile the two very different approaches to sociological research that dominate the field: the positivist, normal science side of the discipline, and the more critically oriented, reflexive tradition. Typically, sociologists aspire to unify these approaches or orientations to social research in some kind of grand, monolithic program or system. In contrast, Burawoy argued that sociology is best conceived and practiced as an ongoing, reciprocal exchange between these two distinctive ways of knowing. It is what Burawoy called a "dialogue" between two sciences. (For a similar analysis with a contrasting solution, see Pierre Bourdieu's (1988) plea for "heterodoxy" in the social sciences.) The point for sociologists like Burawoy or Bourdieu, or Phillips and Knottnerus, is not that every sociologist needs to be simultaneously engaged in both normal and reflexive sociology, or be expert at both qualitative and quantitative methods. The point, rather, is that the field as a whole needs both ways of thinking and knowing, and that all sociologists—no matter what their method of choice, or substantive specialization—need to appreciate the respective contributions of each.

So too, I believe, for the sociological imagination. It is best understood as an active, ongoing, and necessary dialogue between the discipline's contextualizing impulse and its critical orientation. Mills, it is worth noting, had a particularly broad and interdisciplinary sense of the dialogues and interactions required by the sociological enterprise. "The sociological imagination," he wrote in his introduction, "is the capacity to shift from one perspective to another—from the political to the psychological; from examination of a single family to comparative assessment of the national budgets of the world; from the theological school to the military establishment; from considerations of an oil industry to studies of contemporary poetry" (Mills, 1959). Clearly, the sociological imagination is not some analytic system that can be mechanized and codified, but a process, an ongoing, never-ending project that exists only when it is activated in the analysis of the fascinating, multifaceted, ever-changing worlds of human experience and interaction.

Once these basic points are grasped, there is not a great deal intel-lectually standing in the way of anyone putting into practice this won-derful, dynamic, bifocal way of thinking about the lives that we lead and the worlds that we live in. But still, this may be easier said than done—especially if we aspire to the imaginative sociological heights achieved by a virtuoso like C. Wright Mills. Which brings us to the question: how, exactly, can we cultivate and refine the sociological imagination so broadly conceived? What steps can us ordinary and aspiring sociologists take to develop and sustain our own sociological imaginations?

## Cultivating the Sociological Imagination

Near the end of the appendix that concludes *The Sociological Imagina-tion,* C. Wright Mills poses the same essential question: "But, you may ask, how do ideas come? How is the imagination spurred to put all the images and facts together, to make images relevant and lend meaning to facts?" Mills's answer is disheartening at first but ultimately, I believe, useful, inspiring, and empowering.

What is disheartening is that Mills says that there is no real answer to the question. All he can do, he says, is to "talk about the general con-ditions and a few simple techniques which have seemed to increase my chances to come out with something" (1959: 211). His response, ironically, is so personal and particular as to seem almost asociological. Far from losing his sociological senses, however, Mills is making two points. One is that the sociological imagination is, ultimately, an intensely personal project—which is to say, the creative, synthetic act of a thinking, reflect-ing, synthesizing human being. On this point Mills argues it is better to have "one account by a working student of how he is going about his work, than a dozen 'codifications of procedure' [his quotation marks] by specialists who often as not have never done much work of consequence" (1959: 195). In addition, I think Mills means to suggest that the act of imagining the world in sociological terms—even when he does it—is somewhat less mysterious and magical than we may think, more about method and routine than anything else. And in fact, in seeing how Mills uses his own example to direct and guide the aspiring sociologist on how to go about her or his work, the sociological imagination not only takes on deeper meaning and shape, we are also provided with some practical, preliminary steps—methodological guides, essentially—for doing our own sociological imagining.

Mills offers both some specific techniques, as well as some basic ob-servations about one's working environment. On the latter front, he talks about the need to surround yourself with "a circle of people who will talk and listen" (1959: 201), people who will stimulate, engage, and push you to articulate and develop your ideas about the world. In addition, Mills says that the aspiring sociologist must refuse the conventional separation of work life from private life. This latter point is a bit counterintuitive for sociologists whose first lessons have been that the world is larger than themselves and that they therefore need to avoid the danger of overgeneralizing from one's own personal experience. For Mills, however, in order to understand the world around you, it is best to start with what you know, or think you know, and then to subject those ideas and that experience to ongoing, systematic reflection and examination. The deep assumption here is that sociologists are not outside the object of their study but rather part of it, and that their comprehension and explanation is better pursued by engaging (often critically) this reality rather than running from it. The sociological imagination is, in these respects, "a choice of how to live as well as a choice of career" (196).

Mills's reflections on his own scholarly habits and practices are more expansive and concrete. Indeed, the bulk of the appendix is Mills's attempt to "report in some detail" how he "goes about [his] craft"—and it is here that the work is most valuable. Though not delineated explicitly as such, there are at least three working guidelines that can be culled from these pages:

*Learn from existing materials.* Much as Mills insisted that the sociologist needed to trust her instincts and intuitions, he also realized that there is no need to constantly reinvent the wheel. Sociology, in Mills's view, is a fundamentally collective, communal enterprise, one in which every practitioner is not only allowed but expected to borrow from and build upon existing theory, data, methods, and understandings.

*Be relentless in pursuit of your topic and put your ideas to the empirical test.* For Mills, the sociological imagination is and must be relentless and expansive—asking questions about topics and questions in new ways, searching for more data and information, subjecting ideas to multiple types and layers of testing and analysis, conducting many inquiries and studies. "Good work in social science today is not, and usually cannot be, made up of one clear-cut empirical 'research.' It is, rather, composed of a good many studies which at key points anchor general statements about the shape and the trend of the subject" (1959: 202). Mills specifically recommends working out the design of a whole set of empirical studies on any research question, even those that may not be conducted. "Although you will never get the money with which to do many of the empirical studies you design, it is necessary that you continue to develop them. For once you lay out an empirical study, even if you do not follow it through, it leads you to a new search for data, which often turns out to have unexpected relevance to your problem" (205).

*Write constantly and keep a journal.* Mills spends the bulk of his appendix talking about the need for systematic recording and reflection of ideas in writing. Indeed, he begins by stressing the importance of what he simply calls "keeping a file." "You must set up a file, which is, I suppose, a sociologist's way of saying: keep a journal. Many creative writers keep journals; the sociologist's need for systematic reflection demands it" (1959: 196). Writing serves many different intellectual purposes according to Mills, but at its root the regular, systematic writing and reflection contained in a journal or intellectual "file" is both where and how the sociological imagination is created, cultivated, and made manifest. Writing is, for Mills, the sociological imagination in practice.

Of all Mills's suggestions, this advice about the need for systematic writing and reflection may be most revealing and important. For it is in his descriptions of the writing process that sociology emerges as so much more than the mindless application of theory or technique ("codifications of procedure" by specialists, as Mills describes them in one place). In and through the process of rendering sociological thought in material form, in other words, sociology clearly becomes a craft as well as a science, an intellectual project that requires active, ongoing interpretation, systematic attention to data, creative reflection and reevaluation. and the like.

What is also original and inspiring in these pages are the implicit points and taken-for-granted assumptions bound up in Mills's conception of "intellectual craftsmanship" itself. One of those is the need to take yourself and your work seriously; to see, as Mills did, that your work is intimately bound up with your life, and to work as diligently and systematically as possible on the former always in service of the latter.

Even when produced by a C. Wright Mills, sociological understanding is not an act of creative brilliance, much less the result of outright genius that cannot be explained, reproduced, or recreated. The act of imagining the world sociologically is more akin to how Dan Chambliss (1989) memorably described the accomplishment of athletic excellence: as the result of much hard, boring, mundane work. Similarly, it seems to me that Mills is reminding us that sociological excellence and insight requires a great deal of hard work and discipline, dedication to a craft that has a lineage and established techniques but that exists only in its application and practice on a social world and under unique and variable historical conditions (for additional cases, see Hammond 1964).

## Conclusion

This essay has been an attempt to reinvent and reinvigorate—to reclaim or win anew—the pursuit we call sociology by focusing on contemporary uses and meanings of C. Wright Mills's infectious, evocative phrase "the sociological imagination." What I believe is at stake in this, ultimately, is the heart and soul of sociology itself, a field that has so much potential to help human beings understand and explain the worlds that they live in, but that all-too-often deteriorates into specialized subfields of "experts" relying upon codified techniques or abstract theories and talking only to themselves. There is obviously a great deal more that could and should be said about the ongoing, reclamation project that is the sociological imagination. For example, we could talk about sociology's status and role in an increasingly interdisciplinary and yet specialized academic environment. I would also love to get into the question—raised under the banner of public sociology in recent years (cf. Burawoy, 2004)—of how to cultivate this distinctive way of thinking and knowing for broader and bigger public audiences. (On this score, we once again have no better role model than Mills himself, whose books found audiences far beyond the sociological fraternity.) But in terms of wrapping up this initial foray into the topic, let me highlight one final point on which C. Wright Mills may be distinguished from his and many of our contemporaries.

In trying to capture the reciprocal, interactive dynamic between context and critique that I believe is the sociological imagination, I borrowed from a parallel argument that Michael Burawoy made about cultivating an ongoing dialogue between positive and reflexive modes of sociological investigation. Burawoy and Mills have a great deal in common, but one point on which they diverge is their attitude toward the label of science. Burawoy insists on seeing all of the different dimensions of sociological research and practice as scientific. Mills was far more ambivalent. As he wrote in an early footnote: "I feel the need to say that I much prefer the phrase 'the social studies' to 'the social sciences'—not because I do not like physical scientists ... but because the word 'science' has acquired great prestige and rather imprecise meaning. I do not feel any need to kidnap the prestige or to make the meaning less precise by using it as a philosophical metaphor" (Mills, 1959: 19). Indeed, in depicting sociological work as "intellectual craftsmanship" I believe Mills was, not only trying to avoid the pretensions and truth claims so often associated with "science," but was also suggesting that the kind of knowledge and understanding we produce using our sociological imaginations is unique—in its production, in its substance, and in its contributions to the world. (For a recent similar argument, see Robert Alford's (2005) depiction of sociology as a craft.)

I understand that there is a danger here—that in emphasizing sociology's creative dimensions, its critical roots, and craftsman-like practices, we may unintentionally minimize the capital role of theory, methodological rigor, and analytic systematicity in all of our work, not to mention undermine our larger public and professional standing. This would almost certainly be a mistake. Who, after all, does not believe in the power of "science" in our modern world? Isn't the claim to science key to our legitimacy, our attempts to speak with authority in the public realm? Indeed, one of the great appeals of the Web and Part/Whole Approach championed by Bernie Phillips and his colleagues is its attempt to organize and systematize Mills's unique way of shuttling up and down and across ladders of conceptual abstraction and empirical documentation in his concrete research and writing. Still, I think the risk of following Mills in this terminological territory may be worth it, if only to better capture and convey all the work involved in the ongoing project of understanding and explaining the world in sociological terms.

## Note

Thanks especially to Peter and Patty Adler, Kathleen O. Slobin, Monte Bute, Bernie Phillips, and David Knottnerus. As with other contributors to the Web and Part/Whole Approach, my engagement with "the sociological imagination" stands in contrast to interventions such as those collected in Rhonda Levine's 2005 volume or a later (2006) Mills tribute conference in New York that emphasize Mills's contributions to more radical visions of sociology and social science, focusing especially on his economic and political analyses. While I am extremely sympathetic to these projects (for additional review essays by Joya Misra, Anthony Orum, Immanuel Wallerstein, and Eduardo Bonilla-Silva, see *Contemporary Sociology,* March 2006), my focus here is more oriented toward reinvigorating the discipline as a whole without respect for specific ideological or substantive implications. What goes along with this alternative critical standpoint or perspective—what emerges from it quite naturally, in fact—is a social-change agenda. Some folks really push for this; others don't. Indeed, this is the face of Mills that many sociologists consider to be the most important and powerful. What I am not agnostic about is that good, imaginative sociological work should have real world social change possibilities and applications. If it doesn't, it is more than likely out of touch with reality and has probably deteriorated into philosophy or political ideology. For a slim and engaging volume on the uses and abuses of utopian thought, see Rothstein, Muschamp, and Marty (2003).

## References

Alford, Robert P. 2005. *The Craft of Inquiry: Theories, Method, Evidence.* Oxford: Oxford Univ. Press.

American Sociological Association. 2006. "A Symposium on Rhonda Levine's Enriching the Sociological Imagination." *Contemporary Sociology* 35 (2): 105-114.

Becker, Howard S. 1998. *Tricks of the Trade: How to Think About Your Research While You're Doing It.* Chicago: Univ. of Chicago Press.

Bourdieu, Pierre. 1988. "Vive La Crise! For Heterodoxy in Social Science." *Theory and Society,* 17: 773-787.

Burawoy, Michael. 1998. "Critical Sociology: A Dialogue between Two Sciences." *Contemporary Sociology* 21: 12-20.

———. 2004. "Public Sociologies: Contradictions, Dilemmas, and Possibliities." *Social Forces* 82 (4): 1603-1618.

Calhoun, Craig J. 1995. *Critical Social Theory: Culture, History, and the Challenge of Difference.* Cambridge, Mass.: Blackwell.

Chambliss, Daniel F. 1989. "The Mundanity of Excellence: An Ethnographic Report on Stratification and Olympic Swimmers." *Sociological Theory* 7 (1): 70–86.

Gusfield, Joseph R. 1990. "Sociology's Critical Irony: Countering American Individualism." In *Sociology in America,* ed. Herbert J. Gans. Newbury Park, Calif.: Sage Publications.

Hammond, Phillip E, ed. 1964. *Sociologists at Work: The Craft of Social Research.* New York: Basic Books.

Johnson, Allan G. 1997. *The Forest for the Trees: Sociology as Life, Practice, and Promise.* Philadelphia: Temple Univ. Press.

Kincaid, Harold. 1996. *Philosophical Foundations of the Social Sciences.* New York: Cambridge Univ. Press.

Levine, Donald N. 1988. *The Flight from Ambiguity: Essays in Social and Cultural Theory.* Chicago: Univ. of Chicago Press.

Levine, Rhonda F., ed. 2005. *Enriching the Sociological Imagination: How Radical Sociology Changed the Discipline.* Boulder, Colo.: Paradigm Publishers.

Mills, C. Wright. 1959. *The Sociological Imagination.* London: Oxford University Press.

Phillips, Bernard. 2001. *Beyond Sociology's Tower of Babel: Reconstructing the Scientific Method.* New York: Aldine de Gruyter.

———. 2008. *Armageddon or Evolution? The Scientific Method and Escalating World Problems.* Boulder, Colorado: Paradigm Publishers.

Phillips, Bernard, and Louis C. Johnston. 2007. *The Invisible Crisis of Contemporary Sociology: Reconstructing Sociology's Fundamental Assumptions.* Boulder, Colo.: Paradigm Publishers.

Phillips, Bernard, Harold Kincaid, and Thomas J. Scheff. 2002. *Toward a Sociological Imagination: Bridging Specialized Fields.* Lanham, Md.: University Press of America.

Rothstein, Edward, Herbert Muschamp, and Martin E. Marty. 2003. *Visions of Utopia.* London: Oxford Univ. Press.

Wrong, Dennis H. 1990. "The Influence of Sociological Ideas on American Culture." In *Sociology in America,* ed. Herbert J. Gans. Newbury Park, Calif.: Sage Publications.

# CHAPTER 3

# Putting It All Together

## Toward Increasing Sociology's Relevance to Ecological Research

*Debbie V. S. Kasper*

Global climate change. Species extinction. Desertification. Water scarcity. This list of gloomy, but familiar, terms includes some of the major challenges facing the world's citizens today—challenges which are typically thought of as "environmental problems." While this label is not necessarily incorrect, it is incomplete. These problems, environmental though they be, are in large part products of the organization of human social life. Despite increasing recognition of the need to study the interrelations between humans and the natural environment, the social sciences continue to play a minimal role in ecological research (Endter-Wada et al., 1998). "Environmental problems" tend to be viewed as the result of discrete physical events, while the ongoing social practices that create them are largely ignored (Beamish, 2002). As is becoming increasingly apparent, this attention-bias acts as a tremendous hindrance to addressing socioecological problems in a meaningful way.* This style of thinking is the logical consequence of a dominant paradigm that discourages the recognition of interconnections: between people in society and between human society and nature.

This disciplinary blind spot has had the overall effect of placing "environmental problems" largely beyond the perceived domain of sociological research. Consequently, our understanding of the true nature of these problems—and their socioecological causes and consequences—is very limited. Research which increases that understanding and provides insight into possible solutions must attend to more than just physical causes and effects. In need of further examination is the nature of the relationship of humans with their physical environment. How people relate to their ecological contexts is a product, albeit always unfinished, of a complex combination of influences (social, cultural, and biological, for example) that shape the ways they perceive, act, and react within their environments. In other words, what people *do* within their socioecological contexts *both influences and is influenced by* how people *think* and *feel* about them. These mutually influencing processes, at the same time, work to shape the environments within which societies develop. It is in finding ways to more adequately study these processes that social science will realize its potential for contributing to socioecological research.

A forward-thinking and open-minded approach is essential to the success of such an undertaking. The "Web and Part/Whole Approach" is one such attempt to facilitate a more complex and comprehensive understanding of some of the most serious contemporary problems (Phillips, 2001; Phillips, Kincaid, and Scheff, 2002). The advocates of this approach have been working to bridge the widening gulfs between sociologists by highlighting their fundamental commonalities underlying the formal structure of a hyperspecialized discipline. Their more recent works direct our attention explicitly to the necessity of recognizing and incorporating into social science attention to the complex interactions between physical, biological, and social structures (Phillips and Johnston, 2007). Their disappointment with the failure of sociological methodologies to take such complexities fully into account motivates their continuing efforts. It is in this spirit that I seek to study socioecological problems in a way that advances our understanding of them and informs efforts to address them.

In what follows, I bring together two movements (usually relegated to their respective disciplinary corners) that strive to propel sociological thinking to a new level—one that emphasizes relations, interdependence, and ongoing process, abandoning modern mechanistic worldviews. I highlight their key conceptual contributions, the integration of which, I argue,

---

*I use "socioecological" to refer to the problems and phenomena most often labeled simply "environmental" and to make implicit the interactive relations between human social life and the ecological contexts within which it necessarily takes place.

will help to advance the project of sociology in general and socioecological studies, in particular. The first, *relational process theory*, refers to an approach that is intended to upgrade sociology's conceptual tools, enabling us to more satisfyingly think about, talk about, and study the social as relational processes. *Environmental sociology* attends to relational processes, but demands explicit attention to the relations between societies and their ecological contexts. It too is critical of outmoded patterns of modern thinking, specifically of seeing human society as somehow exempt from the natural laws and ecological limits that govern other organisms. I pay particular attention to their respective concepts, *habitus* and *human exemptionalism*, and their value for sociological thinking. Finally, I introduce the notion of *ecological habitus* derived from the integration of these contributions as an example of a useful concept with which sociology can more effectively study the complex array of relations that pertain to the ecological outcomes of human social life.

## Relational Process Theory: Rethinking the "Individual-Society Problem"

As Mills stated nearly fifty years ago, "social science deals with problems of biography, of history, and of their intersections within social structures" (1959: 143). The trick in sociology has been, and remains, figuring out how to think about, talk about, and study those intersections. Dominant explanations of how society works have been criticized for attributing more influence to either "social structures" or "individual agency," but they seem to have equal trouble dealing with the dynamic points of contact between the two. Conceptualizing the relationship between people and their social worlds remains a problem within sociology and "must be regarded as a core preoccupation of contemporary social thought" (Elliot, 1999: 7). Although there have been a number of important advances toward this end, they have not effected significant change in the discipline. It is on these advances that I focus next.

Among the encouraging variety of attempts to more adequately explain the relationship between people and the societies they comprise, there are important commonalities. In general, they do not view social change as an exception nor as the result of the overpowering force of *either* "individuals" *or* "society." The phenomena of interest, rather, are the complex figurations of interdependent relationships. In explicating this approach, I will refer primarily to the works of Norbert Elias, Pierre Bourdieu, and Anthony Giddens. Although there are others that could reasonably be included here, these three have explicitly and systematically worked to illuminate and overcome what they see as sociology's most fundamental problems. My selection should not be taken as an unrestricted endorsement of these authors' works in their entirety, but only as the most expeditious way to present their similarly alternative approaches, thus far little explored. Highlighting common aspects of their respective projects—Elias's *figurational sociology,* Bourdieu's *theory of practice,* and Giddens's *structuration theory*—I hope to convey their meaning and import for social research.

Foundational to the works of Elias, Bourdieu, and Giddens is the claim that the modern Western subject/object dualism is the largest barrier to a clearer understanding of the social (Elias, 1991b: 7; Bourdieu, 1990: 25; Giddens, 1984: xx). An analysis of subject/object dualism provides a context for understanding why sociology thinks like it does and is therefore a necessary reflexive exercise. Elias, Bourdieu, and Giddens are sensitive to how this conceptual heritage influences approaches to social research and, most notably, distorts our understanding of the concepts "individual" and "society." The terms, as they are commonly used, tend to connote not only distinction, but antithesis. This is simply erroneous, for, as Elias points out:

> There is no zero-point of the social relatedness of the individual, no 'beginning' or sharp break when he steps into society as if from outside as a being untouched by the network and then begins to link up with other human beings.... [T]he individual always exists, on the most fundamental level, in relation to others, and this relation has a particular structure specific to his society." (1991a: 27)

The underlying assumption in the proposed framework is that society cannot be understood through the mechanistic study of its components in isolation, because they do not exist or operate in isolation. Talking about things like social structures, individuals, and social classes as if they were real things that have independent existences leads to what Elias calls "process-reduction," the lamentable tendency of science to present what was observed as mobile and changing as something changeless and eternal (1978: 114). The "present forms of sociological analysis make possible the separation of interrelated things into individual components—'variables' or 'factors,'" the relationships of which appear as an afterthought, "tacked on later to intrinsically unrelated and isolated objects" (Elias, 1978: 116). It is necessary to make relations, not independent objects, the point of commencement. A very brief foray into the works of Elias, Bourdieu, and Giddens—and their efforts to elucidate relations, interdependence, and processes through the introduction and use of alternative concepts— conveys the general thrust of relational process theory and its import within the context of the Web and Part/Whole Approach.

Elias uses the concept of *figuration* to refer to the changing pattern created by interdependent participants in activities of exchange. It serves as a tool that not only eases the constraint to think and talk about individual and society as antagonistic, but illuminates other forms of interdependent relations, as well (1978; 1991a). This sort of relational thinking, Bourdieu admits, presents a genuine challenge. It is currently easier for people to think in terms of visible realities than in terms of relations, but this is precisely the type of thinking that must be fostered (1989). Bourdieu's use of the terms *habitus* and *field* make interactive relations of exchange implicit in ways of thinking about people and the various contexts within which they develop. Critical of traditional notions of "structures" improperly viewed as permanent, wholly external to people, and sources of constraint only, Giddens intends to portray structures as also enabling and as continually produced through social action. He emphasizes the recursive character of social life, introducing the notion of *duality of structure* to convey the idea that structural properties of social systems are both the medium and the outcome of the practices they organize. Examining social phenomena from the standpoint of interdependent relations, Elias, Bourdieu, and Giddens make their processual nature more clear.

As Phillips and Johnston (2007) point out, the complexity of sociological analyses has been limited by the discipline's failure to appreciate all of the dimensions of social life, especially the physical and biological structures that interact with and influence it. In response to what they saw as a glaring paradigmatic flaw, environmental sociology set out to illuminate the discipline's neglect of the environmental context in relation to which societies necessarily exist and develop.

## Environmental Sociology and the Human Exemptionalism Paradigm

Environmental sociology emerged as a critique of the modern Western worldview and the anthropocentrism it encouraged. Its initial aim was to draw attention to the discipline's longstanding Human Exemptionalism Paradigm (HEP) under which humans are viewed as completely distinct from nature and exempt from the natural laws that govern other organisms (Catton and Dunlap, 1978; 1980). Sociology, they argued, tended to focus on cultural factors as the main determinant of societal development and change, while neglecting relevant ecological variables. Environmental sociology was a call for sociologists to recognize the relations, interactions, and processes between human social life and the bio-physical world. In short, it intended to introduce and begin to realize what the pioneering authors called a "New Ecological Paradigm" (NEP).

Emerging out of a reflexive awareness of sociology's limiting paradigm, this movement also focused on the HEP as an important foundation of the modern Western worldview more generally. Not only an academic concern, scholars have identified this distorted worldview as the source of many contemporary "environmental problems" (Benton, 1994; Catton and Dunlap, 1978; 1980; Clark and York, 2005; Dickens, 2004; Foster, 1999;

Freudenburg, et al., 1995; Goldman and Schurman, 2000; and Redclift and Woodgate, 1994). The failure to recognize the essential connections between humans and the wider environment, they argue, has resulted in many unsustainable social practices and to an overwhelming ignorance of their long-term consequences. The general invisibility of the sorts of *socioecological* problems just beginning to come into public focus are largely attributable to this shortsightedness. It would be reasonable to presume that such serious problems might jolt us out of delusions of independence, but this seems not to be the case. The HEP continues to thrive in the United States, apparent in linear systems of consumption and waste, abiding faith in eternal growth, and blatant disregard for the local and global consequences of energy and resource usage.

This is not surprising when we see that even in sociology the concept of human exemptionalism, now thirty years old, remains widely unfamiliar, except within the narrow domain of "environmental sociology." In their analysis of introductory sociology texts published between 2000 and 2003, Lewis and Humphrey find that neither the Human Exemptionalism Paradigm (HEP) nor *any* of what they deem key concepts in environmental sociology are cited (Lewis and Humphrey, 2005: 163–165). A search of the *full text* of all peer-reviewed social science journals in the online database Cambridge Sociological Abstracts turns up only six invocations of the term "human exemptionalism" in American journals (not counting Lewis and Humphrey), all authored by people generally classified as "environmental sociologists."

While there are important works that incorporate the physical- and biological-context dependence of human social life (Lenski, 2005; Massey, 2005; Phillips and Johnston, 2007), the discipline still tends to operate under the outmoded assumptions of the HEP (Beamish, 2002; Dunlap, 1997; Lewis and Humphrey, 2005; and Woodgate, 1997). The persistence of this paradigm continues to limit the apparent relevance of sociology for researching socioecological problems, as well as being at the root of and perpetuating these very problems.

If the social sciences are to play a more important role in better understanding the origins of socioecological problems, then they must develop both the inclination and the means to more effectively examine the ongoing relationships between how people think about their ecological contexts and what they do within them. Environmental sociology complements process sociology by explicitly adding the ecological dimension to the study of social relations. Humans not only exist within interdependent relations with other people, but people and their societies are inextricably connected with the ecosystems on which they depend and with which they are always engaged in mutually influencing processes. Making sociology more relevant to the study of some of today's most serious problems requires a greater openness between specialized fields of inquiry and an integration of the knowledge developed within these fields and within other disciplines. In what follows, I introduce the notion of *ecological habitus,* the product of combining attention to relational processes and the inclusion of society's ecological contexts. Before discussing its meaning and usefulness in research, however, I must first discuss the concept from which it derives: *habitus.*

## Habitus

Habitus is an alternative to the troubled concepts individual and society, where the former is isolated from and in opposition to, but mysteriously part of the latter. Bourdieu and Elias employ the concept of habitus to pull us out of that thought trap and to highlight the *social* nature of what *appear* to be purely individual characteristics. Habitus is a conceptual tool that enables us to more accurately view people as beings in social relationships in which the ongoing interactive processes of creation, maintenance, and change are implicit. Described as "social personality structure" (Elias, 1991a: 201) and "socialized subjectivity" (Bourdieu and Wacquant, 1992: 126), one cannot conceive of habitus as an independent entity as one *can* presently do with the concept of individual. Habitus only makes sense in relation to the unique combination of contexts in which it continuously develops and acts. Although it solidifies with age, "habitus never ceases entirely to be affected by his changing relations with others throughout his life" (Elias, 2000: 377). "An *open system of dispositions,*" habitus "is constantly subjected to experiences, and therefore constantly affected by them in a way that either reinforces or modifies its structures" (Bourdieu and Wacquant, 1992: 133). This "system of dispositions"— somewhat stable and yet always open to change—is what provides the sense of continuity and stability in society for which neither objectivism nor subjectivism alone can account (Bourdieu, 1990: 54). The concept of habitus reflects the dynamic *duality of structure* (different from dualism), where structure is understood as not "external" to people, but as the rules, resources, and sets of relations that have been internalized to some extent—although they can also "stretch away" in time and space beyond the control of individual actors—and is both constraining and enabling (Giddens, 1984: 25-28). Given the linguistic limitations that inspired the notion of habitus in the first place, it should not be surprising that habitus can be difficult to define in concise terms.

Bourdieu describes the habitus as "the durable and transposable systems of schemata of perception, appreciation, and action that result from the institution of the social in the body" (Bourdieu and Wacquant, 1992: 126-127). Elsewhere, he explains that habitus is a structuring structure and a structured structure (1984:170). It is a "structure" because it is a perceptible system of dispositions, resulting from the entire set of conditions in the experience of a life. It is "structured" in that it enters into and develops within preexisting systems of value, meaning, stratification, resource distribution, and so on, and internalizes—to a greater or lesser degree—these through active socialization processes and practices. Habitus is "structuring" because it always participates in the maintenance, change, elimination, or creation of these systems via perceptions and practices in everyday life.

The point of habitus is to provide a term with which to reference the proper object of social science: neither individuals nor groups, but "the *relation between two realizations of historical action,* in bodies and in things" (Bourdieu and Wacquant, 1992: 126). In everyday language, we might more easily think of habitus, as Elias does, as "second nature," which seems to be innate in a person, but is actually embedded in and developing out of social and physical contexts (1991a; 1996). Social class and its manifestation as lifestyle, for instance, appear and are often mistaken for an expression of characteristics inherent to a person or group. Bourdieu uses habitus to demonstrate the processual nature of social class. He is interested in how "the practices engendered by the different habitus appear as systematic configurations of properties expressing the differences objectively inscribed in conditions of existence in the form of systems of differential deviations which, when perceived by agents endowed with the schemes of perception and appreciation necessary in order to identify, interpret, and evaluate their pertinent features, function as lifestyles" (Bourdieu, 1984: 170). In other words, not being able to see or account for the countless conditions that influence the development of one's habits, standards, preferences, and tastes, people take these sets of characteristics to be somehow automatically associable with identifiable social categories.

Likewise, Elias uses the concept of habitus "to overcome the problems of the old notion of 'national character' as something fixed and static" (1996: ix). He compares social habitus to language, describing it as "both hard and tough, but also flexible and far from immutable. It is, in fact, always in flux" (Elias, 1991a: 209). "A process-sociological study, and a familiarity with the investigation of long-term processes," Elias argues, "are needed to explain the differences of individual habitus" in different regions, nations, and cultures (1991a: 210). Attuned to the processes of social stability and change, he identifies a peculiar type of habitus problem that is poorly understood: the "drag effect." He describes a situation in which the dynamic of social development processes is tending to advance beyond a given stage toward another within which the people affected by these changes "cling to the earlier stage in their personality structure, their social habitus" (1991a: 211). Whether, and how quickly, these processes bring about a more or less radical restructuring of this habitus—or whether the social habitus of individuals slows down or blocks this dynamic—depends on the relative strength of the social shift and the deep-rootedness of the habitus. It is only through the constellation of these circumstances that a society is significantly transformed (1991a).

Habitus sidesteps the dilemmas of the old "structure versus agency" debate; it expresses both the *necessity* and *freedom* in the human condition. Bourdieu maintains that it was developed to destroy the circular and mechanical models that assume that structures produce individuals through whose practices structure is reproduced. "Social agents are determined only to the extent that they determine themselves," Bourdieu argues (Bourdieu and Wacquant, 1992: 136). Stated differently, the social field only exerts influences on habitus through relations undertaken by social agents as self-conscious and practical beings. To avoid overstatement, it must also be added that such beings (i.e., us) operate via varying levels of discursive and practical consciousness, as well as unconscious motivations and cognitions (Giddens, 1984: 7). People are always exercising agency through life practices, but it is not always in ways that are intended, explainable, or well understood.

The concept of habitus is an important advancement in the understanding of social processes; it widens our scope beyond the focus on specific variables whose "effects" are to be studied in isolation, and it forces us to acknowledge the continuous flow of simultaneous and mutual influence between people and their contexts. While the concept does not necessarily exclude ecological factors, neither are they obvious, especially given sociology's history of operating under the human exemptionalism paradigm. The concept of habitus, I argue, is particularly useful for exploring socioecological phenomena. I introduce the concept of *ecological habitus* (not independent of the overall habitus in reality) as a useful heuristic device for understanding a subset of ecologically relevant characteristics of habitus.

## Ecological Habitus

Currently, it seems that citizens are more likely to identify specific factors in politics, economics, and technology as determinants of current environmental crises than to recognize a more amorphous and durable factor that is produced in concert with them: lifestyle. Long neglected in both sociology and the public arena (no public figure wants to "pull a Jimmy Carter"), lifestyle—and the conditions that generate it as well as the conditions it generates—remains unexamined and therefore relatively unproblematic in U.S. society. Public discourse about environmental problems tends to portray policy change, economic incentives and disincentives, and technological fixes as the only options for dealing with current and potential troubles. Implicit in politicians' (and some of the more popular environmentalists') statements is the assumption that our style of life need not and will not change. There is a powerful tendency for U.S. citizens to see the American way of life (or at least the comfortable version of it) to be somehow preordained and immutable. Replacing Elias's words "single state" with "American lifestyle" in the following passage conveys it well:

> "The compulsion exerted by the social habitus attuned to the [American lifestyle] appears to many people today as so overwhelming and ineluctable that they take it for granted as something inherent in nature, like birth or death. They do not think about it. As a subject of research this habitus and its constraints largely lie fallow. They are part of the reality of social existence. The idea that they could change is regarded as naïve" (1991a: 228).

The truth, of course, is that the lifestyle of any contemporary culture is not inherent in nature but is created by humans within certain biological, social, and ecological circumstances. It can change and inevitably will change as the circumstances surrounding it are transformed. The concept of ecological habitus will help to make the dependent nature of lifestyle—often invisible—visible, along with its causes and consequences. It will also encourage the understanding of lifestyle as not simply a matter of individual choice with ramifications only for the individuals living them, but as the product of practical and interactive relations to socio-ecological contexts (as well as the other contexts within which human life unfolds).

Ecological habitus refers to the embodiment of a *durable yet changeable system of ecologically relevant dispositions, practices, perceptions, and material conditions—perceptible as a lifestyle—that is shaped by and helps to shape socioecological contexts.* Adapting Bourdieu's representation of habitus in *Distinction* (1984: 171), ecological habitus can be effectively depicted by specifying some of the basic terms (see Figure 3.1). By simply adding "ecological" in bold, I indicate the aspects of habitus in which I am interested. For instance, by adjusting the phrase to read "(**ecologically**) classifiable works and practices," I refer to those works and practices that can be classified *on an ecological basis.* (See Figure 3.1.)

Situating the numerous ecologically relevant aspects of habitus on a continuum from, say ecologically supportive to antagonistic, can provide insight into the overall state of one's ecological habitus. I also added an underlying socioecological context to serve as a reminder of the constant presence of this set of influential and influenced conditions, shared by several people at once. The dotted lines around the edges

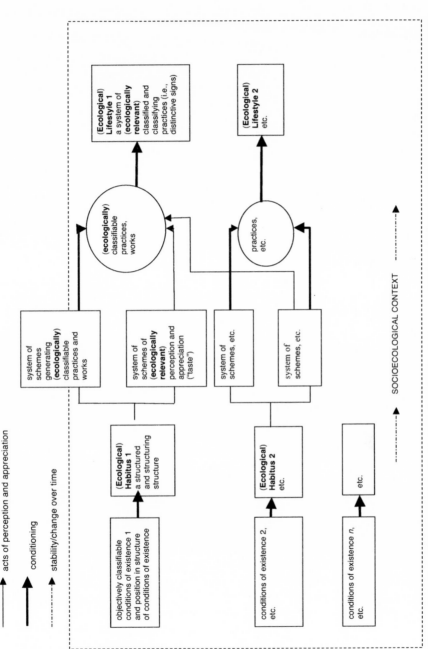

Figure 3.1 Conditions of existence, ecological habitus, and lifestyle (adapted from Bourdieu, 1984: 171)

indicate its openness, that it is one of many identifiable and related contexts in which habitus develops, and the dashed arrows represent the processes of stability and change over time as a result of socioecological interactions.

Returning briefly to the overall theme of the book, I would like to situate ecological habitus in the context of the Web and Part/Whole Approach specifically. In correspondence with the primary goals of this approach, the concept of ecological habitus is intended to: 1) make visible and comprehensible some of the important phenomena contributing to major ecological crises; 2) alert us to the paradigms (both cultural and academic) that affect both these efforts and the status of the ecological crises themselves; 3) clarify the multiple dimensions of human life that contribute to these problems and that will require transformation in attempting to solve them; 4) recognize, employ, and contribute to relevant work in a wider selection of research areas, disregarding the conventional segregation within and between disciplines; and 5) focus on connections and relationships, rather than isolated facts, in exploring and portraying socioecological phenomena.

## Toward Applications of "Ecological Habitus"

The concept of ecological habitus grew out of a recent research project. In response to a mountain of scholarship that calls for paradigm change among academics, I became interested in the more practical question of how a shift from the human exemptionalism paradigm to one in which ecological priorities are integral might occur in societies. I identified ecovillages as communities in the process of realizing such an alternative paradigm and wanted to investigate the theoretical and practical contexts in which they do so. As part of this research I visited eight ecovillages in five eastern U.S. states and participated in an ecovillage design course at an internationally renowned Ecovillage Training Center. I found that ecovillagers exhibited worldviews and practices that, in many ways, are distinctively different from people living in mainstream cities and towns (Kasper, 2008). They exercise an expanded notion of community, one that includes not only the human community, but also the "land community," that is, also the soils, waters, plants, and animals (Leopold, 1949: 204). Moreover, they tended to express an ethical obligation to care for this wider community. Most interesting were the conversations that provided insight into the development of this view and its associated practices. It was clear that community members perceived their paths of ecological enlightenment to be ones of ongoing evolution. Despite a wide range of ecological sensibilities prior to joining, ecovillagers exhibit a distinctively ecological consciousness in what they say and do; that is, they display a certain type of ecological habitus. But *how* did this happen?

Questions like this have long puzzled sociologists; environmental sociological literature is full of studies that attempt to identify and measure the effects of some independent variable, such as "attitudes" or "beliefs," on "environmental behavior." While these works have provided some useful insights into why people behave in certain ways, they tend to focus on the discrete effects of separate variables, remaining unable to contend with the complexity of relational processes among attitudes, beliefs, behaviors, and the various other conditions within which they develop. Simply put, they lack the necessary theoretical and conceptual framework to be able to account for relational processes.

In the ecovillages, I identified a number of ways in which particular worldviews and practices are both consciously and unconsciously encouraged. Explicit community intentions, rules, the physical structure of homes and communities, social interaction practices, and outreach efforts all foster specific ways of thinking about, acting within, and relating to the land community. In complex ways, attitudes, beliefs, and behaviors (among other things) interactively develop within numerous sets of conditions; they cannot be fully understood simply as independent or dependent variables. The result of this interweaving of structures, conditions, and habitus is a distinctive type of ecological habitus: one that thinks about and interacts with its ecosystem, and the larger environment, in supportive ways. Closer study of the sorts of conditions and circumstances that are likely to facilitate the production of certain types of ecological habitus will be increasingly necessary in dealing with socioecological problems. A helpful innovation, then, would be a tool for "measuring" and conveying the overall state of ecological habitus (whether a person or group), but speculation about the nature of such a tool would take us well beyond the scope of this chapter.

## Conclusion

I have discussed two critical movements, elucidating the ways in which relational process theory and environmental sociology are aligned with and complement the Web and Part/Whole Approach and its overarching goal of effecting a paradigm shift. The practical implications of such a paradigm shift are what interest me here, especially the possibilities it creates for sociology to contribute to a better understanding of the world's most pressing socioecological problems. The problems themselves have been identified; it is the processes that underlie them that are not well understood. The abstract concepts and theoretical frameworks presented here—such as figuration, structuration, and human exemptionalism paradigm—are essential for recalibrating our view of the social. More concrete concepts like habitus and ecological habitus can be operationalized and observed in countless ways, thus contributing both to studies of *particular* problems and to our *general* understanding of social processes.

Human societies are inextricably connected to their physical environments. And, whether we are conscious of it or not, human actions always have chains of consequences. The greater the scale of the action—determined in part by population and available technology—the grander the scale of the consequences. As the search for ways to alleviate our growing socioecological problems expands, so does the need for a more adequate understanding of the environmental repercussions of what we do. The state of a person's (or society's) ecological habitus influences everyday behaviors, and thus the consequences of them for the wider world. Strategies that encourage seeing the fuller complexity of human social life are essential steps toward a social science that is more widely deemed socially relevant.

## References

Beamish, Thomas D. 2002. *Silent Spill: The Organization of an Industrial Crisis.* Cambridge, Mass.: MIT Press.

Benton, Ted. 1994. "Biology and Social Theory in the Environmental Debate." In *Social Theory and the Global Environment,* ed. Michael Redclift and Ted Benton. New York: Routledge, 28–50

Bourdieu, Pierre. 1977. *Outline of a Theory of Practice,* trans. Richard Nice. Cambridge: Cambridge Univ. Press.

———. 1984. *Distinction: A Social Critique of the Judgment of Taste,* trans. Richard Nice. Cambridge, Mass: Harvard Univ. Press.

———. 1988. "Vive la Crise!: For Heterodoxy in Social Science." *Theory and Society* 17: 773–787.

———. 1989. "Social Space and Symbolic Power." *Sociological Theory* 7: 14–25.

———. 1990. *The Logic of Practice,* trans. by Richard Nice. Stanford, Calif.: Stanford Univ. Press.

Bourdieu, Pierre, and Loïc Wacquant. 1992. *An Invitation to Reflexive Sociology.* Chicago: Univ. of Chicago Press.

Catton, William R., Jr., and Riley E. Dunlap. 1978. "Environmental Sociology: A New Paradigm." *The American Sociologist* 13: 41–49.

Catton, William. R., Jr., and Riley. E. Dunlap. 1980. "A New Ecological Paradigm for Post-Exuberant Sociology." *American Behavioral Scientist* 24: 15–47.

Dunlap, Riley. 1997. "The Evolution of Environmental Sociology: A Brief History and Assessment of the American Experience." In *The International Handbook of Environmental Sociology,* ed. Michael Redclift and Graham Woodgate. Northampton, Mass.: Edward Elgar, 21–39.

Clark, Brett, and Richard York. 2005. "Carbon Metabolism: Global Capitalism, Climate Change, and the Biospheric Rift." *Theory and Society* 34: 391–428.

Dickens, Peter. 2004. *Society and Nature.* Cambridge: Polity Press.

Elias, Norbert. 1978. *What Is Sociology?* trans. Stephen Mennell and Grace Morrissey with a foreword by Reinhard Bendix. New York: Columbia Univ. Press.

———. 1987. *Involvement and Detachment,* ed. Michael Schröter and trans. Edmund Jephcott. Cambridge: Basil Blackwell.

———. 1991a. *The Society of Individuals,* ed. Michael Schröter and trans. Edmund Jephcott. Cambridge: Basil Blackwell.

———. 1991b. *The Symbol Theory,* ed. with an intro. by Richard Kilminster. London: Sage Publications.

———. 1996. *The Germans: Power Struggles and the Development of Habitus in the Nineteenth and Twentieth Centuries,* trans. and pref. by Eric Dunning and Stephen Mennel. New York: Columbia University Press.

———. 1998. *On Civilization, Power, and Knowledge,* ed. and intro by Stephen Mennell and Johan Goudsblom. Chicago and London: University of Chicago Press.

———. 2000. *The Civilizing Process: Sociogenetic and Psychogenetic Investigations,* trans. Edmund Jephcott, ed. Eric Dunning, Johan Goudsblom, and Stephen Mennell. Malden, Mass.: Blackwell Publishers.

Elliot, Anthony, ed. 1999. *Contemporary Social Theory.* Oxford: Blackwell Publishers.

Endter-Wada, Joanna, Dale Blahna, Richard Krannich, and Mark Brunson. 1998. "A Framework for Understanding Social Science Contributions to Ecosystem Management." *Ecological Applications* 8: 891–904.

Foster, John Bellamy. 1999. "Marx's Theory of Metabolic Rift: Classical Foundations for Environmental Sociology." *American Journal of Sociology* 105: 366–405.

Freudenburg, William R., Scott Frickel, and Robert Gramling. 1995. "Beyond the Nature/Society Divide: Learning to Think about a Mountain." *Sociological Forum* 10: 361–392.

Giddens, Anthony. 1976. *New Rules of Sociological Method.* New York: Basic Books.

———. 1979. *Central Problems in Social Theory.* Berkeley: Univ. of California Press.

———. 1984. *The Constitution of Society: Outline of the Theory of Structuration.* Berkeley: Univ. of California Press.

———. 1987. *Social Theory and Modern Sociology.* Stanford, Calif.: Stanford Univ. Press.

Goldman, Michael, and Rachel A. Schurman. 2000. "Closing the 'Great Divide': New Social Theory on Society and Nature." *Annual Review of Sociology* 26: 563–584.

Kasper, Debbie Van Schyndel. 2008. "Redefining Community in the Ecovillage." *Human Ecology Review* 15: 12–24.

Lenski, Gerhard. 2005. *Ecological-Evolutionary Theory.* Boulder, Colo.: Paradigm Publishers.

Leopold, Aldo. 1949. *The Sand County Almanac: And Sketches Here and There.* Oxford: Oxford Univ. Press.

Lewis, Tammy, and Craig Humphrey. 2005. "Sociology and the Environment: An Analysis of Coverage in Introductory Sociology Textbooks." *Teaching Sociology* 33: 154–169.

Massey, Douglas S. 2005. *Strangers in a Strange Land.* New York: W.W. Norton and Company.

Mills, C. Wright. 1959. *The Sociological Imagination.* New York: Oxford University Press.

Phillips, Bernard. 2001. *Beyond Sociology's Tower of Babel.* New York: Aldine de Gruyter.

Phillips, Bernard, Harold Kincaid, and Thomas J. Scheff, eds. 2002. University Press of America, Inc.

Phillips, Bernard, and Louis C. Johnston. 2007. *The Invisible Crisis of Contemporary Society.* Boulder, Colo.: Paradigm Publishers.

Redclift, Michael, and Graham Woodgate. 1994. "Sociology and the Environment: Discordant Discourse?" In *Social Theory and the Global Environment,* ed. Michael Redclift and Graham Woodgate. London and New York: Routledge, 51–66.

Sewell, William H., Jr. 1992. "A Theory of Structure: Duality, Agency, and Transformation." *American Journal of Sociology* 98: 1–29.

Woodgate, Graham. 1997. "Introduction." In *The International Handbook of Environmental Sociology.* Ed. Michael Redclift and Graham Woodgate. Northampton, Mass.: Edward Elgar, 1–21.

# CHAPTER 4

# C. Wright Mills and Education

*J. I. (Hans) Bakker*

> *Gnothi seauton!* (Greek for "Know thyself!")
> Educating was originally and fully focused on matters of gnosis.
> *(Davis, 2004, as cited by Upitis, 2003: 2)*

> In ancient Greek thought, gnosis emerges as a word to suggest a special or hidden kind of knowledge—but Greek philosophers do not establish a rigid distinction between gnosis and episteme.
> *(Paranjape, 2002: 3)*

## Introduction

IN ORDER TO SET THE STAGE, Mills (1959) is briefly reviewed following the introduction and the outlining of the chapter's key idea.[1] His discussion of the craftsmanship involved in utilizing the sociological imagination is based on an intuitive grasp of sociology as a calling.

Next, that sense of craftsmanship is then applied to education in the social sciences and history. There are at least eight major teaching options (Davis, 2004) and Mills's approach tends to be more metaphysical and intuitive than scientific. For Mills, the mature scholar is an independent thinker and public intellectual, but not a positivist scientist.

From this application to education in the social sciences and history, the idea is extended to education more generally, with some thoughts on the education of body and spirit as well as mind. The "new sociological imagination" requires moving beyond certain limitations in Mills's way of thinking about our discipline. Previous discussions of the idea have not been adequate (Fuller, 2006).

## Key Idea

The key idea in this chapter is that a web approach requires us to be open to the complex interrelatedness of various kinds of knowledge and learning. Hence, while C. Wright Mills is in some ways a model for pedagogy, we should also be aware of some of the limitations of Mills's rhetorical dismissal of abstracted empiricism (AE) and grand theory (GT). A combined Web and Part/Whole Approach can encompass not only an expanded version of Mills's sociological imagination but also that which is valuable in empirical research and theoretical speculation.

One such structure is dichotomy. Dichotomization is separation into two parts (Greek *dikha* + *tomie,* two parts). One example would be "black" versus "white." Most Aristotelian-based logic and Enlightenment science tends to be based on dichotomies. Something either is A or it is not (not A).

The other structure of thinking is weblike. The key to the web approach is to examine ideas as having many linkages. It is a more "ecological" or "evolutionary" approach that involves looking at the ways in which ideas branch out over time. The simplified form of the web approach to thinking involves bifurcation. The term is derived from the Latin (*bi + furca*) and means "two-pronged" or "forked." In other words, the simplest web is a fork in the road. But a web involves not just one fork; it involves many forks, like the branches on a tree.

The key difference between a web-bifurcation approach and a dichotomized approach is that dichotomies tend to appear to come out of nowhere, while a web or bifurcation involves paying attention to interlinkages. At the very least, if we have a fork in the road we know where we have come from; we know the path that led us to that split. The two prongs are not simply polarities in some kind of absolute "space." As the saying goes, if you come to a fork in the road, take it! But when you take it you know where you have taken it, and (usually) why. Even if it was just a whim (like tossing a coin), you know a reason why that particular choice was made. It is concretely situated.

Therefore, after having briefly reviewed C. Wright Mills's polar opposition between AE and GT in this chapter, I will move on to Mills's stress on the importance of craftsmanship in education in sociology. This section examines Mills's ideas in terms of their more general relevance, not just for sociology and other social sciences but also for all disciplines.

## Mills's Sociological Imagination:

When Charles Wright Mills (1916–1962) put out his famous book *The Sociological Imagination* in 1959, he had already published seven books. He also had published two major "classic" articles (Mills 1940; 1943) when he was still a graduate student. Two of his books were coauthored with Hans H. Gerth. The Gerth and Mills (1946) volume is frequently cited by those who wish to cite Max Weber, and it is clear that some of Weber's ideas concerning "domination" (*Herrschaft*) influenced Mills significantly. However, the Gerth and Mills book published in 1953, *Character and Social Structure,* is not nearly as famous or widely read and cited today as the 1946 book. *The* Gerth and Mills (1946) book is the Weber volume. The translations would have been mainly done by Gerth since Mills does not do any further scholarly work involving translation from German into English. Mills's three most famous single-authored books are *The New Men of Power* (1948), *White Collar* (1951), and *The Power Elite* (1956). They examine labor leaders, the new middle class, and the elite.

Since Mills died early, at age forty-two, he did not leave a large number of additional works after *The Sociological Imagination* came out. (He died in 1962, and the book was published in 1959). Randall Collins calls *The Sociological Imagination* Mills's "most important contribution" (Collins and Makowsky, 1998: 238). But that judgment could be challenged. It *is* his definitive statement on the nature of theory and methodology. Even if he had lived to a ripe old age, it is not likely that he would have significantly modified the views expressed in that succinct (234 page) book. It does present his views on the "craft" of sociology. But it is more of a work of polemic than a balanced assessment of others' views. Mills was in some ways a "utopian" thinker (Horowitz, 1983), an American variant of Ancient Greek thinkers like Plato. His progressive, radical ideology was based on an intuition of justice and not necessarily a carefully thought out philosophy.

Perhaps most carefully read by graduate students of my generation (the 1960s Vietnam War era "baby boomer" generation) were chapters 1, 2 and 3. Also frequently consulted by students writing a thesis was "Appendix" on "Intellectual Craftsmanship." But it is highly likely that many students did not have time to really read Chapters 4–10 carefully. It may have been different in another era, but I doubt it. In fact, it is highly likely that today Mills's famous book is more frequently cited than read. Everyone has heard of his famous argument that "personal troubles are public issues." It even became a rallying cry for the Feminist Movement of the 1970s (i.e., "the personal is political"). But one can question to what extent Mills's caustic and strident arguments concerning Parsons and Lazarsfeld, and their students, served for serious intellectual debate.

I will briefly review the main thrust of the book for those who may never have actually read it or who may have read it so long ago that the main thesis has been somewhat forgotten. The principal contention that Mills presents is that sociology as a discipline was suffering from two evils. He labeled those two destructive tendencies "Grand Theory" (GT) and "Abstracted Empiricism" (AE). He did not utilize those words in any kind of neutral manner. Instead, they are terms of derision. Mills uses the two labels in a thoroughly rhetorical manner. He has nothing good to say about either GT or AE. They are thoroughly misleading ways to do sociology and social science generally. A student who is sucked into either GT or AE is likely to go off the right path and never find his way back again.

I say "his" because Mills wrote in the late 1950s when the idea of giving equal voice to women had not yet become fully integrated. Mills, who rode a motorcycle to work at Columbia University in New York City, was a man's man, at least on paper. He reminds me a bit of Norman Mailer, but also of the Beat Poets. He does not attempt to integrate the Feminist Revolution in his writing style. His prose is Hemingwayesque. Sociology is a man's discipline, and a man who wants to become a sociologist should regard it as a kind of heroic journey of discovery. The GT or AE routes are not recommended. They in fact are viewed by Mills as inferior and likely to lead one astray altogether. Most sociologists today are vaguely aware of this, but they nevertheless tend to use the terms "grand theory" and "abstracted empiricism"—if they use them at all—in somewhat softened ways. They become more like heuristic Ideal Types (or, Ideal Type Models) than rhetorical labels. But Mills did not attempt to be neutral about them. He used them as terms of derision, and he did not pull any punches in his mockery of them. That is part of the reason the book caught on.

Who could resist Mills's famous chapter 2 on "Grand Theory" where he "translates" the words of Talcott Parsons? Few graduate students had sufficient sophistication to be able to refute the one-sided attack on Parsons's theory. He does say: "In this translation, I must admit, I have not been altogether faithful; I have helped out a little because these are very good ideas" (Mills, 1959: 29). But the impression left on most readers is that most of what Parsons wrote was unnecessarily verbose and could easily be distilled into ideas that are found in many textbooks. For those of us who struggled with Parsons's prose and attempted to make sense of the various subtle shifts in emphasis in Parsons's architectonic system,

Mills's "translation" felt like a breath of fresh air. He suggests that "... one could translate the 555 pages of *The Social System* into about 150 pages of straightforward English," and "The result would not be very impressive" (Mills, 1959: 21). There is certainly a grain of truth in the assertion that a précis of Parsons's books would serve a useful purpose.

However, what is missing from Mills's analysis of "Grand Theory" (GT) is any attempt to apply some of the same rhetorical techniques to some of the classical social and sociological theorists: Kant, Hegel, Nietzsche, Marx, Max Weber, Simmel, Pareto, Durkheim, Mead, DuBois, Addams, Nightingale, Martineau, Marianne Weber, and so forth. The one and only example of the excesses of GT is Parsons. So, Mills is not entirely fair. He cites Franz Neumann's (1942) *Behemoth* as an example of how to do it right; but, Neumann's analysis has not been all that influential in sociological theory. It is an excellent historically based analysis of the financing of the National Socialist (Nazi) Party, but it is mostly known by specialists. Few sociologists would list Neumann as a leading classical sociological theorist, even though his work is cited by authors like Barrington Moore Jr.

Indeed, when Mills chooses his heroes he chooses some of the better known classical sociological theorists. But he never makes that more sophisticated argument that at times Marx, Weber, and Durkheim are just as obscure as Parsons. Marx's *Capital* (volumes I, II, and III) and *Theories of Surplus Value* (volumes I, II and III) are often summarized in one short volume. Weber's *Economy and Society* (1968/1920) consists of two major parts, with part II actually the one that was written first and with part I sometimes contradicting part II. Durkheim is often quite straightforward in his writing style, but it would be possible to summarize the central thrust of *The Elementary Forms of Religious Life* (1995/1912) in one short paper. Mills does not bother to point any of that out. Hence, the confusion which still exists as to exactly what the term grand theory is supposed to mean. In this chapter, I will always use the term as Mills uses it, hence it will frequently be symbolized by the use of GT. Mills's GT is not the final word on the general concept of higher levels of abstraction in theory. Indeed, one basic aspect of the combined Web and Part/Whole Approach is the explicit understanding that the highest level of abstraction may include the Whole and may, therefore, not always be immediately reducible to simple commonsense, everyday-life prose. The term GT is a rhetorical label. It is "the Other" in Mills's schema. As such it serves a useful purpose if, and only if, we can accept Mills's positive statement of belief in "Classical Theory."

The additional "Other" for Mills is "Abstracted Empiricism" (AE). He makes it perfectly clear that anyone who does AE is likely to be too enamored with the techniques ("method" in the narrow sense). He is particularly strong in his opposition to those who are the second generation AE researchers. While the originators, particularly Paul Lazarsfeld, may have a wide education and a genuine understanding of what they are leaving out in their utilization of reductionistic scientific techniques, the average graduate student utilizing cross-tabulation or regression of secondary data frequently does not have that wider grasp. Being a GT is bad because it means speculating in arbitrary ways and creating numerous pigeon holes that have little or no relationship to any empirical information. But being an AE is even worse because it requires hardly any sophistication about the pressing concerns of sociology as a discipline. The average AE researcher is more interested in solving little puzzles than in really grappling with important topics. It is a routinized and bureaucratized way of doing sociology. It results in "public opinion" polls which are only one step removed from advertising, according to Mills (1959: 51). The procedures can be learned with ease, but the use of such techniques simply results in research that has no relevance whatsoever to the sociological imagination as Mills conceives of it. Like Grand Theory, Abstracted Empiricism is mainly useful for ideological purposes. It has no "critical" component. Mills is not happy with Samuel Stouffer's four volumes (See, for example, Stouffer et al., 1949) on the U.S. military during World War II and much prefers studies such as Alfred Vagts's *History of Militarism*. (Of course, today no one in sociology reads Vagts; but, every textbook mentions Stouffer's study as a breakthrough work.) Mills is particularly concerned with the way in which AE tends to be an approach to sociology that requires a large team of researchers and an administrative apparatus to keep things organized. He favors the single researcher who is both theorist and methodologist. That is, Mills favors the kind of work that, by and large, he himself did, and which made him famous. (Presumably he might also have liked Erving Goffman's insightful work for the same reason, since Goffman did all his research more or less by himself, but Goffman is never cited by Mills.)

In chapter 6 on "Philosophies of Science" Mills returns to his dichotomy and examines AE in terms of the implicit positivism or natural science orientation to epistemology that AE tends to utilize. He points out that, in his opinion, it is not too difficult to get all of the different styles of social science together if we merely consider the problem from a very abstract "philosophical" perspective. But, he states, "... the pertinent question is: suppose we do 'get them together' in one or another grand model of inquiry—of what use is such a model for work in social science, for the handling of its leading tasks?" (Mills, 1959: 119–120). It is his clear intention that it should be the leading tasks that should dictate the way in which we do sociology and not any abstracted philosophy of science. The leading tasks, according to Mills, do not get done using either GT or AE. Instead, what is required is a genuine sense of craftsmanship.

Note that Mills's rhetorical style is a dichotomization between AE and GT. He does not discuss those two abstractions as part of a web, or even as a matter of a branching. He thoroughly rejects both. But he does not as fully develop the third alternative, which he labels the sociological imagination. The sociological imagination, as discussed by Mills, is to a large extent a reliance on intuitive knowing. It is a form of gnosis. I will discuss the spirit of his key idea in terms of a more refined understanding of "Gnosticism" (King, 2004) and that will lead into a fuller conceptualization of education and the body, particularly in terms of *hatha* yoga, gymnastics, calisthenics, and athletics. That is, if Mills is to be taken seriously then we have to view the sociological imagination in Socratic terms and situate Greek philosophy historically. I will not attempt to do that in any complete fashion here. But I do want to point out that Mills presents only a part of the picture. He does not utilize a fully "web-based" approach. I conclude that the synthesized Part/Whole and Web Approach can help to lead to a pedagogy that will emphasize the integration of mind, body, and spirit. A fully integrated approach to teaching requires awareness of all eight of the models of teaching and education that Davis (2004) discusses. Any pedagogy that is restricted to merely one of those eight styles is bound to be unnecessarily restrictive.

I wish to make the fundamental point that Mills's book is largely polemical and therefore does not serve as a complete analysis of what the sociological imagination is or can become. A more complete understanding requires a combined Web and Part/Whole Approach to a pedagogy directed at more than just sole authored Classical Theory and Methods and more than just "the mind" by itself. Just as it requires a web approach to understand Mills's implicit pedagogy, it also requires a Web and Part/Whole Approach to be able to move beyond Mills's limitations to a broader vision.

## Education

While not based directly on Brent Davis's (2004) *Inventions of Teaching: Genealogy,* I nevertheless feel in retrospect that Davis's book is a good way to frame what I am trying to clarify. I will not try to summarize the details of his book here. I will merely provide a very brief overview. Davis, holder of a "Canada Research Chair" in Mathematics Education and the Ecology of Learning at the University of Alberta, Edmonton, makes a crucial distinction between two basic "structures of thinking."

Davis's (2004) ingenious discussion of metaphors of teaching looks at two major forks in the road: Metaphysical and Physical thinking. If we choose the Metaphysical path then we are led to teaching as based on epistemologies of gnosis or episteme. If we choose the Physical path then we are led to a model of teaching that emphasizes intersubjectivity or interobjectivity. Those four branches have further subbranches. The main options that Davis (2004) presents are that teaching can mainly be about:

1. Drawing out
2. Drawing in
3. Instructing
4. Training
5. Facilitating
6. Empowering
7. Occasioning
8. Conversing

He makes it very clear that his approach to models of teaching is not an exhaustive or all-inclusive typology. "A better model [of the models] to illustrate the crossing and recrossings of sensibilities would be something more weblike" (Davis, 2004: 5). He chooses to ignore the finer branches. But his general model of teaching allows me to make a generalization about C. Wright Mills and teaching.

I believe that Mills's (1959) *The Sociological Imagination* tends to argue implicitly in favor of a model of education that is ultimately a metaphysical one. Moreover, I think that Mills was mainly interested in teaching as a form of "Drawing Out." That is, he wanted to get students to rely on their intuitive understanding. To put it in one word, Mills advocates the goal that the Greek philosophers refer to as *gnosis*. The term is difficult to translate. At the conclusion of this chapter, I hope to have made it clear why I believe that Mills is ultimately a great deal more like Socrates, who is reported to have said, "Know Thyself!" (*gnothi seauton*). Mills's "Socratic" approach to knowledge is both his strength and his weakness. We can get an appreciation for the way in which Mills's emphasis on intuitive knowledge is interconnected with other forms of knowledge—and of teaching—if we do not think in terms of simple dichotomies but instead focus on branches of the complex web that was American social science in the 1950s. A web approach will reveal more about Mills's implicit pedagogy than a more linear approach.

## Education for Body, Mind, and Spirit

To some extent that broader vision of teaching would involve all eight of the teaching strategies that Davis (2004) discusses. Mills was not a narrow thinker, and he had a broad understanding of many things. It would be incorrect to try to pin a label on him. He takes up many arguments and is quite multifaceted in his approach. There are hints of this throughout his books. Mills deserves great credit for making the phrase "the sociological imagination" a part of every sociologist's vocabulary, but we should not simply take his arguments in favor of *his version* of the sociological imagination at face value. I will, therefore, contrast Mills's Sociological Imagination (SI) with a more inclusive Web orientation to the sociological imagination *writ large*.

If we do not simply accept Mills's statements at face value but extract from his classic book that which is of lasting value—somewhat in the same way as Croce tried to distill Hegel—then we find an enthusiastic argument in favor of a sociological imagination that is not merely a matter of using one's analytical skills. Sociology, for Mills, is not just a cognitive task, a limited bureaucratic role. It is not a nine to five job. For Mills it is a calling. The word "calling" (Weber's *Beruf*) does not appear in the Index. But it seems clear enough that for Mills there is almost a religious significance to being a social scientist. He caustically derides all those who would approach research as merely a matter of applying existing techniques. Part of the reason the book caught on with so many graduate students of my generation in the 1960s was precisely that it severely criticized the very things we were so painfully required to learn: nonparametric statistical tests, regression analysis, factor analysis, and other such techniques. They were *de rigueur*. You could not be a sociologist without those tools in your backpack. Seemingly the only way out was to either become a "theorist" (i.e., know a lot about the history of classical theory) or opt for cultural/social anthropology (where quantitative methods were less emphasized in those days).

Many of us did accept the idea of sociology as a calling. After all, we could almost as easily have become something else. We could have studied any of the humanistic disciplines, like philosophy, or art history. We could have studied one of the professions, like medicine, law, or library science. There were many avenues open to the better-than-average students of sociology in the 1960s in North America and Europe. But we chose sociology. If we did not choose it in order to do AE or GT, then we often chose it in order to do some kind of sociological-imagination-based sociology. I myself was not interested in being a technician. Indeed, when I had the opportunity to specialize in urban planning and architecture, I returned to general sociology. I wanted to pursue the sociological imagination. It is somewhat surprising to me that I really have managed to support myself and my family while still always engaged in the pursuit of that calling.

While there is much that is rewarding about pursuing social science as a calling, it is not always easy to strive to fulfill the sociological imagination. Even if one were to restrict one's attention simply to the sociological imagination in the stereotypical fashion that Mills sometimes reverts to, it would not be easy. But to strive to broaden the sociological imagination even beyond the point that Mills was able to reach is quite challenging. Yet it is a challenge that is worth it. It may be easier to get tenure or promotion by pursuing AE, or even GT (in certain specialized circumstances), the lasting value of striving for the ideal of the sociological imagination is that it makes one's life better.

I wish to illustrate that by one example from my personal experience as a university professor and "teacher." I will start with the example of being a yoga teacher. Then I will use that example to discuss two recent ways in which I learned more about the integration of body and spirit with mind.

I became a yoga teacher almost accidentally as a result of volunteering one summer at a yoga camp, the Sivananda Yoga Centre in Val Morin, Quebec. There are many Sivananda ashrams around the world, but the one situated in the Mont Tremblanc area north of Montreal is where I spent the summer of 1987–88. My son was seven years old and as a "single parent" I wanted to find a way to be able to spend the summer with him that would be productive. A friend suggested I become a camp counselor. My son was allowed to participate in the kids' camp for free. After the kids' camp was over I continued on. I loved the work out doors in the fresh mountain air. Although there were minor irritations, by and large the summer was a great introduction to intense yoga, and by teaching the children yoga I had my first opportunity to teach yoga. I eventually chose to get certification. My "diploma" is from Kripalu Yoga Center in the Berkshires in Massachusetts. It took a month of hard work to get that recognition, but it was one of the best months of my life. I did yoga at least twice a day and at the end I felt physically fit and mentally alert. During the ten-year 1995–2005 period, I taught yoga in a variety of settings, albeit with several interruptions. Teaching yoga exercises (*asanas*) and breathing (*pranayamas*) has made me a much better academic teacher. Yet I did not initially start with yoga as part of a plan to improve my academic teaching. For a long time the two seemed completely separate.

One of the key things I learned about teaching as a result of teaching yoga is that it is very important to "walk the talk." On those days that I clearly had not been keeping up with the stretches and the breathing, I did what I myself considered a lousy job. I could fool some of the students some of the time, but it was quite apparent to me when I was not really doing my best. I had to be physically involved, even if I did not do each and every posture along with the students every time. Moreover, I had to have the right mind set. I have tried to take that into the academic classroom. I have become more aware that it is not just a matter of saying the words. One has to use the "yogic imagination" and come up with ways of "language-ing" the postures that are personally meaningful. For example, it is one thing to go through the motions when teaching the mountain pose and it is quite another to have really felt that mountain pose. If I really have experienced a posture or stretch, then I can teach it. If I cannot get into a posture, I cannot teach it in a way that is really meaningful to most students. (I will probably never be able to teach the scorpion; it is too hard for me to do!) The best teachers of yoga are people who have really had the experience in a personally meaningful way.

Much the same is true of academic teaching in the classroom. Once, when returning from a conference in Vancouver, British Columbia, I gave a very spontaneous and unrehearsed lecture on social stratification. I grasped the significance of the West Coast Native People's symbolic art forms and utilized some Salish and Kwakiutl designs to illustrate the basic notion of "semiosis," the process of communication through signs. I had been lecturing about semiotics and signs for many weeks, but it was only when I fully got into the lecture body, mind, and spirit that I saw some faces light up in the back row. Some of the students had probably understood me before, but that day suddenly a large number of students who had been somewhat apathetic showed a real interest. I linked semiotics to the ways in which genderism, sexism, classism, racism, and all forms of the "idols of tribe" (Francis Bacon) get reified. The idea of "reification" through "symbols" became somewhat more tangible to the students. I never quite recaptured the spontaneity of that lecture when I would repeat some parts of it in other settings, but I was "on a roll" that day.

One of the main reasons that there is a discipline called sociology is because the Industrial and Agricultural Revolutions of the 18th century greatly transformed Europe. The United States Constitution of 1783 is based in large part on the European Enlightenment traditions that were formulated by French, German, and British thinkers in the 18th century. Now the United States still tries to uphold those Enlightenment beliefs to some extent, but there is considerable political confusion. The Jeffersonian ideals have become largely just a memory as agriculture has become the main occupation of less than 3 percent of the population. The yeoman "family farmer" of the 18th century exists largely in the imagination of writers like Wendell Berry and not in everyday reality in Iowa or Missouri. There are a few real family farms left in Vermont and Idaho, but by and large agribusiness has taken over. This is not the place to launch into an extended discussion of the ways in which the United States of the 21st century could not possibly have been imagined by the founders in the 18th century, but clearly much has changed.

Yet what has not changed about the United States (and Canada) is an optimistic sense of open opportunity. The reality, as indicated very well by C. Wright Mills (1951; 1956) may be quite different. But the "American Dream" remains. That is a dream of individual human dignity and worth. The current political and economic climate is one of deep division in part because many people disagree fundamentally as to how best to accomplish that dream. For some it requires going back to fundamental spiritual values. For others it requires changing with the times. But regardless of whether an American citizen lives in a so-called blue or red state, or in a state which some may regard as a "purple" mixture, the goal is much the same. The struggle is about means and not ends. Do we stay with the Protestant Ethic and the Puritan version of the city on the hill? Or do we move to a new age ethic and a postmodern version of the city on the hill? Do we radically conserve or do we radically change?

There are no easy answers. But one thing is clear. Sociology is a discipline well situated to provide detailed theoretical and empirically based analyses of the specifics of the overall problem of stratification and the general direction of history. The ability to move along the "ladder of abstraction" from the most "grand" theories (i.e., not GT in the narrow sense) to the most "empirical" bits of data (i.e., not AE in the narrow sense) is absolutely fundamental. We can build on Mills's vision of a sociological imagination and construct a new and improved version, one that takes into account the importance of a Web Approach (Phillips, 2001) and the significance of a Part/Whole Approach (Scheff, 1997). The *combined* Web and Part/Whole Approach can be a general sociological approach that will help to provide more cogent and useful answers.

One key aspect of that new vision of a city on the hill is to be able to see that terms used to characterize "the other side" are almost always simplistic and always misleading. King (2004: 1-9) asks: "Why is Gnosticism so hard to define?" Her answer is that even the best scholars have used the term in such a way as to obscure its theoretical and historical significance. It never was and never will be a specific "thing" or "historical entity." It never had a single origin and never had distinctive boundaries, despite Adolf von Harnack's excellent work. That did not surprise me. Having read Randall Collins and Michael Makowsky's (1998) masterful book on "philosophies" I fully appreciate that all of the labels we use (e.g., "Buddhism") tend to be reifications. Why should Gnosticism be any different? But what did really surprise me was that King also argues quite cogently that the typological approach associated with Hans Jonas and the demythologizing method of Rudolf Bultmann are also not necessarily heuristic.

It is clear that Mills did not approach his discussion of the sociological imagination in order to discover something new. He had settled convictions. He believed in his intuitive judgments. Like a lawyer making a brief, he wanted to convince the jury, his academic peers, as well as the educated nonspecialist. Mills wrote as a public intellectual who was concerned with academic research bureaucratization (AE) and with empty theorizing based simply on logical pigeon holes (GT). He recommended an alternative he called the sociological imagination. But we do not have to accept *his* definition of that phrase. Instead, if we are truly seeking to build a general sociology that overcomes the unnecessary degree of superspecialization that exists today, we can build on Mills to refine the idea of a sociological imagination. The situation has changed since the 1950s.

We need to be able to visualize both a discipline and an object of study that will make sociology more cogent and more practical. The vision has been opened up by thinkers like Bernard Phillips, Thomas Scheff, and Harold Kincaid. But each of us can contribute to it in our own way, utilizing our own sociological imagination. The cumulative effect could be quite significant. Heaven knows there is a crying need for the kind of "common sense" that goes beyond the run-of-the-mill common sense that C. Wright Mills complained about. It is crucial not to reify our concepts by giving them a meaning that they may never even have had when they were first formulated. It is extremely important that we view theories and methods as "tools" that serve specific purposes in a certain cultural and political-economic context. The social worlds that humanity occupies are a worthy subject for sociological study not limited by unnecessary and premature closure but nevertheless disciplined by a craftsperson-like degree of precision. If we approach sociology as a calling that requires of us participation in body and spirit as well as mind, we will accomplish far more than if we think of sociology as merely a job or a career.

## Conclusion: Open Air:

Mills has allowed us to open a window to the fresh air that a sociological imagination can provide, and the combined Web and Part/Whole Approach of Phillips and Scheff will continue to improve our robust and healthy outlook. It is a question of integrating body and spirit and not just mind in the narrow sense. The true sociological imagination has yet to be fully developed. The next generation of students will have the opportunity to "stand on the shoulders" of such giants as Weber, Parsons, Lazarsfeld, Mills, and many others still alive and working today. We will have the option of utilizing all eight of the approaches to teaching that Davis (2004) elucidates. That will mean specifically that we will not just be involved in teaching from an ontological framework that is purely "physical" and "intersubjective." We will also have open to us an ontological framework that is "metaphysical" and "gnostic."

The physicist and the linguist can also benefit from Mills's analysis, yet few people outside of sociology and political science have ever heard of Mills. A real "education" (as opposed to mere technical training) requires paying attention not only to the mind, but also to the body and the spirit.

# References and Further Reading

Abelson, Raziel. 1967. "Definition." In *The Encyclopedia of Philosophy*. Vol. 2. Ed. Paul Edwards. New York: Macmillan, 314–324.

Bakker, J. I. (Hans). 1993a *Toward a Just Civilization*. Toronto: Canadian Scholars' Press.

——. 1993b. *Gandhi and the Gita*. Toronto: Canadian Scholars' Press.

——. 2005. "Trust and the Civilizing Process." Paper presented at the Symposium on Trust, Risk and Civility. Toronto: St. Michael's College, University of Toronto. Available on line.

Collins, Randall, and Michael Makowsky. 1998. *The Discovery of Society*. 6th ed. Boston: McGraw Hill.

Davis, Brent. 2004. *Inventions of Teaching: A Genealogy*. Mahwah, N.J.: Lawrence Erlbaum Associates.

Durkheim, David Emile. 1995 [1912]. *The Elementary Forms of Religious Life*. Tr. Karen E. Fields. New York: Free Press.

Feldman, Daniel Hale. 2001. *Qabalah: The Mystical Heritage of the Children of Abraham*. Santa Cruz, Calif,: Work of the Chariot.

Fuller, Steve. 2006. *The New Sociological Imagination*. London: Sage.

Gerth, Hans H., and C. Wright Mills. 1946. *From Max Weber: Essays in Sociology*. New York: Oxford Univ. Press.

Griswold, A. Whitney. 1962 [1959]. *Liberal Education and the Democratic Ideal, and Other Essays*. 2nd ed.. New Haven: Yale Univ. Press. [The book consists of essays originally published between 1951 and 1961.]

Horowitz, Irving Louis. 1983. *C. Wright Mills: An American Utopian*. New York: Free Press.

James, William. 1958 [1892, 1899]. *Talks to Teachers on Psychology: and to Students on Some of Life's Ideals*. New York: W. W. Norton.

King, Karen L. 2004. *What Is Gnosticism?* Cambridge, Mass.: Harvard Univ. Press.

Kincaid, Harold. 1996. *Philosophical Foundations of the Social Sciences*. New York: Cambridge Univ. Press.

Lazarsfeld, Paul F., and Morris Rosenberg. 1955. *The Language of Social Research*. Glencoe, Ill.: The Free Press.

Mills, C. Wright. 1940. "Situated Actions and the Vocabularies of Motive." *American Sociological Review* 5: 904–913.

——. 1943. "The Professional Ideology of Social Pathologists." *American Journal of Sociology* 49 (September): 165–180.

——. 1948. *The New Men of Power: America's Labor Leaders*. New York: A. M. Kelley.

——. 1951. *White Collar: The American Middle Classes*. New York: Oxford Univ. Press.

——. 1956. *The Power Elite*. New York: Oxford Univ. Press.

——. 1959. *The Sociological Imagination*. New York: Oxford Univ. Press.

Neumann, Franz. 1942. *Behemoth*. New York: Oxford Univ. Press.

Paranjape, Makarand. 2002. "The Third Eye and Two Ways of (Un)knowing: Gnosis, Alternative Modernities, and Postcolonial Futures." New York: unpublished paper presented at the Infinity Colloquium, 24–29 July 2002.

Phillips, Bernard. 2001. *Beyond Sociology's Tower of Babel: Reconstructing the Scientific Method.* New York: Aldine de Gruyter.

Phillips, Bernard, Harold Kincaid, and Thomas J. Scheff (eds.). *Toward A Sociological Imagination: Bridging Specialized Fields.* Lanham, Md.: University Press of America.

Scheff, Thomas J. 1990. *Microsociology: Discourse, Emotion, and Social Structure.* Chicago: University of Chicago Press.

————. 1997. *Emotions, the Social Bond, and Human Reality: Part/Whole Analysis.* Cambridge, U.K.: Cambridge University Press.

Stouffer, Samuel, et al. 1949. *The American Soldier.* Princeton, New Jersey: Princeton University Press.

Upitis, Rena. 2003. "Making Art, Making Connections." *Journal of the Canadian Association for Curriculum Studies* 1 (2): 1-6.

Weber, Max. 1968 [1920]. *Economy and Society.* Tr. and ed. Guenther Roth and Claus Wittich. Berkeley, Calif.: Univ. of California Press.

## Notes

1.  This version has been reduced from 18,000 words to 6,600 words. Therefore, the full discussion of the relationship between the Greek concept of *gnosis* and the Sanskrit idea of *jnana* will appear elsewhere.

# CHAPTER 5

# Structural Ritualization Theory

## Application and Change

*J. David Knottnerus*

DAILY LIFE IS NORMALLY CHARACTERIZED by an array of social rituals. Such rituals help create stability in social life while expressing various symbolic meanings that give significance to our actions. The basic assumption that rituals are crucial to human behavior is influenced by the arguments of various social scientists including Durkheim (1965/1915), Goffman (1967), Collins (2004), and Warner (1959; 1962) who have used this concept for analytical purposes (for other useful discussions of ritual, see Kertzer, 1988; Douglas, 1970; Turner, 1967; Bell, 1992; Lukes, 1975). Building upon the contributions of scholars such as these I have developed a perspective, "structural ritualization theory (SRT)," which focuses on the role ritual plays in social life. In this chapter, I discuss some of this work and then comment on recent research that addresses the topic of change and applications of the theory.

SRT formally defines ritualization and presents a set of factors to explain various dynamics involving social action and social structure (Knottnerus, 1997). The theory focuses on the role "ritualized symbolic practices" play in social life and the ways they contribute to the creation, reproduction, and/or transformation of social structure. Being formally stated with precisely developed concepts facilitates use of the framework for empirical investigations and a clearer understanding of the processes occurring in these social settings.

To reiterate, SRT focuses on everyday life and the central role rituals play in human behavior and culture. At the same time, I have given increasing attention to how social rituals can operate at different levels of the social order (i.e., micro to increasingly macro levels of analysis). Ritualized behaviors operating in a particular setting can influence the rituals that develop in different contexts (e.g., across different levels of the social order).

SRT parallels in many ways and is informed by the broad scientific approach illustrated by the Web and Part/Whole Approach as described in the Introduction, which calls for a definition of the problem, movement up language's ladder of abstraction, movement down the ladder of abstraction, integrating knowledge, and reflexive analysis. Indeed, these approaches provide an extremely valuable framework for developing and identifying the key components and assumptions that shape a program of theory and research.

To begin with, a scientific approach emphasizes the importance of the concrete (or particulars), such as the complex nature of human transactions and social bonds. SRT directs our attention to one crucial dimension of relationships: rituals. So, the role of ritual in social life is the key concept or research problem addressed by this perspective. In focusing on ritual, research has been directed toward various social topics.

Furthermore, an emphasis on moving up and down the conceptual ladder of abstraction between (a) concrete situations and (b) theory and social process/structure is realized in ritualization theory. This perspective seeks to develop theoretical concepts, which explain the processes by which rituals operate and structure social life, from micro to more macro levels of analysis. At the same time, these abstract concepts are always grounded in empirical research, whether they involve tests or exemplifications.

A broad scientific approach augmented by the web/part-whole perspective and SRT emphasizes the need for cooperative efforts aimed at theory development and synthesis, i.e., integration. Such an orientation also implies openness to using different methodologies and forms of evidence in our research (Knottnerus, 2005). This orientation emphasizes the complexity of social behavior. Theoretical and methodological procedures which generate comprehensive explanatory formulations and bodies of evidence are essential for understanding the complex nature of social reality.

Finally, an emphasis on reflexive analysis is a crucial component of the Web and Part/Whole Approach and a broad scientific orientation. A reflexive analysis of SRT suggests that a number of views in the social sciences and personal circumstances have shaped this approach. Consistent with the arguments of Giddens (1984) I assume that structure and agency are both integral parts of social life with each implicated in the dynamics of the other. Social structure, or the patterned relations between social units, is real and is manifested in myriad ways (for discussions of structure, see Knottnerus and Prendergast, 1994; Chew and Knottnerus, 2002). Yet, agency is also real and must be taken into account. Furthermore, I assume that an important aspect of agency involves the perceptions and symbolic constructs of people that guide and are expressed in their behavior and interaction. My appreciation for this last point, along with my first exposure to the writings of the classic theorists in sociology, occurred during my undergraduate studies at Beloit College and was primarily due to the efforts of a truly exceptional teacher, Dr. Donald Summers. He introduced me to the works of many scholars including various phenomenologists (e.g., Merleau-Ponty, 1962; Berger and Luckmann, 1966) and interactionists.

Influenced by my reading of those such as Durkheim, Goffman, and Simmel, I eventually recognized how ritual provides a valuable tool for analyzing the dynamics involving human agency and structure. Notwithstanding the seminal contributions of scholars such as these, I also recognized that ritual has been undertheorized in sociology, especially in ways that would allow for a precise, systematic investigation of social phenomena based on clearly defined theoretical concepts.

Finally, I should mention that other circumstances have shaped this approach. My appreciation for the importance of science began in my youth partly due to the influence of my parents and my early education in a high-quality public school system. My appreciation for the importance of social inequities and problems in contemporary society was due to a number of factors. Influences in my early life include my family, which provided the encouragement to read widely and a religious upbringing, which, as I understood it, stressed the relevance of our values for real world problems. Lastly, events in U.S. society in the 1960s and early 1970s and my experiences at an undergraduate institution that emphasized critical thought, the importance of knowledge, and the need to apply this knowledge to the world we live in helped shape my desire to change social conditions that inhibit human development

Having identified some of the key ways a scientific approach overlaps with SRT, I will now provide a more detailed description of the theory and more recent work that has relevance for the topic of social change and applications of its principles.

SRT is grounded in a growing number of empirical studies. Reflecting a commitment to multimethod research strategies, various individuals have conducted investigations of ritual dynamics in different social milieus. Studies focus on ritualization occurring in both contemporary and historical settings and U.S. and international contexts. In doing so, the theory attempts to bridge across methods having been applied in the field, in historical research, and in the laboratory. Very different kinds of evidence have been examined including field observations, videotapes of groups, interviews, archival evidence, literary sources, and secondary data.

SRT also involves several extensions of the theory, i.e., different lines of theory and research based upon or related to the original formulation. Succinctly stated, current work is proceeding along six directions: disruption and deritualization, the enactment of ritualized practices in organizations and communities, structural reproduction, strategic ritualization and the role of power, collective ritual events and the role of emotions, and applied research.

To provide more concrete detail about some of this work I briefly discuss several of these lines of research. The first topic addressed by the perspective might seem far removed from the topic of change, but it is actually quite relevant, not only because it examines certain forces that undermine change, but also because it presents some of the key concepts of the theory.

In its original formulation the theory focuses on structural reproduction by emphasizing the importance of groups that are embedded or nested within a more encompassing collectivity such as an informal youth group in a school or a problem-solving group in a bureaucratic organization. The formulation focuses on the ritualized actions performed in a wider social environment that acquire significance for the actor and then become part of the individual's script for his or her immediate world. In this way, although practices are not just "copied," they surface and are expressed in ways that may confirm the pattern of behavior in the wider social environment.

More precisely, a number of concepts allow for an examination of this issue. Briefly stated, ritualized symbolic practices (RSPs) help structure group dynamics. RSPs are standardized, schema-driven actions. "Schema" refers to a cognitive framework. RSPs, therefore, are regularly engaged-in actions that possess meaning and express symbolic themes. They contribute to the patterning of everyday behavior and interaction in various social settings. RSPs refer to the widespread form of social behavior in which people engage in regularized activities when interacting with others. Such practices are found throughout social life and can include ritualized forms of interaction within different subcultures, institutions, and groups of varying size (e.g., patterns of behavior in a youth group, religious practices, family gatherings and celebrations, play and recreational activities).

The original theory emphasizes the social processes by which RSPs in larger social environments influence embedded groups, i.e., bounded groups located in a wider social environment. It is argued that the taken-for-granted ritualized practices of people in such groups are strongly influenced by the regularized patterns of behavior, i.e., RSPs, occurring in the larger social environment, which they are exposed to or engage in. Generally speaking, important or dominant ritualized practices in the larger milieu will, over time, shape the cognitive or symbolic schemas that guide the actions of actors in embedded groups. They become part of the cognitive scripts that dictate their behavior.

Four factors play a part in structural reproduction and ritualization processes more generally. The four factors that influence RSPs are salience, repetitiveness, homologousness, and resources. Salience involves the "degree to which a RSP is perceived to be central to an act, action sequence, or bundle of interrelated acts" (Knottnerus, 1997: 262). This involves the prominence or conspicuousness of a RSP, which can vary. Repetitiveness involves the "relative frequency with which a RSP is performed" (Knottnerus, 1997: 262). The repetition of RSPs can also vary. For instance, in a social setting or domain of interaction, the presence of a RSP might be rare. In other domains, actors may engage in the ritualized practice quite often. Homologousness implies a "degree of perceived similarity among different RSPs" (Knottnerus, 1997: 263). It is possible that different RSPs exist in a social setting, and these actions may display a similarity in meaning and form. The greater the correspondence between them, the more likely they reinforce each other. This enhances the impact of RSPs on actors in a domain of interaction. Finally, resources are "materials needed to engage in RSPs which are available to actors" (Knottnerus, 1997: 264). The greater the availability of resources, the more likely an actor will engage in a RSP. Resources include nonhuman materials such as money and time. They also include human traits like interaction skills, physical strength, and intellectual ability.

Rank is another important concept in the theory. It involves "the relative standing of a RSP in terms of its dominance" or importance (Knottnerus, 1997: 266). According to the theory, rank is a function of repetitiveness, salience, homologousness, and resources. A RSP ranks high if it is repeated often, is quite visible, is similar to other practices, and actors have resources to take part in it. Overall, the higher the rank of the RSP, the greater its impact on the thoughts and behavior of actors, and the greater the likelihood that similar RSPs and social structures will be reproduced in an embedded group.

A growing number of researchers have conducted various studies supporting the argument just presented along with other formulations related to the theory. Experimental tests examining the reproduction of hierarchical social structures in task groups have provided support for the theory (Sell, Knottnerus, Ellison, and Mundt, 2000). In a very different type of study utilizing diaries, autobiographical materials, and historical sources, research has examined the transmission of status structures from owners of slave plantations to slave societies in the antebellum South (Knottnerus, 1999; Knottnerus, Monk, and Jones, 1999). And, in a study using literary texts such as novels, shorts stories, diaries, memoirs, and fictionalized autobiographies, a further instance of such reproduction is found in a historical-comparative analysis demonstrating how female and male youth societies in 19th century French elite schools mirrored the respective institutional systems they were embedded in (Knottnerus and Van de Poel Knottnerus, 1999; Van de Poel-Knottnerus and Knottnerus, 2002). For instance, in 19th century French lycées, male youth re-created many of the ritualized behaviors and relations they were exposed to in their informal, oftentimes secret embedded world. While verbally opposed to the strict regime male youth were exposed to in 19th century French lycées, boys ultimately reproduced these authoritarian, hierarchical arrangements within their own social world. What resulted in their informal, hidden social world was an even more exaggerated version of the social environment in which they were embedded.

What all this research demonstrates is how under certain conditions actors will reproduce the social behaviors and arrangements they are exposed to, even if they do not generate positive, rewarding outcomes and may actually lead to undesirable consequences.

A different line of research focuses more directly on issues related to change, i.e., "disruption and deritualization." This work examines the basic assumption underlying SRT that rituals are a necessary dimension of social behavior. It does this by examining critical situations in which the ritualized practices people normally engage in are severely disrupted. It is argued that those who are able to create new or reconstitute old ritualized practices subsequent to such disruptions are best able to adapt to their immediate situation. In other words, collective and more "individualized" rituals (which are still social in nature) serve as a buffer to disruptive events. Much of this research has examined the accounts of persons interned in concentration camps during the 20th century directing attention to the importance of rituals in these survivors' lives while imprisoned. Such research, which examines the daily lives—"particulars" of people's experiences—clearly reveals the significance of rituals for enabling people to cope with disruptive situations.

The first comparative case study (Knottnerus, 2002) of this issue focused on persons placed in concentration camps in the middle of the 20th century in four different cultures: Germany, Japan, the Soviet Union, and the United States. Evidence concerning actors' experiences in these different cases was obtained from published accounts in the form of diaries, memoirs, autobiographies, and biographies. By reading these accounts and employing certain rules and a coding scheme, I identified different ritualized behaviors that were responses to severe disruptions of prisoners' lives. Various findings have emerged from this research and more recent investigations of Nazi camps. To begin with, we find that all of the accounts, which were authored by survivors of these camps, contain unambiguous references to ritualized practices. While a wide variation exists in the number of references to such practices, the average number of references is large. Moreover, comments refer to a wide variety of ritual types. In looking at all the accounts at least twenty-seven different types of ritual practices are mentioned by internees including, for example, religious practices; holding of classes; talking, story telling, and discussion groups; sports; holiday celebrations; music; and idiosyncratic activities (unique practices peculiar to an individual or group). It is also apparent that these activities take one of three forms: personal/private, informal social, and quasi-formal organizational rituals.

In the aggregate certain ritual types appear to be more common, such as references to religious or musical activities. A closer examination of accounts quickly reveals, however, great differences. Examining the actual comments of just a few of the internees confirms these observations. For instance, while Kitagawa (1967) describes how Japanese Americans engaged in Christian or Buddhist religious services in American camps, Beattie (1946), a war correspondent imprisoned in Nazi camps, repeatedly describes prisoners as taking part in cooking "bashes" and engaging in artistic activities. In contrast, Stajner's (1988) account of life in Siberian labor camps describes instances of ritualized informal interaction involving periodic storytelling, joke telling, and the exchange of memories.

Furthermore, wide variations in accounts are found not only between cultural groups but also among prisoners within each of the four groups. And, large differences exist within the different types of ritualized practices, e.g., individuals describing how they engaged in very different kinds of ritualized sporting activities ranging from sumo wrestling or softball to soccer. Certain individuals also discuss idiosyncratic ritualized activities. For instance, Gill (1988: 360), who survived internment in Auschwitz, states: "I kept to a ritual of washing—although they made water available in the Block washroom only at midnight. All through the summer of 1943 I remember getting up at midnight, which was an effort, and going to wash myself. I know that having a self-imposed routine was a tremendous help." This account illustrates a basic point worth emphasizing: unique, small, and what might appear to be trivial rituals can, under extreme conditions, assume great significance for people providing meaning and stability in their lives.

Lastly, we find that a number of narratives contain quite revealing reflective statements about internees' behavior in these camps. For instance, Herling (1951: 143-44), who was interned in Soviet concentration camps, offers the following observation about those who engaged in various ritualized behaviors such as mending clothes, writing letters, or visiting friends in the barracks in the evening:

All these activities had one quality in common—they imitated the normal occupations of a free life. Our behavior observ[ed] the symbolic ritual of a dimly remembered routine.... The foregoing description, however, applies only to those few prisoners who made some effort to save themselves from complete demoralization. But the majority ... left their bunks during the evening only to fill up the hollowness of their stomachs with a pint or two of the inevitable hot water.... The majority of prisoners ... deluded themselves that this suicidal form of relaxation strengthened the organism of their bodies.

In essence this research suggests that disruptions can differ, some being extremely severe and of a coercive nature, and they can negatively impact individuals and groups in various ways. When people experience disruptions, the reconstruction of RSPs enables people to adjust to this situation. Moreover, these ritual processes appear to be a fundamental part of human life occurring in very different cultures. Although, the form such rituals take are exceedingly varied.

This research has also led to studies examining other kinds of situations that fall under the categories of disruption and deritualization. These include disasters (Thornburg, Knottnerus, and Webb, 2007; forthcoming), displaced youth during the cultural revolution in China (Wu and Knottnerus, 2005; 2007), and a laboratory experiment studying disruptions in group interaction (Sell, Knottnerus, and Adcock, unpublished manuscript). A growing body of findings suggests, again, the importance of ritualized practices in facilitating people's ability to cope with adverse conditions.[1]

Interpreted in a different way, what this research suggests is that ritualized behaviors can be interrupted, can break down, can be reconstituted, and sometimes can change. And, when this occurs these changes can involve the reenactment of ritual practices that may greatly differ in both their nature and their consequences. In other words these newly created practices can range from having deleterious personal or social effects to their facilitating human survival and personal/social development. In regard to the latter possibility, reconstituted rituals may have beneficial or restorative consequences. This observation leads to the following proposal that once principles are well established and investigated, the next step would be to use this knowledge to alleviate undesirable social conditions. Such applied or change-oriented efforts, grounded in a theoretical understanding of social life, could involve the development of interventionist techniques and policy recommendations.

While my efforts in this regard are quite recent, I would like to briefly describe one study which has just been completed and highlight several other projects that have potential relevance for the issue of change. The first investigation, conducted by Ulsperger and Knottnerus (2007, forthcoming; see also chapter 9 in this volume by the same authors), examines nursing homes in the United States. In this investigation we employ SRT to analyze the occupational rituals shaping the daily lives of staff in nursing homes. To study this issue we analyzed the content of literary sources focusing on everyday activities in nursing homes. The findings clearly show that the bureaucratic nature of nursing homes influences workers' cognitions and behaviors. Most importantly, evidence reveals that bureaucratic ritualized practices unintentionally result in abuse and neglect of residents.

For example, the greatest number of references was to staff separation and hierarchy, which concerns dividing lines between levels of staff. Repeated references were made to distinctions between staff involving different ranks of nurses, training certifications, and medical, administrative, and nonprofessional personnel. Most salient were discussions of work duties as they relate to the employment hierarchy. Staff members are to focus on specific work duties, and not others. What this results in, however, is that if a worker does not complete the task, it may well never be carried out. For instance, in one facility it was the activity director's responsibility to serve coffee to residents in the cafeteria. Residents confined to their rooms were denied this small treat because aides would not respond to their requests to bring them coffee, since it was not their duty. And, the same pattern was evident in other cases such as high-level staff ignoring abuse of residents, because it was not technically their duty to deal with direct care.

Many references are also made to rules concerning the ways people carry out job-related activities. Indeed, some suggest that workers are overwhelmed by regulations and that rules override compassion. Formal rules shape routine and oftentimes quite personal behavior whether the rules involve feeding or residents not being allowed to bathe by themselves (even if they are capable of doing so). In other words, with this emphasis on rules, workers tend to lose sight of the original goal of the long-term care facility. The focus drifts away from providing care to ensuring staff do not deviate from official guidelines. Furthermore, this emphasis on rules sometimes leads to an informal mindset among some employees such as aides that places the greatest value on carrying out one's duties in an efficient manner even if this involves abusive techniques, e.g., over-medicating residents.

The upshot is that in various ways bureaucratic culture facilitates ritualized practices and cognitions, which place bureaucratic goals over resident requirements, oftentimes leading to their maltreatment. Such ritualized behaviors become part of the daily social fabric of the organization.

Of course, while rituals can have negative consequences, they can also lead to positive outcomes enhancing personal/social development and well being. In that regard, SRT discusses not just structural reproduction but also ritual change or what is referred to as "transformative structural ritualization" (Knottnerus, 1997). It is argued that ritual dynamics can also create new behaviors and social structures. And, one way this can occur is through the support for new RSPs in formal organizations. In regard to nursing homes various possibilities exist for countering the negative impact of bureaucratic rituals through the promotion of alternative rituals. While this issue is discussed in greater depth in the chapter on physical abuse in nursing homes, I can mention a few of these recommendations here.

Administrators and other concerned professionals could become more formally aware of and deemphasize bureaucracy. Supervisors could push for an open dialogue about bureaucratic procedure and consequences. By facilitating awareness among staff in nursing homes about how such conditions exist, the first step would be taken toward reducing some of the unfavorable features of bureaucracy and creating an atmosphere conducive to other work rituals. Another step could involve efforts to counter focusing on specific job activities due to staff separation by training all employees to assist residents with at least small problems, irregardless of their job title and formal duties. Other changes in procedures could require upper-level staff to interact on a daily basis with residents, thereby, enhancing communication, closeness, and care. While these and other recommendations may seem limited in nature their cumulative effect, if implemented, would facilitate new occupational rituals that would personalize residents and workers' relations with them.

As previously noted, several other projects are also of potential relevance for the issue of change. For instance, Thornburg, Knottnerus, and Webb (2007, forthcoming) are investigating how disasters such as earthquakes, floods, or terrorist attacks can severely disrupt the ritualized activities engaged in by people in their daily lives. Such disruptions often affect entire communities and societies. Here too, many questions are raised concerning the ways people's daily practices are interrupted, to what extent they are able to cope with such events, and whether people can adapt to the situation by constructing new or old personal and social rituals. Our research suggests the reconstitution of ritualized activities is crucial to reestablishing social stability after a disaster. Such issues warrant far more research and attention by disaster responders, government agencies, and relief organizations.

Alex Thornburg and I are also investigating how ritualized ways of thinking and acting associated with the marketplace may shape the way we behave in different social arenas. To study this issue, we are examining how consumer rituals may spread from the economic sector to religious institutions, influencing the development of megachurches. We are focusing on how certain aspects of consumer rituals including spectacle and economic and psychological well being may impact how modern religion is practiced and organized. This research should provide a basis for better understanding how certain undesirable consequences associated with this development can be altered or resisted. For instance, it is possible that within some religious organizations smaller closeknit groups could engage in alternative RSPs that express themes emphasized in the organization's religious heritage (i.e., Christian tradition) which are not consumer based.

In sum, research suggests that changes in ritual practices can occur in different contexts and at different levels of the social order. Studies of internees in concentration camps demonstrate the possibility of change in people's personal lives and relations. Research examining nursing homes and megachurches suggest that change in ritual behaviors may occur within different kinds of formal organizations. And disaster research points to the importance of disruptions and the renewal of ritual not only at the individual and interpersonal level but also for entire communities and societies. Looked at a little differently, ritual change can arise from different sources ranging from more personalized, informal efforts initiated by individuals to formal, programmatic attempts to restructure group relations.

Finally, I would offer a few thoughts dealing with SRT, implications for change, and the need for further work. In addressing the topic of change and the development of new rituals, the theory argues that the higher the rank of RSPs (as determined by their salience, repetitiveness, homologousness, and resources), the greater their impact on actors' cognitions, behavior, and relations with others. In other words, the greater the rank or importance of new rituals, the greater the likelihood that the change will be successful and the new practices will endure.

Moreover, the theory suggests that mechanisms should exist that support the new RSPs. Findings from research on structural reproduction indicate that groups embedded in larger social environments will be strongly influenced by the new RSPs, leading to the re-creation of ritualized behaviors and structures in those embedded groups. When change occurs and new rituals are created in groups, which are embedded in larger social environments with different ritualized practices, one might expect the larger milieu will gradually impact the embedded groups resulting in a deterioration of the new rituals. One of the implications of this research is that once new ritualized behaviors develop in groups embedded in wider social environments containing different practices, it cannot be assumed that those new behaviors will continue indefinitely on their own. Mechanisms of some sort should also be present that will facilitate and reinforce the new practices.

What these mechanisms might be has not been addressed in previous work, but it is quite likely that different factors could contribute to the maintenance of ritual practices. For instance, at the personal level periodic self-reflection and appraisal could provide a technique for individuals to monitor ritualized practices and sustain the motivation to engage in them. Possible social factors would include the use of sanctions by organizations that reward or punish actors for engaging in ritual practices. Another technique would involve the reeducation of group members to reinforce new ritual activities. Other social dynamics could also be involved such as special collective events that generate emotional intensity, commitment to new group rituals, and group solidarity (Knottnerus, forthcoming). Additional social dynamics might involve legitimation processes, which validate newly developed ritual enactments. It is issues such as these that will be addressed in future research as I focus more on applications of SRT, ritual change, and the transformation of culture and social organization.

In conclusion, the goal of SRT is to contribute to the explanation of ritual in everyday life and culture. The theory and research discussed here, which shares a number of important assumptions and goals with a broad scientific approach augmented by the web and part/whole perspective, seeks to expand our understanding of the universal occurrence of rituals among humans and the social dynamics surrounding them. At the same time, this body of work has a number of implications for people's social and personal lives and how changes in them may be brought about. The present paper represents a first effort aimed at framing this discussion and developing a more focused and comprehensive examination of this topic.

## Notes

1. For additional research utilizing the theory, see Knottnerus, Ulsperger, Cummins, and Osteen 2006; Guan and Knottnerus 1999; 2006; Knottnerus and Berry 2002; Varner and Knottnerus 2002; Knottnerus and LoConto 2003; Mitra and Knottnerus 2004; forthcoming; Ulsperger and Knottnerus 2006; Edwards and Knottnerus 2007).

## References

Beattie, Edward W., Jr. 1946. *Diary of a Kriege*. New York: Thomas Y. Crowell.
Bell, Catherine. 1992. *Ritual Theory, Ritual Practice*. Oxford: Oxford Univ. Press.
Berger, Peter, and Thomas Luckmann. 1966. *The Social Construction of Reality*. Garden City, N.Y.: Doubleday.
Chew, Sing C., and J. David Knottnerus, eds. 2002. *Structure, Culture and History: Recent Issues in Social Theory*. Lanham, Md.: Rowman & Littlefield.
Collins, Randall. 2004. *Interaction Ritual Chains*. Princeton, N.J.: Princeton University Press.

Douglas, Mary. 1970. *Natural Symbols*. New York: Vintage.

Durkheim, Emile. [1915] 1965. *The Elementary Forms of the Religious Life*. New York: Free Press.

Edwards, Jennifer, and J. David Knottnerus. 2007. "The Orange Order: Strategic Ritualization and Its Organizational Antecedents." *International Journal of Contemporary Sociology* 44:179-199.

Giddens, Anthony. 1984. *The Constitution of Society: Outline of the Theory of Structuration*. Berkeley: Univ. of California Press.

Gill, Anton. 1988. *The Journey Back from Hell: An Oral History. Conversations with Concentration Camp Survivors*. New York: William Morrow.

Goffman, Erving. 1967. *Interaction Rituals: Essays on Face-to-Face Behavior*. Garden City, N.Y.: Anchor Books.

Guan, Jian, and J. David Knottnerus. 1999. "A Structural Ritualization Analysis of the Process of Acculturation and Marginalization of Chinese Americans." *Humboldt Journal of Social Relations* 25:43-95.

———. 2006. "Chinatown Under Siege: Community Protest and Structural Ritualization Theory." *Humboldt Journal of Social Relations* 30:5-52.

Herling, Gustav. 1951. *A World Apart*. Trans. Joseph Marek. New York: Roy Publishers.

Kertzer, David I. 1988. *Ritual, Politics, and Power*. New Haven, Conn.: Yale Univ. Press.

Kitagawa, Daisuke. 1967. *Issei and Nisei: The Internment Years*. New York: Seabury Press.

Knottnerus, J. David. 1997. "The Theory of Structural Ritualization." In *Advances in Group Processes*. Vol. 14, ed. Barry Markovsky, Michael J. Lovaglia, and Lisa Troyer. Greenwich, Conn.: JAI Press, 257-279.

———. 1999. "Status Structures and Ritualized Relations in the Slave Plantation System." In *Plantation Society and Race Relations: The Origins of Inequality*, ed. Thomas J. Durant Jr. and J. David Knottnerus. Westport, Conn.: Praeger, 137-147.

———. 2002. "Agency, Structure and Deritualization: A Comparative Investigation of Extreme Disruptions of Social Order." In *Structure, Culture and History: Recent Issues in Social Theory*, ed. Sing C. Chew and J. David Knottnerus. Lanham, Md.: Rowman & Littlefield, 85-106.

———. 2005. "The Need for Theory and the Value of Cooperation: Disruption and Deritualization." *Sociological Spectrum* 25:5-19.

———. Forthcoming. "Collective Events, Rituals and Emotions." *Sociological Inquiry*.

Knottnerus, J. David, and Phyllis E. Berry. 2002. "Spartan Society: Structural Ritualization in an Ancient Social System." *Humboldt Journal of Social Relations* 27:1-42.

Knottnerus, J. David, and David G. LoConto. 2003. "Strategic Ritualization and Ethnicity: A Typology and Analysis of Ritual Enactments in an Italian American Community." *Sociological Spectrum* 23:425-461.

Knottnerus, J. David, David L. Monk, and Edward Jones. 1999. "The Slave Plantation System from a Total Institution Perspective." In *Plantation Society and Race Relations: The Origins of Inequality*, ed. Thomas J. Durant Jr. and J. David Knottnerus. Westport, Conn.: Praeger, 17-27.

Knottnerus, J. David, and Christopher Prendergast, eds. 1994. *Recent Developments in the Theory of Social Structure*. Greenwich, Conn.: JAI Press.

Knottnerus, J. David, Jason S. Ulsperger, Summer Cummins, and Elaina Osteen. 2006. "Exposing Enron: Media Representations of Ritualized Deviance in Corporate Culture." *Crime, Media, Culture* 2:177–195.

Knottnerus, J. David, and Frederique Van de Poel-Knottnerus. 1999. *The Social Worlds of Male and Female Children in the Nineteenth Century French Educational System: Youth, Rituals and Elites*. Lewiston, N.Y.: Edwin Mellen Press.

Lukes, Steven. 1975. "Political Ritual and Social Integration." *Sociology* 9:289–308.

Merleau-Ponty, Maurice. 1962. *Phenomenology of Perception*. New York: Routledge & Kegan Paul.

Mitra, Aditi, and J. David Knottnerus. 2004. "Royal Women in Ancient India: The Ritualization of Inequality in a Patriarchal Social Order." *International Journal of Contemporary Sociology* 41:215–231.

———. Forthcoming. "Sacrificing Women: A Study of Ritualized Practices Among Women Volunteers in India." *Voluntas: International Journal of Voluntary and Nonprofit Organizations*.

Sell, Jane, J. David Knottnerus, and Christina Adcock. Unpublished manuscript. "Disruptions in Task Groups: When Does Disruption Lead to Disorder?"

Sell, Jane, J. David Knottnerus, Christopher Ellison, and Heather Mundt. 2000. "Reproducing Social Structure in Task Groups: The Role of Structural Ritualization." *Social Forces* 79:453–475.

Stajner, Karlo. 1988. *Seven Thousand Days in Siberia*. Trans. Joel Agee. New York: Farrar, Straus & Giroux.

Thornburg, P. Alex, J. David Knottnerus, and Gary R. Webb. 2007. "Disaster and Deritualization: A Re-interpretation of Findings from Early Disaster Research." *Social Science Journal* 44:161–166.

———. Forthcoming. "Ritual and Disruption: Insights from Early Disaster Research." *International Journal of Sociological Research*.

Turner, Victor. 1967. *The Forest of Symbols: Aspects of Ndembu Ritual*. Ithaca, N.Y.: Cornell Univ. Press.

Ulsperger, Jason S., and J. David Knottnerus. 2006. "Enron: Organizational Rituals as Deviance." In *Readings in Deviant Behavior*, 4th ed. Ed. Alex Thio and Thomas C. Calhoun. Boston: Allyn and Bacon, 279–282.

———. 2007. "Long-term Care Workers and Bureaucracy: The Occupational Ritualization of Maltreatment in Nursing Homes and Recommended Policies." *Journal of Applied Social Science* 1:52–70.

———. Forthcoming. "The Social Dynamics of Elder Care: Rituals of Bureaucracy and Physical Neglect in Nursing Homes." *Sociological Spectrum*.

Van de Poel-Knottnerus, Frederique, and J. David Knottnerus. 2002. *Literary Narratives on the Nineteenth and Early Twentieth-Century French Elite Educational System: Rituals and Total Institutions*. Lewiston, N.Y.: Edwin Mellen Press.

Varner, Monica K., and J. David Knottnerus. 2002. "Civility, Rituals and Exclusion: The Emergence of American Golf During the Late Nineteenth and Early Twentieth Centuries." *Sociological Inquiry* 72:426–441.

Warner, W. Lloyd. 1959. *The Living and the Dead: A Study of the Symbolic Life of Americans* (Yankee City Series). New Haven, Conn.: Yale Univ. Press.

———. 1962. *American Life: Dream and Reality.* Rev. ed.. Chicago: Univ. of Chicago Press.

Weber, Max. 1946. *From Max Weber: Essays in Sociology.* Tr. Hans Gerth and C. Wright Mills. New York: Oxford Univ. Press.

Wu, Yanhong, and J. David Knottnerus. 2005. "Ritualized Daily Practices: A Study of Chinese 'Educated Youth.'" Shehui (Society) 6:167–185.

———. 2007. "The Origins of Ritualized Daily Practices: From Lei Feng's Diary to Educated Youth's Diaries." Shehui (Society) 1:98–119.

CHAPTER 6

# Harry Braverman and the Working Class

*Frank W. Elwell*

In 1974 Harry Braverman published *Labor and Monopoly Capitalism,* an analysis of the impact of capitalism on work in the 20th century United States. Using the concepts and theories developed by Marx in the first volume of *Capital,* Braverman's book was a biting critique of the growing degradation of work in America. A large part of Braverman's argument centered on the "deskilling" of jobs in a capitalist economy in a systematic effort to more efficiently control and coordinate the labor force to maximize profit. Braverman then documents the growth of working-class occupations from 1900 to 1970 using U.S. Census data. This chapter briefly reviews Braverman's argument and data and then extends the analysis through 2001 to determine the validity of the Braverman/Marxist critique.

Harry Braverman was born on December 9, 1920, in Brooklyn, New York. His parents were Jewish-Polish immigrants. His father was a shoe worker. Attending Brooklyn College for one year, Braverman was forced to withdraw and find employment for economic reasons (he was not to return to college until the early 1960s; he received a Bachelor of Arts degree from the New School for Social Research in 1963). It was during his single year of college as a young man when he first became exposed to Marx and socialism. Shortly after, he joined the Young People's Socialist League.

At the age of 16 (1937) Braverman found work at the Brooklyn Naval Yards as a coppersmith apprentice, where he worked until 1941. It was in this trade that Braverman got a sense of the impact of science-based technology on jobs. He was drafted toward the end of the war and was "sent by the Army to Cheyenne, Wyoming, where as a sergeant he taught and supervised locomotive pipefitting" (Foster, 1998: x). In about 1947 he moved to Youngstown, Ohio, with his wife, Miriam, finding work as a steelworker. Fired from one company "at the instigation of the FBI," Braverman managed to find work at others (Foster, 1998: x).

From his early year in college on, Braverman continued his commitment to socialist ideology and to organizations devoted to the establishment of these ideals. He became a member of the Socialist Workers Party (SWP) and attended a six-month course of Marxist study at their Trotsky School in the early 1950s. But there were deep divisions in the SWP in the early '50s. In 1953, Braverman left (or was expelled from) the SWP and became a coleader with Bert Cochran of a splinter group, the Socialist Union. It was at this point that he began coediting and writing for their paper, the *American Socialist,* under his party name, Harry Frankel. While working and writing for this paper, he worked out many of the ideas later expressed in *Labor and Monopoly Capitalism.*

When the *American Socialist* folded after some seven years, Braverman moved into book publishing, becoming an editor for Grove Press in 1960. At Grove he edited *The Autobiography of Malcolm X,* and later became a vice president and general manager at Grove Press until resigning in 1967 "when the president of the company refused to publish a book by Bertrand Russell on American war crimes in Vietnam" (Livingston, 2000: para 7). Braverman then became the director of Monthly Review Press and worked there until his death from cancer on August 2, 1976, at the age of 55.

My own working-class credentials are not nearly so impressive. My father worked his way through college in the 1930s, becoming a mechanical engineer, but he married and raised his nine children in accordance with working-class values. Only three of us went on to college (none of the girls). It was while working my way through college—as a dishwasher, a waiter, an ice cream man, and finally as a bun catcher[1] in a factory bakery—that I got a sense of how the working class is treated in the United States; very poorly indeed. My first paper as a graduate student in sociology for a class on symbolic interaction was titled "Labeling and the Working Class." The thesis of the paper was that there was a dark side to the American success ethic: people who do not "make it" economically are labeled as inferior and are treated as either lacking intelligence, ambition, or both. Consequently, they are treated as inferiors at work and discriminated against and mocked in life. Fast forward several years; I was looking for a modern day Marxist to profile for a book on social theory; I ran across a reference to Harry Braverman's *Labor and Monopoly Capital,* bought a copy and read it, and was simply awed by his mastery of both Marx and class in America.

This chapter is based upon the chapter I completed on Harry Braverman for *Sociocultural Systems: The Contemporary Expression of Classical Theory* (Elwell, forthcoing). Braverman's overall theory is taken directly from Karl Marx. His problem—a study of the objective conditions of the working class—is identical to the task Marx set for himself in *Capital.* The value of Braverman's book is not in extending Marx's analyses or in combining Marx's insights with others. Rather, the value of the work is that it applies Marx's analyses to American society in the first two-thirds of the 20th century and, further, renders Marx's analyses truly accessible to a modern audience. It is a very successful work on both counts.

Braverman begins his analysis by pointing to a contradiction in the literature on work. There is the widespread belief and assertion that modern occupations are more demanding in terms of technical skills, educational levels, and training. So entrenched is this belief that it is rarely questioned or examined. However, even some of the same people making these assertions are reporting widespread dissatisfaction with work—the hours, the pace, the lack of meaningful participation—as evidenced by low morale, high absenteeism, and early retirement (Braverman, 1974/1998: 3). These two views, he points out, are somewhat contradictory. More surprising still, there is little attempt in the literature to reconcile these differences. Work, Marx (and thus Braverman) asserts, is central to the human animal. It is through work that men and women realize their very humanity. Widespread dissatisfaction with such an essential activity is a very serious issue indeed.

Worker dissatisfaction presents itself to management, Braverman explains, as "a problem in costs and controls, not in the humanization of work" (Braverman, 1974/1998: 36). Braverman brings his extensive and unique life experiences—worker, foreman, publisher, social activist, socialist intellectual—to his study of the "dynamic underlying the incessant transformation of work in the modern era." In *Labor and Monopoly Capital,* Braverman details the achievement of capitalist management in gaining control of the labor process—both social organization and technology—to maximize profitability. While most will not agree with Braverman on every count, the book will give many an appreciation for the devastating effects of the detailed division of labor on human life and the role of capitalism in spreading this division.

Braverman carefully documents 20th century business history to show that the dedication to maximize profits is the core principle organizing work under a capitalist system. The corollary to the drive to accumulate capital is the need for control over the labor process. Capitalists gain control of the labor process by separating the design and execution functions within the internal division of labor and monopolizing the former in the hands of management. This separation allows management to better control the pace and direction of the labor process. The process also constantly creates a class of unskilled workers lacking independence, dignity, and bargaining leverage—a class totally "dominated and shaped by the accumulation of capital."

## The Working Class

The heart of Marx's critique of capitalism beats in his analysis of the effect of the capitalist mode of production on the working class. Braverman carries on this tradition. Under capitalism, workers become a "labor force," just another factor of production, another commodity to be purchased. Controlling costs, maximizing productivity, and amassing more capital are the overriding goals of the enterprise. To do this the capitalist class has created jobs that use men and women in inhuman ways, separating their labor power from their critical faculties (Braverman, 1974/1998: 96). That the process is repugnant to the workers is apparent from the high absentee rates, widespread job dissatisfaction, early retirements, and alienation. The thrust of the critique, however, does not rely upon such indicators but rather upon the objective conditions of work itself. Real skill is replaced by manual dexterity, conception and thought is removed from execution, control of action and pace is removed from the worker and placed in management.

The process of turning workers into commodities is continually being extended into more areas of the economy. Further, each succeeding generation has to be acclimated to the new mode of work; each has to be socialized to overcome the initial revulsion to the ever-more-detailed division of labor, the consequent rending of human beings. This ever-widening process, Braverman claims, becomes a permanent feature of capitalist society (Braverman, 1974/1998: 96). Laborers are increasingly seen as machines, machines that can be readily adapted to the requirements of most any job. This view of man as a machine, Braverman says, has become more than a mere analogy. For the capitalist class, the laborer as machine is how the class has come to use labor; it is how it has come to view humanity (Braverman, 1974/1998: 124).

Many in the media and academe equate the working class with traditional blue-collar labor, that is, manual occupations in the goods-producing industries. The conventional wisdom is that this working class is a small and shrinking minority in modern societies—that we are rapidly moving into a "postindustrial" world. In this new world almost everyone is becoming professional or at least "white collar," and average pay and working conditions of the working class that remains have made them part of the middle class, part of the bourgeoisie.

Supporters of such conventional wisdom point to the decline of manufacturing jobs and the rise of white-collar work in offices and in the new service industries. When the academicians write of white collar they call forth images of managers, computer programmers, and accountants. When they write of the rise of service occupations they call forth images of lawyers, physicians, and dietitians. The reality, according to Braverman, is far different.

There have been tremendous gains in productivity among manufacturing industries. The tasks of designing the product, laying out the steps of production, coordinating the tasks, selecting the materials, scheduling the processes, calculating costs, and keeping records are all removed from the factory floor and placed in the office. By dividing the labor in such a detailed manner the capitalist gains productivity, a less skilled and thus less costly workforce, and total control over the production process (Braverman, 1974/1998: 86). The application of more sophisticated technology to the production process leads to further gains in these areas. Overall, the gain in productivity means that the capitalist can now employ fewer workers to produce a certain level of output (Braverman, 1974/1998: 86).

However, this increase in the productivity of labor has been somewhat offset by a tremendous increase in the scale of production (it is the scale of production, you will recall, that makes such innovations economically feasible). Consequently, employment in production industries has not declined in absolute numbers, but it has declined in terms of its *relative* size (Braverman, 1974/1998: 163-164). Braverman gathers data that demonstrates that workers in manufacturing, construction and other goods-producing industries (excluding agriculture) have grown from about 14 million workers in 1920 to slightly over 23 million in 1970. However, their proportion of the working population has declined from about 46 percent in 1920 to only 33 percent of the workforce in 1970.[2]

If you equate working in production industries with working class, it would appear that the working class is indeed a small and shrinking minority. Braverman, however, defines the working class in much broader terms. The working class, he claims, consists of those who come to the labor market with nothing to sell but their labor (Braverman, 1974/1998: 261). That labor is systematically exploited and degraded by the capitalist system. To enable growth in profit, businesses break skills down to simple tasks, automate where economically feasible, and manipulate the speed of production. These processes do not just occur in manufacturing operations, Braverman adds, but throughout the capitalist economy.

While the first separation of conception and execution of tasks occurs between the factory and the office, the second occurs within the office itself. In the United States, the proportion of clerks and administrative assistants in the working population climbed from 2 percent in 1900 to 18 percent by 1970 (1974/1998: 204). While traditionally classified as "white collar," Braverman points out, the vast bulk of these jobs involve minimal skills and initiative and garner wages and benefits roughly equivalent to manual occupations.

The number of service workers, he reports, rose from 1 million at the turn of the century to some 9 million by the 1970 census. While there are a couple of occupations in this grouping that require some educational credentials and extensive on-the-job training (for example, police supervisors, detectives, and firefighters), most are low skill, low paying, and often temporary. Some examples of the types of jobs encompassed in the service classification are janitors, chambermaids, busboys, dishwashers, childcare workers, and the like. Skills required for the majority of these jobs are minimal. The pay, Braverman reports, is the worst average of all census job classifications. To this group Braverman adds retail sales workers and cashiers, people with the same skills and compensation as the majority of service workers. In 1970, Braverman reports, there were a total of 3 million such workers (1974/1998: 253).

According to Braverman's figures, the percentage of the workforce engaged in essentially rote manual occupations, with little skill, educational requirements, autonomy, or decent compensation has been growing each decade since 1900 (1974/1998: 262). (See table 6.1.) He arrives at these figures by adding up the number of people working as operatives and laborers, craftsmen, clerical workers, and service and retail sales workers for each census year from 1900 to 1970.[3] Beginning in 1900 at slightly over 50 percent of the labor force, he notes that this group rises to 69 percent in 1970.[4] An advanced capitalist society, one supposedly based on scientific technology and higher education, seems to be predicated on the exploitation of a significant proportion of its working population.

Braverman asserts that work in monopoly capitalist economies has become very polarized, with a few people having all of the technical expertise and managerial control over a largely unskilled and uneducated workforce. As conception and execution are separated, more and more technical expertise is concentrated in fewer hands. Braverman estimates that, at most, only 3 percent of the 1970 workforce consisted of such technical specialists as engineers, architects, draftsmen, designers, natural scientists, and technicians. It could be, Braverman allows, that many managers who are primarily technical specialists have been excluded from this list. But it is also true that a portion of those on the list include those "whose jobs are confined to the repetition of simple activities that are rapidly learned and do not encompass any true conceptualization or planning functions" (Braverman, 1974/1998: 166–167).

Table 6.1 Working Class (in millions) 1900–2001

| | 1900 | 1910 | 1920 | 1930 | 1940 | 1950 | 1960 | 1970 | 1983 | 2001 |
|---|---|---|---|---|---|---|---|---|---|---|
| Operatives and laborers | 7.3 | 9.9 | 11.5 | 13.0 | 14.4 | 15.5 | 16.4 | 18.1 | 16.1 | 17.7 |
| Craftsmen | 2.9 | 4.0 | 5.0 | 5.7 | 5.6 | 7.3 | 8.0 | 9.5 | 12.3 | 14.4 |
| Clerical workers | 0.9 | 2.0 | 3.4 | 4.3 | 5.0 | 7.1 | 9.6 | 14.3 | 16.4 | 18.5 |
| Service and sales workers | 3.6 | 4.9 | 4.9 | 7.3 | 8.8 | 8.7 | 10.6 | 13.4 | 21.3 | 29.7 |
| Total workers | 14.7 | 20.8 | 24.8 | 30.3 | 33.8 | 44.6 | 55.3 | 66.2 | 80.8 | |
| Total "active" or "experienced labor force" | 29.0 | 37.3 | 42.2 | 48.7 | 51.7 | 57.9 | 64.5 | 80.0 | 100.1 | 135.1 |
| *Workers (as percent of total "labor force")* | | | | | | | | | | |
| Percentage | 50.7 | 55.8 | 55.8 | 62.2 | 65.4 | 66.7 | 69.1 | 69.1 | 66.0 | 60.0 |

Source: Braverman, 1974/1998, p. 262; For 1983 and 2001, U.S. Census Bureau, Statistical Abstract of the United States: 2002, Table no. 588.

In addition to this 3 percent, Braverman acknowledges that there are a significant number of individuals engaged in lower levels of management as well as professional specialties. He estimates that this middle level accounts for about 20 percent of occupational employment in 1970 (Braverman, 1974/1998: 279). However, Braverman points out, these occupations should not be equated with the old middle class of independent entrepreneurs of an earlier capitalist era (1974/1998; 279). Most are wage earners dependent upon the corporations or government for their employment. Unlike the old middle class, they are part of the exploitation system. Taking their character from both capitalist and worker, he says, they take part in the expropriation of surplus from the workers, but have the same dependent characteristics as other workers, with only their labor to sell. The sheer productivity of the working class and the expropriation of the resulting surplus make the number of middle-level managers possible. Further, Braverman asserts, this group is prone to the very same rationalization techniques as other labor as soon as a great enough mass is gathered to make economical a detailed division of labor and automation (Braverman, 1974/1998: 281–282).

Braverman appears somewhat uneasy about the size of this middle stratum and its import for the Marxist analysis of capitalism.[5] But, as Braverman points out, class is part of a dynamic process, always changing and often difficult to encapsulate into neat theories and formulas. Nor does science require theory to explain all (Braverman, 1974/1998: 282–283).[6]

## Labor in Hyperindustrial Capitalism

There have been a number of changes in the structure of the American workforce since Braverman wrote his treatise in the 1970s. Recall that Braverman demonstrated that workers in manufacturing, construction, and other goods-producing industries (excluding agriculture) grew from about 14 million workers in 1920 to slightly over 23 million in 1970. However, he found that their proportion of the working population had declined from about 46 percent in 1920 to only 33 percent of the workforce in 1970. Data computed since Braverman indicate that the proportion of employment in manufacturing and construction has declined even further, going to 29 percent in 1980, and to 22 percent in 2000. Absolute numbers involved in manufacturing alone have actually declined in that time period, from about 22 million to about 20 million, or about 15 percent of the total employed population (U.S. Census Bureau, Statistical Abstract of the United States, 2002, Table 591). While employment in manufacturing, agriculture, and public administration declined between 1980 and 2000, employment in the service industries climbed from about

29 million workers (29% of the workforce) to about 49.5 million workers or 37% of the workforce.[7]

Table 6.1 also presents Braverman's breakdown of occupational classifications computed for the years 1983 and 2001. As can be seen, while Braverman's working class has continued to grow in terms of absolute numbers (with the exception of "Operatives and Laborers"), going from 80 million workers in 1970 to 100 million total workers in 1983, and 135 million in 2002, the percentage of working-class occupations as part of the total labor force has declined over these years. The proportion of working-class occupations goes from a high of 69.1 percent of the total American labor force in 1960 and 1970 to 66 percent in 1983 and down to 60 percent in 2001.

So, for the first 70 years of the 20th century, Braverman found that the percentage of the American workforce engaged in manual and clerical occupations, with little skill, educational requirements, autonomy, and compensation, has been growing each decade (1974/1998: 262). However, this trend has been halted and reversed in the latter third of the century. Although it should be pointed out that even today the working class is still a majority (60 percent) of the employed population in hyperindustrial society,[8] the trend now seems to be in the opposite direction. How far this trend can go is open to question. Can an industrial society (or a hyperindustrial society) exist without a significant portion of the working population engaged in manual or clerical labor? Is a bureaucratic-hyperindustrial society even possible without the bulk of the people engaged in detailed division of labor—isn't such a society defined by this very division? Can a capitalist society long exist without exploiting a significant portion of its working population?[9]

While all segments of the working class have increased in terms of absolute numbers over the last decade, it is interesting to note the differences in the relative numbers among the four basic categories. Only one category experienced a proportionate decline, that of "Operatives and laborers." This group numbered some 15.5 million in 1950, or some 27 percent of the total workforce. By the year 2001 this group stood at 17.7 million, a slight rise in absolute numbers, but only 13 percent of the total workforce. "Craftsmen," the skilled and semiskilled portion of manual labor, also experienced a slight proportional decline. In 1950, this group numbered 7.3 million (13 percent); by 2001 they were at 14.4 million or 11 percent of the workforce.

"Clerical" and "Service and sales workers" both experienced rapid growth in the last half of the 20th century. The "Clerical" group has gone from 7.1 million workers in 1950 (12 percent of the workforce) to 18.5 million workers in 2001 (14 percent of the workforce). In 1950 "Service and sales workers" numbered 8.7 million (15 percent); by 2001 this group stood at 29.7 million (or 22 percent of the workforce).

What can account for these changes? It would appear that the bulk of the proportional decline of the working class is due to the relatively slow growth in the number of manufacturing jobs in the United States. These manufacturing jobs have been slow growing due to automation and international trade now bringing many goods from other countries, and many low-skilled American manufacturing jobs have been exported or "outsourced."[10]

Compared to manufacturing, it is far more difficult to automate most personal service work. Besides, it is seldom economical to replace a small number of minimum wage unskilled laborers in a single location with technology. Compared to goods-producing jobs, it is also more difficult to ship many of these jobs overseas to cheaper labor markets (though by no means impossible with some of these occupations, like telephone service representative). And this is what accounts for much of our legal and illegal immigration. If you cannot have the services provided from cheaper overseas labor markets, another option is to import cheaper foreign laborers.

Clerical work stands somewhat intermediate to manufacturing and service working-class occupations. The personal computer has made it relatively inexpensive to "automate" typing and filing services even in small offices. The use of such technology greatly improves the productivity of the workers who remain. While some clerical work can again be shipped overseas to lower-wage markets, particularly with the current worldwide surplus of broadband and satellite access, many foreign labor markets still do not have the English skills, American cultural knowledge, or the wage differentials, to offset the inconvenience of offshoring such occupations.

Manufacturing jobs (combining "Operatives and laborers" and "Craftsmen" in table 6.1) have been in some proportional decline in U.S. society since 1970, accounting for 34 percent of the total workforce in 1970, 28 percent in 1983, and 24 percent in 2001. What has replaced these jobs? As just reported, some of the jobs have been replaced by clerical and service and sales workers, although the proportionate growth in these areas has not been great enough to offset manufacturing declines. The bulk of the growth in American jobs is mainly attributable to the rapid growth of "Managerial and Professional Specialty" occupations, to which we now turn.

Braverman estimates that by 1970, some 20 percent of the workforce was engaged in lower levels of management and professional specialties. By 1983, the "Managerial and professional specialty" occupations accounted for some 23,592 million of the employed, or 23 percent of the employed population. By 2001 these occupations had ballooned to 31 percent of the employed population.[11] Add to this the Technical and Sales Occupations (nonretail and nonclerical) and the figures go to 31 percent of all employment for 1983 and 39 percent for 2001.[12] Clearly this middle level of employment has grown dramatically since Braverman's time (U.S. Census Bureau, Statistical Abstract of the United States, 2002, Table No. 588. for 1983 and 2001 figures.)

Within the broad category of "Managerial and professional specialty," the fastest growth was experienced among "Executive, administrative, and managerial" occupations (EAM) and the "Professional Specialty" areas. EAM grew from 11 percent of the workforce in 1983 to 15 percent in 2001. Braverman, of course, would attribute the growth in these occupations as further evidence of centralization of coordination and control. The "Professional specialty" categories grew from 13 percent of the total workforce in 1983 to 16 percent in 2001. Within the professional specialties, which include such occupations as health diagnosing (physicians and dentists), college teachers, librarians, lawyers, entertainers, and athletes (the latter three being very uneven in terms of prestige, pay, and benefits), the proportions stayed remarkably stable over the two decades. Teaching (at all levels) is by far the largest professional specialty area, with approximately 30 percent of all specialty employment; health-care specialties (including registered nurses, pharmacists, therapists, and physician assistants) is second with approximately 20 percent of all employment within the professional-specialties category (U.S. Census Bureau, Statistical Abstract of the United States, 2002 Table No. 588. for 1983 and 2001 figures).

Recall that Braverman estimated that only 3 percent of the 1970 workforce consisted of technical specialists such as engineers, architects, draftsmen, designers, natural scientists, and technicians. A similar computation of occupational data for 1983 and 2001 shows slight growth in the concentration of technical expertise. In 1983, about 3.5 million individuals had such occupations (3.5 percent of the total workforce). By 2001 this number had climbed to 7.3 million (4.7 percent) (Statistical Abstract of the United States, 2002, Table 588). Interestingly, computer scientists accounted for the bulk of this growth, a technical expertise almost unknown in the 1970 census. Excluding their numbers the concentration of technical expertise for both 1983 and 2001 is at Braverman's estimate of about 3 percent of the labor force (Braverman, 1974/1998; U.S. Census Bureau, Statistical Abstract of the United States, 2002 Table No. 588. for 1983 and 2001 figures). To conclude, the workforce of hyperindustrial society is not completely congruent with that of industrial society. As is necessary for a more complex technological infrastructure and a more bureaucratic structure, there are a higher proportion of executives, managers, and professionals in the workforce. Some of these positions, no doubt, are given high degrees of latitude and freedom; some are highly paid and prestigious as well. However, contrary to the postindustrial dreamers, these elite do not (nor can they ever) make up the bulk of the society. The economy still depends on a large working-class population. The bulk of these jobs are unskilled or semiskilled occupations, with an increasing proportion in sales and personal services. While the proportion of the population engaged in goods production has declined somewhat, the number of service and sales workers has remained strong and is projected to remain so. And the unemployed and the underemployed—the industrial reserve army of Marx and Braverman—are all still very much with us.

Because our economic system is one of capitalism, a great part of the sociocultural system (as well as the world-system) is organized around a need to expand capital. It is this drive that is a major force behind the ever-more-detailed division of labor; the adoption of computers and other technologies to replace workers; globalization and outsourcing; immigration; the commodification of social life; the degradation of work and workers; the economic, political, cultural polarization within and between societies; and rising tides of alienation and anomie. Contrary to Braverman, however, I do not assert that capitalism is the only force at work causing these changes. Capitalism is an economic system that must be placed within the sociocultural web of population, technological and environmental relationships, bureaucratization, nationalism, consumerism, the advance of science, and rationalization. These forces—never alone but always in interaction with one another (sometimes reinforcing, sometimes contradicting)—are the stuff of sociology.

## Notes

1. One of my better job titles, though the job itself was hell. It consisted of being stationed at a table placed at the end of a conveyer belt; packages of buns would then slide on the table from the belt. My job was to grab one package with my right, one with my left, balance two packages in between, and slide the four of them into the plastic tray for transport to the stores. The trays were stacked 14 high.

2. There are two main types of employment tables that need to concern us. The first, just remarked upon, divides workers up in terms of their industry of employment. This table looks at the number of employees by industry, but it includes all occupations within these industries. So, for example, employment in "Manufacturing" would include, not only the blue-collar production worker on the assembly line, but also the service worker sweeping the shop, the executive who runs the personnel department, and the secretary typing and filing the executive's correspondence.

The other type of employment table of interest looks at employment by occupational classification. There are six broad classifications used by the U.S. Census Bureau. "Managerial and professional specialty," "Technical, sales, and administrative support," "Service occupations," "Precision production, craft, and repair," Operators, fabricators, and laborers," and "Farming, forestry, and fishing." There are many subcategories under these categories.

The difference between employment in industries and occupations can be striking. While some 37% of the 2001 workforce were employed by service industries, only 14% of all employed persons were actually working in service occupations. These figures (and many more from the U.S. Census as well as other government sources), available at your local library and through the Internet, are especially useful in that they are records of change over time in industries and occupations.

3.   Braverman admits that the methodology is somewhat crude. It is intended as a rough computation, based on Census data gathered for other purposes, and is therefore not ideal for this exercise. There will be some occupations included in his working class estimate who are paid closer to a managerial scale, and in which the occupation enjoys a degree of autonomy. However, there will be other occupations excluded from his estimate, particularly in some of the technical fields, that have little autonomy or compensation.

4.   It should be emphasized that these figures do not include agriculture, a significant occupation in 1900 (in terms of numbers). Braverman argues that while the compensation for such an occupation was uneven (although often low), the autonomy and skill were very high indeed.

5.   According to Karl Marx (and thus Braverman), as capitalism develops the working class is supposed to become progressively de-skilled, exploited, and larger as former capitalists and the middle stratum of self-employed small businessmen are absorbed into its ranks. Eventually, the vast majority of people within capitalist society become workers (95 percent is a figure often given) with just a few capitalists at the top. Then, comes the revolution.

6.   Hyperindustrial society, one supposedly based on scientific technology and higher education, seems to still be predicated on the exploitation of a significant proportion of its working population.

7.   Again, these figures are for the number of employees by industry, but they include all occupations within these industries. As mentioned in note 2, for example, employment in "Manufacturing" would include not only the blue-collar production worker on the assembly line, but also the service worker sweeping the shop, the executive who runs the personnel department, and the secretary typing and filing the executive's correspondence.

8.   Marxists are insistent that their brand of social science is truly scientific.

9.   In accordance with Wallerstein and other world-systems theorists, it could well be that the recent growth of globalization has allowed capital to exploit labor on a worldwide scale, thus allowing for a larger proportion of elite and middle classes in some core countries, and a significant pool of degraded labor in peripheral and semi-peripheral countries.

10.   In the latter case, only the location of the exploitation of workers has changed. Sweatshops in third-world countries, where workers are compensated pennies on the dollar and environmental and worker safety laws are minimal, now are the basis of profit of many companies.

11.   From 1983 to 2001 the total labor force grew from 100,834,000 to 135,073,000, or by 34 percent. In that same time period, the growth of the Manager and Professional Specialty categories grew from 23,592,000 to 41,894,000 or by 77 percent.

12.   Again, these figures are rough estimates only. There are, of course, some people excluded from the estimate that should be included, and others who are included that should not be there. Also, it should be pointed out, this middle stratum includes some self-employed workers who would be more akin to the older middle class. In 2001 self-employed "Managerial and professional specialty" as well as "Technical, sales, and administrative support" numbered about 5 million. The absolute numbers of self-employed in these two categories have been remarkably stable since 1990.

13.   It is interesting that the new computer specialties should account for the bulk of the growth in technical expertise in the last 20 to 30 years. The application of computing technology to factory and office is widely credited with a tremendous boost in productivity. Computerization is a tremendous aid in extending the reach of supervisory personnel as well as the professional; it is a tremendous aid in precision technology as well as in the routinization of tasks. Millions have lost jobs (or never been hired) due to

the increasing application of computer technology to the office and the factory. Millions more in other occupations have had their skill requirements lowered because of the application of this technology—and consequently their pay. For all this, the real technical expertise of the computer industry is in the hands of about 2.75 million computer scientists and programmers, or about 2 percent of the total labor force.

## References

Braverman, Harry. 1974[1998]. *Labor and Monopoly Capital: The Degradation of Work in the Twentieth Century.* New York: Monthly Review Press.

Foster, John Bellamy. 1998. "Introduction to the 1998 Edition of Monopoly Capital." In Harry Braverman, *Labor and Monopoly Capital: The Degradation of Work in the Twentieth Century.* New York: Monthly Review Press, ix–xxiv.

Livingston, Michael G. 2000, September 29. *Harry Braverman: Marxist Activist and Theorist.* Retrieved July 11, 2007, from Marxist History: http://www.marxists.org/history/etol/newspape/amersocialist/harry_braverman.htm.

Mills, C. Wright. 1959 [1976]. *The Sociological Imagination.* New York: Oxford Univ. Press.

U.S. Census Bureau, Statistical Abstract of the United States. 2002. Tables No. 588 and 591.

# CHAPTER 7

# The Web Approach to State Strategy in Puerto Rico

*Vince Montes*

SOCIAL MOVEMENTS AND CONTENTIOUS ACTION are indicators of larger processes and structures in a given society. Therefore, this field should not simply be concerned with the many nuances of contentious behavior and its relationship with state repression. Without the goal of developing an understanding of the full complexity of the state and its role in society, we are often left with interpretations that view dormant periods of contentious action as reflections of harmonious societies, or that states only rear their heads in times of contentious action as a response to threats or attack. Consistent with C. Wright Mills's web approach systematized by Phillips (2001), this paper attempts to link seemingly unconnected sets of problems due to the highly bureaucratic social sciences. Rather than just focus on traditional modes of state repression, the web approach analyzes a vast array of strategies that states utilize to maintain their authority.

The Puerto Rican case illustrates how the United States has utilized strategies that are most pervasive. Contexts in which inequality prevails and where grievances have not been adequately met are ideal for measuring changes in state strategy over time. The United States is reliant on various facilitative types of strategies to hinder contentious action. This chapter applies a web approach to the U.S. governmental strategy in Puerto Rico by linking traditional and nontraditional modes of state repression (e.g., police/military, the legal system, and crime control) to various facilitative modes (e.g., elite promotion, political process manufacturing, social-aid provisions, employment distribution, and the use of the military as a vehicle for social integration). This approach allows a broader understanding of the more permanent and ongoing role of the state.

## Theoretical Implications

The impact of state repression on contentious behavior has long been of interest for social movement scholars (Tarrow, 1998; McAdam, 1982; Tilly, 1978). My intention here is to address how we have underconceptualized the state in our quest to understand its role in hindering contentious action. The importance that state repression plays in either neutralizing or instigating resistance has been firmly established (Davenport, Johnston, and Mueller, 2005). However, other state strategies have dropped out of that analysis. States are not limited to repression because they have at their disposal a multitude of other strategies. My approach does not reduce the significance of state repression, but argues that it is but one aspect of state strategies. Mills's study of the sociology of his time revealed a consistent pattern of "dealing in a fragmentary way with scattered problems" (1943: 166). For Phillips, "the web approach to the scientific method [can be used] for integrating available sociological knowledge" (2001: 79). The web approach can "organize diverse phenomena and concrete connections to particular phenomena" (Kincaid, 2002: 132).

### Building on a Nontraditional View of State Repression

By expanding the analysis of state repression, we can begin to view the state as an active and permanent actor in the noncontentious population. Although this view of the state is often reserved for non- or less-than-democratic states (Boudreau, 2005), state repression should be analyzed not only during periods of mobilization, but as a constant process that includes noncontentious times. The underlining assumption has been that the United States has a nonrepressive state because it has a democratic type of government. This underlying bias has influenced U.S.-based social movement theory (Davis, 1999: 594–595; Osa, 2001: 211). For example, rarely is the United States state analyzed as repressive. It has however been analyzed as having repressive periods, usually explained as a direct response to heightened levels of contentious action. In a more nontraditional view of repression, the targets of the state are not necessarily contenders, and repression is not always contingent on actual increases in contention. States also engage in a constant program to prevent the formation of contentious action.

Lawrence argues that by the late 1960s, due to increases in contention in the United States, the government began adopting a counterinsurgency strategy of permanent repression (2006: 6). This strategy moved away from the traditional belief that insurgency is the occasional and erratic behavior of exploited or oppressed people to the idea that "just because you can't see rebellion doesn't mean it isn't there. It really is happening. The state's enemies are gathering forces. . . ."(Lawrence, 2006: 6). A shift away from the more liberal notion of the state as a benign arbiter serving the greater good is needed in order to develop a framework that can objectively analyze the state. States should be seen as calculated thinking machines that employ strategies which include repression to ensure the status quo of social arrangements. There appears to be some progress in the inclusion of counterinsurgency activities in research on state repression.

More recently, Cunningham (2004) illustrates that state repression in the United States goes beyond overt operations; he argues that FBI and their COINTELPRO operations need to be factored into an analysis of state repression. The study of counterintelligence in the United States has not been the focus of social-movement scholars. A less traditional view of the state allows us to see state repression in both its overt and covert manifestations. These actions also impact the general public in many ways such as distorting movements with slander and disinformation that criminalizes contentious actors. The general public is also impacted when repressive laws (e.g., patriot acts) meant to target dissidents affect entire populations. Another significant aspect in the nontraditional mode of state repression is crime control. Oliver, for example, argues for the extension of the concept of state repression to include incarceration, because of the role that prisons played as repressive agents on black males in the United States during the Black Power Movement in the early 1970s (2004). The extension of state repression beyond "subversive" targets has not been the focus of social-movement research. However, research by Parenti (1999) and Wacquant (2005) suggest the importance of crime control as an aspect of state repression.

## Expanding the Facilitation Concept

Similar to state repression, facilitation is an aspect of state strategy that aims to hinder the mobilization of contentious action. In Tilly's model, states are engaged simultaneously in the repression, facilitation, and toleration of social movements (1978: 100). He defined facilitation as any action by a state that lowers the cost for contentious action such as when states provide publicity, legalize membership, provide payoffs, or provide protection by sending in troops to promote a group's actions (Tilly, 1978: 80). The concept of facilitation has largely been absent in the analysis of state repression, and when it is applied it is often interpreted as being merely the flip side of repression. Yet, when this concept is applied in the above context it has limitations in range and temporality, because states also use facilitative strategies on aggrieved populations that are not engaged in contentious actions. And once a contentious period has run its course, facilitation like repression of certain groups is no longer the focus of analysis.

Facilitation targets specific contentious groups or actions (selectively) and larger sections of the general public (nonselectively). By looking at facilitation as more of a hegemonic strategy designed to win over and/or to manufacture the consent of aggrieved and oppressed people, we see its relevance in maintaining a particular political order. After all, the aim of facilitation is to foster a sense of loyalty through the implementation of various forms of co-optation that are not limited to the leadership or elite promotion of contending groups or actors. But facilitation can also be seen as directing aggrieved and oppressed peoples' claims to a political process. States do indeed respond to challengers by also absorbing their demands and facilitating their entry into the polity (Tarrow, 1998: 82).

In the Puerto Rican case, as we will see below, facilitation is multifaceted and largely anchored in the social structure of control. The facilitative modes, at times, are not easily detected because of the unequal relationship in which the dominant group is able to promote its interest and manipulate the political reality of this relationship. However, facilitation is readily observed in the co-optation of elite and large sectors of the aggrieved population by the use of social-aid provisions, employment, and the military as a vehicle for social integration. Much of the above is what has historically kept the political arrangement afloat while denying fundamental issues such as the right for self-determination and democracy.

## The Repressive Modes

The repressive modes in Puerto Rico include the U.S. military and police, the legal system, and crime control. These modes have been selective and nonselective, and they are rooted in the structure of control.

### Military and Police

The U.S. military in Puerto Rico has often been seen as innocuous and not as a repressive force. Yet, the U.S. military is probably the most pervasive and ominous of all the repressive modes, due to the colonial context of Puerto Rico. The consolidation of U.S. hegemony in Puerto Rico was gradual, influenced by complex structures and processes. But the reorganization of the repressive apparatus was the earliest approach of the United States undertaken by the military regime (Bosque-Perez, 2001: 5). Although the degree of the U.S. military presence on the island (e.g., number of bases, troops, and military readiness) varied due to being a part of the U.S. geopolitical strategy, the U.S. involvement in maintaining the political arrangements on the islands by preventing and neutralizing mobilization was consistent.

The U.S. War Department established several military organizations that engaged in surveillance as well as a strategy aimed at furthering a pro–United States sentiment (Bosque-Perez, 2001: 7). In 1899, the Puerto Rican Regiment was established as part of a policy to utilize native troops to generate local sentiment and because native troops have geographical knowledge that could aid in disposing of "evil" (i.e., native resistance) (Rodriguez-Beruff, 1983: 22). Puerto Ricans were made citizens when the U.S. Congress passed the Jones Act of 1917, which also made them available for the U.S. draft at the onset of World War I. The United States also established a National Guard branch in Puerto Rico in 1919 (Rodriguez-Beruff, 1983: 25). According to Rodriguez-Beruff, the Guard was established when the existing internal forces of repression (i.e., the Puerto Rican Regiment and the police) were no longer considered sufficient against the emerging working-class movement (1983: 25). Then, in the 1920s, the Citizens Military Training Camps were created as a result of concern for "growing Bolshevistic tendencies among the working class youth" (Rodriguez-Beruff, 1983: 24). The Guard was considered from the beginning along with the Puerto Rican Regiment and the Reserve Officers' Training Corps program at the University of Puerto Rico as not only instruments for internal security but instruments for shaping pro-U.S. ideology.

The U.S. military occupies approximately 13 percent of the land and has control of all waterways in Puerto Rico at no cost (Cripps, 1974: 58). There are approximately eighteen military bases with forty-eight U.S. National Guard armories in thirty different communities (see National Guard in Puerto Rico in references). In the 1980s, these military installations had approximately 10,243 full-time active military and civilian personnel stationed on them (Garcia Muniz, 1993: 57). Currently the numbers are approximately 16,000 U.S. Army, Air Force reservists, and National Guard (Rosenberg, 1999). Coming up with accurate military figures in Puerto Rico is problematic because Puerto Rico is a part of a military network system that is subordinate to the U.S. military command in the Western hemisphere (Lindsay-Poland, 2004). This system is responsible for operations in Latin American and the Caribbean, from military intervention, to covert actions, drug interdiction, and homeland defense. These figures do not include the other federal agencies that have departments on the island such as the FBI, DEA, CIA, and other agencies like the Coast Guard that are also stationed on the island.

This military presence on the island has historically served as a constant reminder and deterrent to local resistance: a show of United States' military strength as compared to Puerto Rico's military weakness. In the 1930s, for example, amid deteriorating socioeconomic conditions and political discontent, the Nationalist Party (a proindependence organization) emerged to challenge the U.S. authority in Puerto Rico. Labor strikes were also prevalent at the time, and strikers clashed routinely with strikebreakers and police (Fernandez, 1996: 116; Dietz, 1986: 163, 164, 173). There were eighty-five strikes or actions from July to December of 1933 (Dietz, 1986: 163). The United States responded by building up its repressive capacity (e.g., appointed an ex-military administrator and provided advance weaponry to police) in Puerto Rico and then repressed the Nationalist Party (Rodriguez-Beruff, 1983: 35). Throughout the 1930s, many rank and file Nationalists were arrested. In 1937, the police opened fire on Nationalists, their families, and their supporters, killing twenty-one and wounding more than one hundred fifty at a demonstration against the arrest and harassment of the Nationalists (known as the "Ponce Massacre") (Steiner, 1974: 226-7).

The U.S. military also played a direct role in suppressing the Nationalists' uprising in 1950. The Nationalists responded to the United States and the Popular Democratic Party's efforts to establish commonwealth status for Puerto Rico by launching an uprising (Maldonado-Denis, 1972: 195). The Nationalists seized seven towns on the island and declared independence for Puerto Rico and attempted to assassinate President Truman in Washington, D.C., in order to call international attention to the colonial situation in Puerto Rico (Maldonado-Denis, 1972: 196). The United States responded with a deployment of the U.S. National Guard, 272 policemen, 4,017 soldiers, and 4 U.S. military planes to assist the troops (Helfeld, 1964: 36). With air support, machine guns, bazookas, and tanks the U.S. military and police recaptured the towns. A highly repressive period followed with mass arrests. Puerto Ricans during 1950 to 1954 were also arrested for violation of the Puerto Rican version of the Smith Act (*La Mordaza*) (Bosque-Perez 2005: 32). The FBI and local police in the early 1960s increased their actions by becoming more aggressive in their objective to neutralize mobilization. For example, FBI memos illustrate how the FBI used a campaign of "dirty tricks" to create divisions and distrust among proindependence organizations and to discredit its leadership (Churchill and Vander Wall, 1990: 63-90). The intelligence division within the island's police force was reorganized and provided additional resources to "fight against subversives" (Bosque-Perez, 2001: 23). In 1973 and in 1974, the U.S. National Guard on the island was deployed amid widespread and sustained contentious action, e.g., acts of sabotage and vandalism crippled many vital services. This period included many labor strikes and other contentious actions. There was also an upsurge in armed proindependence organizations that targeted U.S.-based companies and the U.S. military installations (Montes, 2003).

It was discovered in 1987 that the FBI and the local police had "subversive" dossiers on about 75,000 Puerto Ricans deemed as a threat. These dossiers go back to the early days of the U.S. occupation. These dossiers were not only on members of proindependence and radical workers, but also included large sections of the Puerto Rican population (Bosque-Perez, 2005: 24). In the 1960s, prior to the mobilization, the FBI's COINTELPRO operations were active in a campaign to disrupt the proindependence organizational efforts as well as labor leaders on the island and in the United States (Bosque-Perez, 2001; Churchill and Vander Wall, 1990; Gautier Mayoral, 1983: 431-450). Counterintelligence can also be seen in the 1978 Cerro Maravilla incident in which counterintelligence police murdered two activists. There was also a string of unsolved murders of activists, and many cases in which supporters were simply imprisoned because of their activism (Bosque-Perez, 2001: 32). In addition, in 1985, 200 FBI agents raided Puerto Rican activists' houses and businesses throughout the island in an attempt to intimidate supporters of independence, and they arrested people alleged to be connected to the Los Macheteros (an underground armed proindependence organization) (Fernandez, 1996: 246-247). The network of both traditional and nontraditional modes of repression composed of the U.S. military and various police forces on the island has played a significant role in enforcing Puerto Rican's identification with the United States by undermining nationalist sentiment.

## Legal System

The legal system in Puerto Rico is overseen by the U.S. federal courts and has operated more in a traditional capacity of state repression. In 1936, for example, Albizu Campos and other Nationalists were charged and convicted with the wartime Sedition Act of 1918; they spent almost a decade in the federal prison (Berríos Martínez, 1997). This act was a part of a larger effort to restore "order" and to criminalize political dissent on the island during the 1930s. The legal system in 1947 enacted the Taft-Hartley Act as a means to hinder the development of a radical labor movement (Dietz, 1986: 223). In 1948, in anticipation of a Nationalist Party's mobilization with the release Albizu Campos (leader of the Nationalists) from prison and the university strike in 1947, Law 53 was implemented. This antisubversive law was based on the U.S. Smith Act and was modified for Puerto Rico as a result of the increase of contention on the island (Silen, 1971: 77). Law 53 and to some extent the Taft-Hartley Act were designed to heighten a repressive atmosphere on the island, and was used repeatedly in the 1970s and 1980s against Puerto Ricans in the United States and in Puerto Rico in a response to a growing movement and the emergence of clandestine proindependence organizations (Deutsch, 1984: 1183; Gautier Mayoral, 1983). The United States used the federal grand jury to intimidate the movement's support base and to isolate their support (Deutsch, 1984: 1186). As a result, several Puerto Ricans and non–Puerto Ricans were incarcerated for refusing to cooperate with the grand jury investigation of armed proindependence organizations. The U.S. legal system also applied federal laws on such seditious conspiracy to arrested members of the armed organizations, thereby increasing the sentence length and further criminalizing the movement.

The United States and the mass media absolutely denied the political nature of Puerto Rican opponents and portrayed them as criminals and terrorists. According to Ward, during the late 1960s, the Movement for Puerto Rican Independence (MPI) was accused of being connected with the armed groups and as a result several of its members were arrested (1981: 84–85). Thus, being a Puerto Rican political dissident meant to engage in a certain degree of high-risk behavior. According to Cripps, many people did not join proindependence supporters because they were afraid of reprisals (1974: 103). From the 1930s, the late 1940s to the early 1950s, to the arrest of members of the armed organizations as well as other proindependence political activists from the 1960s to the 1980s, the United States had used its courts to criminalize proindependence activists. The enactments of repressive laws in Puerto Rico have followed specific periods of increased contention and have also been used preemptively. This cursory historical observation of the legal repressive mode illustrates how this traditional mode criminalized dissidents.

## Crime Control

The contemporary pervasive Western view is that law enforcement and prison systems and more specifically crime control are politically neutral. Parenti's (1999) and Wacquant's (2005) studies help us to understand crime control as a repressive mode. Parenti argues that during the late 1960s and the early 1970s, the U.S. state felt threatened by internal and external forces mobilized to challenge U.S. authority (1999: 4–5). There was also an increase in illicit drug use and a rise in crime rates, which U.S. authorities saw as connected to a breakdown in the normative order; therefore, the authorities developed a series of strategies to combat these threats (Parenti, 1999: 4–5).

Although social movement scholars do not include crime control in their analyses of state repression, the state clearly made little distinction between nonpolitical crime (e.g., illicit drug use and property crimes) and contentious action against the state. The result was a fortified state that developed an extensive crime-control strategy. By 1967 the federal government and states spent billions of dollars to reshape a "new" rationalized police model, which included the militarization of the police with advanced technology for surveillance, weapons, and specialized programs (e.g., SWAT teams), to build up the "soft" side of crime control, community policing (Parenti, 1999: 6). According to Parenti, the "war on drugs" became the Trojan Horse for the increased federal involvement in policing (e.g., making drug offenses federal offenses, increasing federal agency involvement, and loosening constitutional rights) that continues today (1999: 10).

As the new crime-control policies took hold in the aftermath of a very contentious period, the incarceration rates by the mid-1970s began to peak (Parenti, 1999; Wacquant, 2005). According to Michael Tonry, the architects of the so-called war on drugs were aware that this war would be fought mainly in minority areas of U.S. urban cities, which would result in a disproportionate number of young blacks and Latinos being incarcerated (Wacquant, 2005: 21). For Wacquant, the ghetto as an institutional form is based on closure and power whereby a population is deemed dishonest and dangerous and is at once secluded and controlled (1998: 143). The percentage of prison inmates convicted for drug-related offenses went from 5 percent in 1960, to 9 percent in 1980, to one-third in 1995 (Wacquant, 2005: 19). Even though black men only comprised 7 percent of the population their incarceration rate was nearly doubled to 55 percent in 1995 (Wacquant, 2005: 21).

According to Wacquant the penal system has partly supplanted the ghetto as a mechanism for racial control with the upheaval of the 1960s and the deindustrialization of the economy (2005: 19). Parenti also has a larger explanation that linked the United States with changes in the economy; the domestic racial and class rebellion was the impetus for moving away from the politics of the carrot to the politics of the stick (1999: 240). In other words, the above economic changes prevented employment as an effective mode for facilitation. Parenti argues that the new state strategy was designed to keep a lid on a potentially explosive situation (1999).

Puerto Rico has many features of a classic colony, but also operates in many ways similar to a state in the United States because it is subjected to federal laws. As a result, crime control in Puerto Rico is under the command of the U.S. federal government, which includes its agencies, such as the FBI, DEA, and the U.S. military. A U.S.-led crime-control policy in Puerto Rico has the potential of being merely an instrument of repression designed to maintain the political arrangement.

In many ways the treatment of Puerto Ricans in Puerto Rico parallels the treatment of minority groups (including Puerto Ricans) in the United States. Puerto Rico appears to have some of the characteristics of a ghetto. For O'Neill and Gumbrewicz, Puerto Rico is a "country of minorities" with high rates of unemployment, crime, and incarceration rates, and it is especially on the receiving end of the "get tough" laws against drug-related transgressions (2005). In fact, Puerto Rico has approximately 48 prisons (Guadalupe-Fajardo, 2000), and in 2005 the incarceration rate was 386 per 100,000 (total 15,046) (World Prison Population List, 2005). Puerto Rico is one of the main points of entry for drug trade into the United States; it was designated in 1995 a High Intensity Drug Trafficking Area and accordingly receives additional DEA resources. The U.S. federal "war on drugs" has impacted Puerto Ricans in various ways such as in undermining the Puerto Rican Constitutional ban on the death penalty and on wire tapping (O'Neill and Gumbrewicz, 2005). During the late 1980s and then from 1992 to 2000 under the program of *Mano Dura,* the U.S. National Guard was used in a zero-tolerance approach to crime. The Guard was used to occupy public-housing projects in Puerto Rico and virtually put neighborhoods under siege (Rosa, 2005). In 1989 the U.S. Congress authorized the use of the Guard to support drug interdictions and other counterdrug activities.

Overall, the rise in crime may in fact be connected to the failures of the politics of the carrot (e.g., social aid and employment), which is what we will explore below.

## Facilitation Modes

Similar to state repression, the facilitative modes are multifaceted, both selective and nonselective, and are largely anchored in the structure of U.S. control in Puerto Rico. Facilitation is designed to foster loyalty that can produce a particular type of stability over time by the implementation of various forms of co-optation.

### Elite Promotion and the Political Process

Puerto Rico's elite and political process grew out of colonial circumstances of its national development. The political process has historically operated within the sphere of external control, and it is within this restriction that Puerto Rico's political parties operate. The political process provides the island elite and their political parties an arena in which to exercise their limited power. This in turn has brought about a sense of legitimacy to the political arrangement because it provides an appearance of participatory democracy.

During the 1930s, amid economic depression and increased levels of contentious action, the United States repressed the Nationalist Party and the labor movement while it gravitated toward Luis Muñoz Marin. Muñoz Marin was perceived by the United States as the more "suitable" choice because of his willingness to work with the New Deal Administration. He became the primary benefactor of the New Deal provisions in Puerto Rico and in him Roosevelt found someone in the political arena he could trust to help usher in economic reform as well as help stabilize a politically volatile situation (Morales Carrion, 1983: 230). The New Deal came to Puerto Rico in the form of reconstruction (public works) and relief programs (food and direct-aid distribution) in order to relieve poverty. By mid-1934, an estimated 35 percent of the population was receiving aid (Trias Monge, 1997: 96; Dietz, 1986: 147). In 1938, Muñoz Marin, helped establish the Popular Democratic Party (PPD) and became its leader. The PPD was successful in creating popular appeal with its focus on immediate social improvements, land reform, and its appeal to Puerto Rican nationalism (Lapp. 1995: 171). The PPD gained a rural support base and even gained proindependence supporters from both inside and outside of this party (Maldonado-Denis, 1972: 154). As a result of his broad-based appeal, the PPD won a majority in the island's senate in 1940 and Muñoz Marin became the president of the senate. In 1944, the PPD won control in both houses and in 1948 Munoz Marin became the first-elected governor in Puerto Rico. In 1947, U.S.-appointed governor Rexford Guy Tugwell and members of the PPD drew up Operation Bootstrap, a new economic program designed to promote industrialization through the establishment of an export-oriented economy that would attract U.S.-owned manufacturing companies to the island. Operation Bootstrap was credited with increases in the standard of living and provided employment and for a time served to quiet the colony. Yet, other factors had also contributed to the economic improvements, such as increases in U.S. federal aid to the island and a large economic-based emigration off the island to the United States during and after World War II. In an attempt to meet a United Nations' mandate to decolonize territories in 1946, the U.S. Congress passed Public Act 600 in 1950, which granted Puerto Ricans the legal framework for the creation of commonwealth status (Garcia-Passalacqua, 1984: 125). Although the political status of Puerto Rico fundamentally remained the same, the United Nations did remove Puerto Rico from the list of non-self-governing countries. More importantly, the PPD received a type of legitimacy as the leading political party in Puerto Rico, and to a large extent this formalized Puerto Rico/U.S. relations.

The evaporation of the Operation Bootstrap "miracle" became very apparent by the mid-1960s as U.S. corporations began to flee to countries with cheaper labor. In fact, poverty became so pervasive that by 1966 approximately one-third of the population on the island received surplus food from the Department of Agriculture (Maldonado-Denis, 1972: 172–173). There was also a global rise in radical and anticolonial movements in this period that challenged colonial powers, and Puerto Rico was no exception. A proindependence mobilization remerged in this period to challenge the legitimacy of the United States that was met with various forms of repression. As a result, the case of Puerto Rico was debated at the United Nations, which called into question Puerto Rico's political status. The United States and the PPD responded by attempting to short circuit a U.N. resolution by holding a nonpolitically binding plebiscite in Puerto Rico.

Amid these events, there was division among the elite (e.g., division within the PPD as well as within the traditional statehood party); this resulted in changes in the voting alignment. In 1968, after twenty years, the PPD lost its hold on the governor's office. The New Progressive Party (PNP), a new prostatehood political party that campaigned on a "Statehood is for the Poor" platform won its first governor's election during political and economic uncertainty. To a large extent, not to minimize serious political differences between the two parties, the PNP became a partner in the political arrangement on the island, and since 1968 both parties have rotated in and out of the governor's office. It is important to understand that political parties in Puerto Rico are not mere puppets of the United States, but are active participants in sustaining their own positions of power by cooperating closely with the United States.

## Social-Aid Provisions

Piven and Cloward's (1971) research illustrates how increases in welfare programs in the United States did not follow increases in poverty, but instead followed increases in contention. Piven and Cloward illustrate how the 1930s and 1960s experienced increases in welfare programs, which were used to restore "order" as a result of insurgency, while in the period from 1940 to 1960 (period of stability) welfare assistance was used to reinforce work norms and to maintain a labor surplus (1971). In the case of Puerto Rico, Gautier Mayoral argues that the United States has historically used welfare assistance, not only to relieve massive unemployment, but as a means to maintain its legitimacy (1980: 46).

The political arrangement in Puerto Rico is held together by many parts of a complex state strategy. Electoral systems are often seen as indicators of democratic political processes. However, consent tends to be more a manufactured process because real political power resides in the hands of an external power. The New Deal provisions of the 1930s brought social aid and employment to Puerto Rico. We have also seen how this was the foundation of elite promotion and the generalized appeasement of an impoverished country that also served to legitimize the U.S. presence in Puerto Rico. An influx of U.S. federal social aid along with increased periods of repression certainly appears to have followed increases in contentious action in the 1930s and during the 1970s. However, increases in contention followed a different pattern in the late 1940s and the early 1950s. This period only experienced increases in repression because this was a period characterized by the economic improvements of Operation Bootstrap.

Amid economic decline and rising contention, the United States introduced the food-stamp program to Puerto Rico in 1971 (fully implemented 1974). In 1973, the per capita income was half as small as the poorest state in the United States, with approximately 75 percent of its population eligible for food stamps (Fernandez, 1996). With the climbing unemployment rate and a sluggish economy, food stamps came to Puerto Rico like hurricane relief and served to rescue the entire commonwealth economy (Rivera-Batiz and Santiago, 1996: 16). In fact, Anderson argues that a big part of what maintains the political arrangement between the United States and Puerto Rico is the federal transfers (Anderson, 1988: 3). Puerto Rico has become increasingly dependent on direct federal transfers, such as food stamps. By the early 1980s, billions of U.S. dollars in social aid had come to Puerto Rico (Garcia, 1984: 71), and by 1993 grants amounted to $1 billion (Rivera-Batiz and Santiago, 1996: 15). Recent figures show that around 60 percent of the population is estimated to be living under the poverty level and that the impoverished majority are unable to find enough living-wage jobs, making them more dependent on a gamut of federal entitlements to survive (Gonzales, 2000: 250). According to Garcia-Passalacqua, what is for the U.S. charity is for the elite on the island control and is for the masses survival (1984: 70). He called this a psychology of dependency where the average Puerto Rican feels that the U.S. federal government guarantees their survival (Garcia-Passalacqua, 1984: 8). According to Gonzales, unemployment in the last quarter of a century has rarely dipped below 11 percent and during times of U.S. recessions has surpassed 20 percent (2000: 250). With such figures, it is difficult to overlook the role of social-aid provisions as a part of a state strategy.

## Employment Distribution

The ability of the United States to provide employment has played a large part in its facilitation mode. During the economic depression of the 1930s, as illustrated above, the rise in contentious action resulted in the ushering in of social aid as well as public-works programs. The primary design of Operation Bootstrap was not a model for industrializing a Puerto Rican economy, but to provide U.S.-based corporations a competitive advantage in the global economy. This was accomplished by enticing U.S. corporations with such benefits as low wages, lack of trade barriers, tax exemptions, and subsidies to move to Puerto Rico (Cordero-Guzman, 1993: 7).

This program fits well with the strategy of facilitation because Operation Bootstrap was also meant to provide some employment to alleviate the bleak economic conditions on the island. According to Carrion, the "political consensus" that the United States and the PPD created in this Cold War climate was largely based on the ability to deliver employment and improvements to the standard of living (1995: 143).

Consistent with modernization theory, policies of controlling population growth were implemented to stabilize the growing rates of unemployment in Puerto Rico that resulted from the displaced agricultural workers. Push/pull factors were in play in the post WWII period: There were demands for cheap labor in the United States while there were labor shortages in Puerto Rico. State policies encouraged Puerto Rican immigration to the United States by implementing policies such as subsidized airfare and advertisement campaigns about employment opportunities and promises of the "American Dream."[1] In addition, as part of growth control during the 1930s and 1940s, the United States and the colonial administration took "aggressive measures in providing contraceptives to the population" (Rivera-Batiz and Santiago, 1996: 32). By 1982, 39 percent of the women in Puerto Rico were sterilized, the highest in any nation in the world (Rivera-Batiz and Santiago, 1996: 33).

By the mid-1960s, the labor movement in Puerto Rico demanded better wages, including the federal minimum wage, while nations such as Taiwan and South Korea became more competitive in gaining U.S. investors (Garcia-Passalacqua, 1984: 39). As a result, many manufacturing jobs began to leave Puerto Rico. U.S. corporations did not invest the profits they earned in Puerto Rico into Puerto Rico; instead most of them accumulated their profits until the end of the tax exemption period (10 years) and then liquidated their profits into other subsidiary companies outside of Puerto Rico (Dietz, 1986: 301). In addition, the decline of labor-intensive manufacturing to capital-intensive industry requires less employees.

The miracle, however, never materialized for many Puerto Ricans who have to contend with high unemployment rates. Gonzales describes two Puerto Ricos: one is the vacation paradise that has the second highest standard of living in Latin America, and the other is a "welfare basket case" that drains $5.3 billion a year in governmental assistance while paying no federal taxes (2000: 246). In the latter, 60 percent of Puerto Ricans live under the poverty level and are confronted with serious social ills, such as high rates of crime, murder, and AIDS (Gonzalez, 2000: 246). In fact, in 2005, the unemployment rate was 10.9 percent, which was more than double that of the United States (Ocasio Teissonniere, 2005: 3).[2] If Puerto Rico had the same employment participation rate as the United States, unemployment would be over 30 percent (Ocasio Teissonniere, 2005: 3).[3]

A shift in the U.S. strategy can be seen as the U.S. attempt to absorb some of the unemployed by expanding the U.S. federal sector on the island. In 1950, employment in the federal sector on the island was 13.9 percent, in 1960 it was 18.5 percent, and by 1970 it had increased to 28.6

percent (Carrion, 1980: 248). Currently, the government has become the largest employer on the island, employing approximately 30 percent of the population, either directly or indirectly (Perez Serrano, 2005).[4] Yet, U.S. corporations continue to take in huge profits off the island, while billions in federal welfare and transfer payments come to the Puerto Ricans yearly to alleviate poverty (Gonzalez, 2000: 251).

## The U.S. Military as a Vehicle for Social Integration

The U.S. military in Puerto Rico is embedded in almost all aspects of Puerto Rican society and cannot be understood only in terms of state repression. The military plays a dual role in socially integrating large sectors of the Puerto Rican population into the "American way of life." Rodriguez-Beruff argues that many of the U.S. military organizations were designed to instill a pro-U.S. ideology and to develop loyal and patriotic U.S. citizens (as opposed to a Puerto Rican nationalism) (Rodriguez-Beruff, 1983: 23). The concept of the military, or more specifically military service, as a vehicle for social integration was used to study how the military serves as a unifying force that brings together separate entities into a nation (Deitz, Elkin, and Roumani, 1991: 2). The U.S. has carried out some nation-building strategies, such as imposing U.S. citizenship and conscription into the military. The problem has been that these state-building strategies have been imposed externally, which is more in keeping with colonialism as opposed to the formation of a democratic federation.

Cripps argued that imposed U.S. citizenship in 1917 was intended to link Puerto Ricans more securely to the United States as well as to curb the growing discontent during the U.S. preparations for World War I (1974: 23). Besides increasing its military numbers by drafting Puerto Ricans, it is clear that the United States intended to use its military as a means to generate loyalty toward the United States (Rodriguez-Beruff, 1983: 24). Citizenship certainly was a very important ideological element in the historical process of producing consent by instilling U.S. values in Puerto Ricans (Rivera Ramos, 1994: 9, 13–14). Knottnerus's research illustrates how ritualized symbolic practices play a role in socializing behavior by creating, reproducing, and/or transforming social structure (2005). The military facilitates by shaping and reinforcing soldiers' group solidarity, allegiance, and commitment to the military group and to the wider social system it represents. This develops through ritualized symbolic practices such as drilling, combat experiences, and parades that impact the cognitions or symbolic thoughts of actors and generate ritual experiences that heighten group allegiance (2005).

Puerto Ricans have a long history of either being drafted or enlisting in the U.S. military. Puerto Ricans have fought in every war since World War I (Gonzales, 2000: 253). One of the results is that this has created a large number of veterans on the island (e.g., 170,000 veterans in Puerto Rico during the 1980s, with about 12,000 of them active in the American Legion (Rodriguez-Beruff, 1983: 25). Veterans are selected for special privileges such as pensions, loans, and medical treatment (Rodriguez-Beruff, 1983: 25). This in turn continues the "ritualized symbolic practice" by keeping a large segment of the population connected to the United States long after their military service ends. Organizations like the American Legion keep the sense of U.S. patriotism alive in many Puerto Rican veterans. The Legion developed as an anticommunist organization to prevent the radicalization of former soldiers by keeping them connected to the military (Campbell, 1997: 4).

Even during wartime, the military offers one of the very few escapes from poverty. This is similar to how it has historically provided economic opportunity to many poor people living in ghettos and rural areas in the United States. Throughout the many decades of the U.S. military presence, the military has used the island for recruitment and has also been a large employer for many Puerto Ricans. In the 1980s, there were more Puerto Ricans from Puerto Rico in the U.S. military per capita than from three-fourths of the United States (Perusse, 1987: 21).

## Some Implications for the Web Approach to National Government Strategy

As the Puerto Rican case illustrates, to conceptualize national government action in terms of traditional modes of government repression is to develop a distorted and skewed analysis that not only simplifies a complex actor, but this simplification may also lead to rationalizing the current political arrangement. It is apparent that leaving out other modes of repression, and excluding facilitative modes yields an analysis that does not inform us about the U.S. government's encroachment in other aspects of Puerto Rican society.

The web approach provides a framework to analyze a national government as a more complex and sophisticated apparatus that has a greater reach than just targeting contenders. This is a reach that is only understood by analyzing areas that are not usually considered to be in the realm of social movement theory. The various modes of facilitation demonstrate a complex system of appeasement and co-optation designed in many ways to win or to manufacture Puerto Rican consent to the U.S. authority. By analyzing government repression along with other state strategies such as facilitation in its various forms, we have seen how the entire Puerto Rican population is subjected to a combination of state strategies that are more pervasive and hegemonic than a traditional analysis of state repression would be able to uncover.

# Notes

1. From 1900 to 1940 there was a net outflow of approximately 73,000 for the entire time period, as opposed to an average annual net outflow of 47,000 between the late 1940s and the 1950s (Rivera-Batiz and Santiago, 1996: 45).

2. In the last 25 years, the unemployment rate has rarely dipped below 11 percent and during U.S. recessions has surpassed 20 percent (Gonzalez, 2000: 250).

3. The participation rate, meaning the portion of working-age persons employed or actively looking for work, was 46.4 percent, while in the U.S. it was 66 percent (Ocasio Teissonniere, 2005: 3).

4. There are approximately 320,000 government employees in Puerto Rico (Roman, 2005: 3). Florida, in comparison, has 14 government agencies for 17 million people, while Puerto Rico has 130 agencies for approximately 4 million people (Roman, 2005).

# References

Anderson, Robert. W. 1988. "Political Parties and the Politics of the Status." *Caribbean Studies* 21(1–2): 1–43.

Berríos Martínez, Rubén. 1997. "Puerto Rico's Decolonization" *Foreign Affairs* (November–December). http://www.independencia.net/ingles/frgAffairs.html.

Bosque-Perez, Ramon. 2001. "Political Persecution Against Puerto Rican Activists." Unpublished manuscript.

———. 2005. "Political Persecution Against Puerto Rican Anti-Colonial Activities in the 20th Century." In eds. Ramon Bosque-Perez and Jose Javier Colon-Morera. *Puerto Rico Under Colonial Rule,* Albany: SUNY Press, 13–48.

Bourdreau, Vince. 2005. "Precarious Regimes and Matchup Problems in the Explanation of Repressive Policy." Eds. Christian Davenport, Hank Johnston, and Carol Mueller. *Repression and Mobilization.* Minneapolis: Univ. of Minnesota Press.

Campbell, Alec. 1997. "American Veterans and Class Conflict after World War I." Unpublished paper presented at the New School for Social Research, December 9.

Carrion, Juan Manuel. 1980. "The Petty Bourgeois and the Struggle for Independence." In ed. Adalberto Lopez. *The Puerto Ricans: Their History, Culture and Society.* Rochester, Vt.: Schenkman Publishing Company, Inc.

———. 1995. "Puerto Rican Nationalism and the Struggle for Independence." In ed. Berch Berberoglu. *The National Question: Nationalism, Ethnic Conflict, and Self-Determination in the 20th Century.* Philadelphia: Temple Univ. Press, 133–157.

Churchill, Ward, and Jim Vander Wall. 1990. *The COINTELPRO Papers: Documents from the FBI's Secret Wars Against Dissent in the United States.* Cambridge, Mass.: South End Press.

Cordero-Guzman, Hector R. 1993. "Lessons from Operation Bootstrap." *NACLA* xxvii(3): 7–10.

Cripps, L. L. 1974. *Puerto Rico: The Case of Independence.* Rochester, Vt.: Schenkman.

Cunningham, David. 2004. *There's Something Happening Here: The New Left, The Klan, and the FBI Counterintelligence.* Berkeley: Univ. of California Press.

Davenport, Christian, Hank Johnston, and Carol Mueller. 2005. *Repression and Mobilization,* Minneapolis: Univ. of Minnesota.

Davis, Diane. 1999. "The Power of Distance: Retheorizing Social Movements in Latin America." *Theory and Society* 28: 584–638.

Deutsch, Michael E. 1984. "The Improper Use of the Federal Grand Jury: An Instrument for the Internment of Political Actives." *Journal of Criminal Law & Criminology* 75(4): 1159–1196.

Dietz, Henry, Jerrold Elkin, and Maurice Roumani. 1991. *Ethnicity, Integration, and the Military.* Boulder, Colo.: Westview Press.

Dietz, James L. 1986. *Economic History of Puerto Rico: Institutional Change and Capitalist and Capitalist Development.* Princeton, N.J.: Princeton Univ. Press.

Fernandez, Ronald. 1996. *The Disenchanted Island: Puerto Rico and the United States in the Twentieth Century.* Westport, Conn.: Praeger Publishers.

Garcia Munoz, Humberto. 1993. "U.S. Military Installations in Puerto Rico: Controlling the Caribbean." In eds. Edwin Melendez and Edgard Melendez. *Critical Perspectives on Contemporary Puerto Rico.* Boston, Mass.: South End Press.

Garcia-Passalacqua, Juan M. 1984. *Puerto Rico: Equality and Freedom at Issue,* New York: Praeger Publishers.

Gautier Mayoral, Carmen. 1980. "Interrelation of United States Poor Relief, Massive Unemployment and Weakening of 'Legitimacy' in Twentieth Century Puerto Rico." *Caribbean Studies* 19(3, 4): 5–46.

———. 1983. "Notes on the Repressive Practices by Intelligence Agencies in Puerto Rico." *Revista Juridica de la Universidad de Puerto Rico* 52(3): 431–450.

Gonzalez, Juan. 2000. *Harvest of Empire.* New York: Penguin Books.

Guadalupe-Fajardo, Evelyn. 2000, "The High Price of Hard Time." *Caribbean Business* 28(40): 01, 26,

Helfeld, David M. 1964. "Discrimination for Political Beliefs and Association." *Revista del Colegio de Abogados de Puerto Rico* 25(1) (November): 5–276.

Hernandez, Donna R. 2005. "Iraqi Elections: Lessons from Puerto Rico." *ColorLines,* 2005-2.

Kincaid, Harold. 2002. "Explaining Inequality." In Bernard Phillips, Harold Kincaid, and Thomas J. Scheff (eds), *Toward a Sociological Imagination: Bridging Specialized Fields.* Lanham, Md.: Univ. Press of America, 131–150.

Knottnerus, J. David. 2005. "Structural Ritualization Theory: Current Research and Future Developments." Presented at the Sociological Imagination Group Conference, Philadelphia, August 13, 2005.

Lapp, Michael. 1995. "The Rise and Fall of Puerto Rico as a Social Laboratory, 1945–1965." *Social Science History* 19(2): 169, 199.

Lawrence, Ken. 2006 (1985). "The New State Repression." Portland, Ore.: Tarantula Publishing.

Lindsay-Poland, John. 2004. "U.S. Military Bases in Latin America and the Caribbean." Foreign Policy in Focus. August. http://www.fpif.org/briefs/vol9/v9n03latammil.html.

Maldonado-Denis, Manuel. 1972. *Puerto Rico: A Socio-Historic Interpretation,* Vintage Books.

McAdam, Doug. 1982. *Political Process and the Development of Black Insurgency, 1930–1970.* Chicago: Univ. of Chicago Press.

Mills, C. Wright. 1943. "The Professional Ideology of Social Pathologists." *American Journal of Sociology* 49(2) (Sept.): 165–180.

———. 2000 (1959). *The Sociological Imagination.* Oxford: Oxford Univ. Press.

Montes, Vince. 2003. *Cycles of Protest: Contentious Puerto Rican Collective Action, 1960s–1980s.* Unpublished dissertation, New School for Social Research.

Morales Carrion, Arturo. 1983. *Puerto Rico: A Political and Cultural History,* New York: W. W. Norton.

National Guard in Puerto Rico. http://www.globalsecurity.org/military/agency/army/arng-pr.htm.

Ocasio Teissonniere, Georgianne. 2005. "Stagflation Threatens Puerto Rico's Economy." *Caribbean Business* 33(32): 1, 16.

Oliver, Pamela. 2004. Section on Collective Behavior and Social Movements Invited Panel. "Institutionalization and Revitalization of Social Movements." 99th Annual ASA Meeting, San Francisco, Calif.

O'Neill, LeeAnn, and Jennifer Gumbrewicz. 2005. "Our Forgotten Colony: Puerto Rico and War on Drugs." *The Modern American,* spring: 8–11.

Osa, Maryjane. 2001. "Mobilizing Structures and Cycles of Protest: Post-Stalinist Contention in Poland, 1954/1959." *Mobilization* 6 (2): 211–232.

Parenti, Christian. 1999. *Lockdown America: Police and Prisons in the Age of Crisis.* New York: Verso.

Perez Serrano, Mariella. 2005 "Government Jobs Increased by 6,000 Since January; Growth in Public-Sector Employment Continues While Private Sector Declines." *Caribbean Business* (June 10).

Perusse, Roland I. 1987. *The United States and Puerto Rico: Decolonization Option and Perspectives.* Lanham, Md.: Univ. Press of America.

Phillips, Bernard S. 2001. *Beyond Sociology's Tower of Babel: Reconstructing the Scientific Method.* New York: Aldine De Gruyter.

Piven, Frances Fox, and Richard A. Cloward. 1971. *Regulating the Poor.* New York: Vintage.

Rivera-Batiz, Francisco L., and Carlos E. Santiago. 1996. *Island Paradox: Puerto Rico in the 1990s.* New York: Russell Sage Foundation.

Rivera Ramos, Efren. 1994. "Problems of Self-Determination and Decolonization in the Modern Colonial Welfare State: The Case of Puerto Rico." *Clacso,* 9–20.

———. 2001. *The Legal Construction of Identity: The Judicial and Social Legacy of American Colonialism in Puerto Rico.* Washington, D.C.: American Psychological Association.

Rodriguez-Beruff, Jorge. 1983. "Imperialism and Militarism: An Analysis of the Puerto Rican Case," *Proyecto Caribeno de Justicia y Paz,* Rio Pedras: Puerto Rico.

Roman, Elisabeth. 2005. Can Puerto Rico Taxpayers Continue to Carry Big Government? *Caribbean Business* 33(6): 1, 18.

Rosenberg, Carol. 1999. "Puerto Rico Becoming a Military Hub for U.S." *The Miami Herald*, July 6.

Silen, Juan Angel. 1971. *We, the Puerto Rican People: A Study of Oppression and Resistance*. New York: Monthly Review Press.

Steiner, Stan. 1974. *The Islands: The Worlds of the Puerto Ricans*. New York: Harper & Row Publishers.

Tarrow, Sidney. 1998. *Power in Movement: Social Movements and Contentious Politics*. Cambridge: Cambridge Univ. Press.

Tilly, Charles. 1978. *From Mobilization to Revolution*. Reading, Mass.: Addison-Wesley.

Trias Monge, Jose. 1997. *Puerto Rico: The Trials of the Oldest Colony in the World*. New Haven: Yale Univ. Press.

Wacquant, Loïc. 1998. "A Black City within the White: Revisiting America's Dark Ghetto." *Black Renaissance* 2(1): 141-151.

————. 2005. "The Great Penal Leap Backward: Incarceration in America from Nixon to Clinton." In eds. John Pratt, David Brown, et al. *The New Punitiveness: Current Trends, Theories, Perspectives*. Portland, Ore.: Willan Press.

Ward, Ana Mercedes R. 1981. "The Impact of the Cuban Revolution on the Political Status of Puerto Rico: 1959-1980," Unpublished dissertation, Tulane Univ.

World Prison Population List. 2005. 6th ed. London: King's College London, International Centre for Prison Studies.

# CHAPTER 8

# Macho/Madonna Link?

## Hypermasculine Violence as a Social System

*Thomas J. Scheff*

IT IS CLEAR THAT MEN are much more physically violent than women. But most feminist theory has blamed men rather than develop causal theories. The way in which both men and women contribute to interpersonal and collective systems of violence is considered. In particular, it is hypothesized that hyperfeminine women complement and encourage or tolerate hypermasculine men. To understand the larger system, it may be necessary to study emotional/relational configurations of men and women, in addition to the usual studies of power and domination. Unacknowledged shame seems to play a key role in these configurations. The central hypothesis is that hypermasculine aggression is generated by the suppression of the vulnerable emotions (shame, fear, and grief) and the exaggeration of anger in males. Hyperfeminine women encourage or at least tolerate this behavior because they suppress anger and act out fear. If these ideas are to be tested, they will need to be translated into testable propositions based on clearly defined concepts.

There are by now several studies criticizing feminist theory for blaming men unfairly (Farrell, 1993; Patai, 1993; Sommers, 2001; Levine, 2003; Nathanson and Young, 2006). However, these studies do not take what seems to me the next step, which is to replace blame with concepts that help depict the social system of which men and women form a part. This essay focuses on violent males, and the way in which their emotional/relational ties to women close to them might contribute to their behavior.

This is only a preliminary exploration of ideas that might be first steps toward improving our understanding of gender roles and violence in modern societies. Until they are stated as testable propositions, they will only be illustrative and provisional. The next step would be to clearly link the small parts of individual conduct and social interaction to the large wholes of social institutions (Scheff, 1997; 2006) in terms of a web of clearly defined concepts (Phillips, 2001; Phillips and Johnston, 2007).

## Two Dimensions of Social Systems

Marx's early work implied two basic dimensions of the human condition: power and class, on the one hand, and, on the other, social integration: the emotional/relational polarity. His later work, however, was limited to the first dimension, power and class in political economies. Unfortunately, social science has followed suit, with greed for power and property usually seen as the dominant human motive.

In his early writing, however, Marx gave the two dimensions equal treatment. In 1844 he suggested that the most important human "species" need is *connection* with other human beings. He went on to discuss alienation from the mode of production, others, and self. Although the state of connectedness of actual human bonds is much less visible than power and property, he noted two observable emotional responses to alienation: impotence and indignation (Tucker, 1978: 133–144).

As will be suggested below, feelings of impotence can be viewed as a shame cognate, and indignation as representing a shame-anger blend. Marx himself seemed to link these signals of alienation to violence. In a letter to Arnold Ruge in 1843 discussing German nationalism, Marx wrote: "Shame is a kind of anger turned in on itself. And if a whole nation were to feel ashamed it would be like a lion recoiling in order to spring" (Marx, 1844/1975). This sentence can be seen as prophetic of the next hundred years of German history, particularly the rise of Hitler (Scheff, 1994, chapter 5).

Following the current practice in most social science, analysis of masculine behavior links it to lust for power and domination, with no mention of alienation and its relational/emotional accompaniments. A hint in the latter direction can be found in the work of the psychoanalyst

Alfred Adler (1956). He argued that young children have an intense need for love and connectedness, especially from their parents. If a secure bond is not available, Adler proposed two different responses: an inferiority complex (chronic shame), or *the drive for power*. Since we now know, thanks to child-development studies, that male children get less affection and intimate talk from parents than females, his idea points toward an emotional/relational basis for the hypermasculine focus on power.

## Links Between Hypermasculinity and Violence

Although now in general use in the social sciences, the word hypermasculine is relatively new. It is likely that it was first used by Nandy (1983) in her study of colonialism and gender. At some time it will probably replace the more common usage of *machismo*. The word hyperfemininity is still newer. Although there are by now several studies using the term, including those discussed below, there are many more meanings than is the case with hypermasculinity. Here I will attempt a definition in terms of types of emotions and relationships usually involved. I will begin with an analysis of the much clearer idea, hypermasculinity.

An English general describes the slaughter of his brigade as they moved toward German lines in World War I.

> They advanced in line after line, dressed as if on parade and not a man shirked going through the extremely heavy barrage, or facing the machine gun fire that finally wiped them out. Yet not a man wavered, broke the ranks, or attempted to come back. I have never seen, indeed could never have imagined such a magnificent display of *gallantry, discipline, and determination.* (Emphasis added.) (Goffman, 1967)

The general sees the men's self control as virtuous, but it can also be seen as strict adherence to what my teacher, Erving Goffman, called the "cult of masculinity" (1967, 149–270). The idea of a *cult* of masculinity turns out to be especially fortuitous, as was the case with many of Goffman's seemingly casual formulations. Since a cult points toward culture, hypermasculinity might be explained in terms of social relationships and emotions.

Goffman's chapter "Where the Action Is" (1967, pp. 149–270) is by far the longest of his essays. He proposed that scenes of "action" (risk-taking) are occasions that allow the display of "character," in the sense of establishing one's degree of "courage, gameness, integrity, and composure" (229). Of the four components, Goffman gave most attention to the last. By composure, he meant poise, calmness, and above all, control over one's emotions. "Character contests" are competitions in which risks are taken to determine which actor has the most character, and particularly, control over emotions.

Goffman's discussion implies that it is masculine men that have "character." A man with character who is under stress is not going to cry and blubber like a woman or child might. All occasions are seen as opportunities for one to test one's own character as compared to that of another person or other persons. The hypermasculine pattern leads to *competition,* rather than *connection* between people. Since he didn't consider the link to violence to be described here, Goffman's view of hypermasculinity appears to be a gross error. The image of men commanded into machine-gun fire, and passively accepting the command, is a vision less of courage of the leaders and the men than their stupidity.

## Emotions and Self-Knowledge

A social/emotional approach to conflict runs counter to the rationalism of most current thinking. Most political analysis is "realist": human actions are usually viewed as propelled by material, calculable forces. In world literature, however, there has long been an alternative to narrow rationalism in the quest for self-knowledge: *know thyself.* Classic Greek philosophy proposed that a crucial goal for all human beings was knowledge of self, and by implication, that *human folly is a result of ignorance of self.* This thread forms a central concern in both ancient and modern literature.

The theme is epitomized in *Tasso,* an 18th-century drama: "The gift of the great poet is to be able to voice his suffering, even when other men would be struck dumb in their agony." The conjunction between the suppression of emotions and dumbness may turn out to be more than just an accidental pun, as suggested by the example from WWI above.

Self-knowledge is not just a cognitive matter, but also an emotional one. Discovering one's hidden emotions may be not only the most difficult part of knowing thyself, but also the most important. Knowledge of emotions in self is also closely related to the social realm: awareness of emotions concerns not only one's own, but those of others, and therefore links individual and social matters. To the extent that we are ignorant of our own emotions and those of others, our life is a long sleep.

Boys, more than girls, learn early that vulnerable feelings (love, grief, fear, and shame) are seen as signs of weakness. First at home, then at school they find that acting out anger, even if faked, is seen as strength. Expressing anger verbally, rather than storming, may be seen as weakness. At first merely for self-protection, boys begin suppressing feelings that may be interpreted as signs of weakness.

In Western cultures most boys learn, as first option, to hide their vulnerable feelings in emotionless talk, withdrawal, or silence. I will call these three responses (emotional) *silence*. In situations where these options seem unavailable, males may cover their vulnerable feelings behind a display of hostility. That is, young boys learn in their families, and later, from their peers, to suppress emotions they actually feel by acting out anger whether they feel it or not.

I call this pattern "silence/violence." Vulnerable feelings are first hidden from others, and after many repetitions, even from self. In this latter stage, behavior becomes compulsive. When men face what they construe to be threatening situations, they may be compelled to *silence* or to rage and aggression.

Even without threat, men seem to be more likely to use silence or violence than women. With their partners, most men are less likely to talk freely about feelings of resentment, humiliation, embarrassment, rejection, joy, genuine pride, loss, and anxiety. This may be the reason they are more likely to show anger: they seem to be backed up on a wide variety of intense feelings, but sense that only anger is allowed them. Two studies of alexthymia (emotionlessness; Krystal, 1988, Taylor et al., 1997) do not mention any difference between men and women, but most of the cases discussed are men.

Numbing out fear, particularly, makes men dangerous to themselves and others. Fear is an innate biological signal of danger that helps us survive. When we see a car heading toward us on a collision course, we have an immediate, automatic fear response: *Wake up sleep-head, your life is in danger!* Much faster than thought, this reaction increases our chance of survival, and repressing it is dangerous to self and others. If the sense of fear has been repressed, it is necessary to find ways of uncovering it.

In order to avoid pain inflicted by others, we learn to repress the expressions of feeling that lead to negative reactions from others. After thousands of curtailments, repression becomes habitual and out of consciousness. But as we become more backed up with avoided emotions, we have the sense that experiencing them would be unbearably painful. In this way, avoidance leads to avoidance in an ever increasing, self-perpetuating loop. The idea of social/emotional *feedback loops* may provide the model of motives that can lead toward infinite intensity.

## Shame as the Master Emotion

Pride and shame are not only individual feelings, but also crucial elements in social systems. Genuine pride can be seen to signal and generate solidarity in the sense of connectedness. Shame signals and generates alienation in the sense of disconnectedness. People who are on the same page in each other's presence tend toward authentic pride states; those who are disconnected tend toward shame states.

I use the awkward phrases "pride states" and "shame states," because, as will be discussed below, most of our pride, and almost all of our shame occurs outside of awareness. Especially in English-speaking cultures, these two emotions are usually sensed to be unacceptable, even to one's self.

The emotion of shame can be directly acknowledged by referring to one's inner states of insecurity, or feelings of separateness or powerlessness. But several studies have shown that shame usually goes unacknowledged to self and others. For example, Lewis (1971) used systematic measures of emotion to analyze the recordings of over a hundred psychotherapy sessions. She found that shame was by far the most frequently occurring emotion, but that it was virtually never mentioned by client or therapist.

Acknowledging shame helps connect parties; admissions of feelings of weakness or vulnerability can build solidarity and trust. One is exposing one's deepest feelings. Denial of shame builds a wall between parties. If shame signals are disguised and/or ignored, both parties lose touch with each other. Pride and shame cues give instant indications of the "temperature" of the relationship. Pride means the parties are neither engulfed (too close), a "we" relationship, nor isolated (too far), an "I" relationship, but are emotionally and cognitively connected. Elias called an I-We relationship "interdependence" (1972). Overt shame usually signals engulfment, bypassed shame, and isolation (see discussion of these two forms of shame below).

Unacknowledged shame appears to be *recursive,* feeding upon itself, and causing recursion in other emotions, such as grief and fear. To the extent that this is the case, shame could be crucial in the causation of interminable conflict. One type of loop involves only shame. If it goes unacknowledged, it can loop back upon itself (being ashamed that one is ashamed). For example, persons prone to blushing have told me that when they are conscious of blushing, they fall into a loop of being ashamed of their blushing, and blushing more because they are ashamed, and so on.

Shame can also co-occur with other emotions, such as grief (unresolved grief), fear (fear panics), or anger (humiliated fury) causing unending recursion. Unacknowledged shame seems to foil the biological and cultural mechanisms that allow for the expression and harmless discharge of these elemental emotions. In the absence of shame, or if it is acknowledged, grief may be discharged by weeping, under culturally appropriate conditions of mourning. But if shame is evoked by grief and goes unacknowledged, unending loops of emotions (shame-grief sequences) may occur.

Individuals and groups may be unable to mourn. Volkan (2004) sees this inability as central to what he calls the intergenerational transmission of trauma. He noted that the battle cry for the Serbian attack on Bosnia was a defeat by the Turks 800 years earlier.

If shame is evoked but is unacknowledged, it can set off a sequence of shame alternating with anger. However, shame-shame sequences are probably much more prevalent than shame-anger sequences. Elias's (1978; 1982) analysis of changes in advice manuals over the past five centuries implies that shame-shame sequences are a central core in the development of modern civilization, to the extent that they occur in the socialization of children.

The other, less frequent direction in the dysfunctional management of shame is to mask it with anger. Shame/anger may be interminable in the form of "helpless anger," or in the more explosive form, "humiliated fury." The shame-anger loop could be central to destructive conflict. If one is in a shame state with respect to another, one route of denial is to become angered at the other, whether the other is responsible or not. That is, if one feels rejected by, insulted by, or inferior to another, denial of shame can result in a shame-anger loop of unlimited intensity and duration.

## A Theory of Massive Violence

One difficulty in communicating the new theory is that emotions have virtually disappeared as creditable motives in modern scholarship, as already indicated. One would hardly know they existed from reading the analyses of causes of conflict in the social sciences. When references to emotions are made, they are likely to be abstract, casual, indirect, and brief. For example, emotions are sometimes invoked under the rubric of "nonrational motives," but with little attempt to specify what this category might contain.

Unacknowledged alienation and vulnerable emotions can lead to interminable conflict. Like Watzlawick and colleagues (1967), I propose that some conflicts are unending—any particular quarrel being only a link in a continuing chain. What causes interminable conflict?

There are two forms of interminable conflict, the quarrel and impasse. Both forms may grow out of isolation and unacknowledged shame and other vulnerable emotions. Shame is pervasive in conflictful interaction, but largely invisible to interactants (and to most researchers). I connect the two forms of conflict with the two forms of unacknowledged shame proposed by Lewis (1971); quarrels with the *bypassed* form, impasses with the *overt, undifferentiated* form.

The two forms of shame are polar opposites in terms of thought and feeling. Overt shame involves painful feeling with little ideation, but bypassed shame involves rapid thought, speech, or behavior, but little feeling. Lewis's analysis parallels Adler's (1953), but also represents an immense advance over it. Unlike Adler, she described observable markers for the theoretical constructs, and specified the causal sequence, the unending spiraling of emotion in "feeling traps."

Overt shame is marked by pain, confusion, and bodily reactions: blushing, sweating, and/or rapid heartbeat. One may be at a loss for words, with fluster or disorganization of thought or behavior, as in states of embarrassment. Many of the common terms for painful feelings appear to refer to this type of shame, or combinations with anger: feeling peculiar, shy, bashful, awkward, funny, bothered, or miserable; in adolescent vernacular, being freaked, bummed, or weirded out. The phrases "I felt like a fool," or "a perfect idiot" are prototypic.

Bypassed shame is manifested as a brief painful feeling, usually less than a second, followed by obsessive and rapid thought or speech. A common example: one feels insulted or criticized. At that moment (or later in recalling it), one might experience a jab of painful feeling (producing a groan or wince), followed immediately by imaginary but compulsive, repetitive replays of the offending scene. The replays are variations on a theme: how one might have behaved differently, avoiding the incident, or responding with better effect. One is obsessed.

Lewis (1971) referred to internal shame-rage process as a feeling trap, as "anger bound by shame," or "humiliated fury." Kohut's (1971) concept, "narcissistic rage," appears to have the same effect, since he viewed it as a compound of shame and rage. Angry that one is ashamed, or ashamed that one is angry, then one might be ashamed to be so upset over something so "trivial." The shame part, particularly, is rarely acknowledged, difficult to detect and to dispel. Shame-rage spirals may be brief, a matter of minutes, but can also last for hours, days, or a lifetime, as bitter hatred or resentment.

Brief sequences of shame/rage may be quite common. Escalation is avoided through withdrawal, conciliation, or some other tactic. Wars are generated by a less common process. Watzlawick and colleagues (1967: 107–108) call it "symmetrical escalation." Since such conflicts have no limits, they may have lethal outcomes. In this theory, unacknowledged shame is the cause of revenge-based cycles of conflict [this formulation was anticipated in the work of Geen (1968) and Feshback (1971)]. Shame-rage may escalate continually to the point that a person or a group can be in a more or less permanent fit of shame/rage, a kind of madness.

## Gender Differences in Emotion Management

In my experience, most women express vulnerable emotions more than most men. Certainly they express fear and grief more. The difference between men and women with respect to shame is probably smaller, but with women still more expressive of this emotion, if only obliquely. That is, women seem more likely to review the events of their day, either to themselves or with another person, than men. In doing so, they are likely to encounter one or more of the vulnerable emotions.

On the other hand, more women are inhibited about expressing anger, whether verbally or acting it out. There also seems to be a huge difference between most men and women in feeling and expressing love. Men learn early on from fathers and schoolmates that love, like fear, grief, and shame, is likely to be interpreted as a sign of weakness. It too, is seen as a vulnerable emotion. This difference is represented in a comic episode in the film *Big*. Tom Hanks, a ten-year-old boy magically inhabiting the body of the man he will become, is mystified by the flirtatiousness of a woman who is attracted to him. When he finally understands, he responds by giving her a playground shove.

My impression is that the gender difference in these four emotions is slowly decreasing, as women are being prepared at home and school for careers. This change is clearest with respect to anger; more women are expressing or acting out anger. The change toward the masculine pattern of vulnerable emotions is less clear, and may be quite slow. It seems that even career women still cry much more freely than men and are quicker to feel and acknowledge fear.

## Killing by Men

Men are far more likely to be mass killers than women. An earlier article (Scheff 2003), used the examples of Lt. Calley and Hitler to illustrate my theory of hypermasculine isolation, repression, and violence. Newman (2004) collected information about all mass killing episodes in schools between 1974, when they were unusual, to 2002, when they had become more frequent. All told she found twenty-seven shootings involving twenty-nine boys. (In two of the episodes, there were two shooters). No episode with a girl shooter was found. Women can be as verbally abusive as men, and commit homicides, but are much less likely to commit multiple, and especially, random killings. (The 2006 shooting in the Goleta, California, Post Office by a woman is still a rare occurrence.)

As far as I can tell, none of the boys in the Newman study seemed to have a single secure bond. They were isolated from schoolmates, teachers, and family members as well. One might think at first glance that at least in two of the episodes, the pair of boys who were shooters together might have had a secure bond. There is very little direct evidence, but several comments suggest that the collaborating boys had an engulfed bond, shutting out the world of other possible relationships, and suppressing vital parts of themselves in order to be loyal to the other boy.

Engulfment is often mistakenly seen as a secure bond, but it is always a form of alienation from self.

A 2005 school shooting occurred at Red Lake Senior High School, Minnesota. This particular case is somewhat unusual in that the shooter, Jeff Weise, left a long record of writing on the Internet. On March 21, 2005, he killed seven people and himself. He was a very obese (6 feet, 250 lbs.) sixteen-year-old, whose father had committed suicide ten years earlier. His mother, driving drunk, was brain damaged in an accident in 1999. According to Jeff's online postings, since her accident, she had been beating him mercilessly, and he never stood up to her.

In another posting, he stated "I have friends, but I'm basically a loner in a group of loners. Most of my friends don't know the real me. I've never shared my past with anyone, and I've never talked about it with anyone. I'm excluded from anything and everything they do, I'm never invited, I don't even know why they consider me a friend or I them" (Santa Barbara News–Press, 2005).

This boy was obviously without a single secure bond, rejected continually and relentlessly by everyone around him, including his mother and his so-called friends. It is little wonder that he seemed to be drowning in shame, as indicated in another of his postings: "I really must be fucking worthless...." He had attempted to slit his wrists a year earlier, was seeing a therapist, and was on antidepressants. The news reports provide no information about the number of sessions with the therapist or what transpired in them.

However, the fact that he was on antidepressants suggests yet another rejection, this time by the medical profession. This boy's main problem was that his life was a living hell, which needed immediate intervention, change, and personal attention. Whoever put him on antidepressants may have been guilty of gross negligence and malpractice. Yet providing psychotropic drugs is overwhelmingly practiced in the United States regardless of the social surroundings. In this way, lack of secure bonds is not only interpersonal, but also embedded in the social structure. Men, especially, because of the isolation caused by their training for achievement, suffer more than women from lack of secure bonds.

## Men, Women, and Massive Violence

The difference between men's and women's attitudes toward violence can be seen in the various polls that are relevant to the support of the Iraq war. No matter which poll or the framing of the question; women always express less support for the war. Women are much less keen on violence than men in its collective form. At the level of families, women are also less likely to commit violence than men, especially physical violence.

A recent literature review of responses to stress (Taylor, et al., 2000) finds that women, much more than men, are likely to "tend and befriend" rather than fight or flight. The attachment/networking response seems to be more alive in women than in men. The tend/befriend can be viewed as the default variant for females, an important modification of Cannon's idea of fight or flight.

The silence/violence pattern seems to be the corresponding variant for males. The violence part obviously corresponds to fight. But the silence part is equivalent to flight, if withdrawal includes not just physical flight, but also withdrawal in its psychological sense. The Taylor et al. "tend/befriend" pattern for women, when combined with the silence/violence pattern for men, suggests that the fight/flight response is crucially modified by culture-driven gender differences, hence the cult of masculinity.

The silence/violence model can be applied to the masculine mystique in general. Hypermasculine men are silent about their feelings to the point of repressing them altogether, even anger (Acting out anger seldom resolves it). Repressing love and the vulnerable emotions (grief, fear and shame, the latter as in feelings of rejection or disconnection) leads to either silence or withdrawal, on the one hand, or acting out anger (flagrant hostility), on the other. The composure and poise of hypermasculinity seems to be a recipe for silence and violence.

This formulation might explain the enormous energy that seems to propel gratuitous violence. Isolation from others blocks the working through of repressed emotions. Isolation, when combined with the recursive nature of shame, might set up what can be seen as a doomsday machine, experienced by individuals and groups as an unbearable amount of pain and hostility.

Collins (1990; 2008) also notes the vast energy that goes into wanton violence, such as the slaughter of noncombatant men, women, and children in villages by U.S troops during the Vietnam War. His explanation is in terms of what he calls a "forward panic." That is, he suggests that like the backward panics that occur in theater fires, the killing was set off by runaway fear. The theory outlined here proposes that it is a special kind of fear that sets off rampages, since it is unacknowledged. My theory also adds several other components to the model: social isolation of individual killers, the other two vulnerable emotions (grief and shame), and the acting out of anger.

It may be impossible to understand collective conflict, especially gratuitous wars like Vietnam and Iraq, as long as we ignore its emotional/relational components. It seems particularly applicable to the followers of hypermasculine leaders. The leaders' desire for power and property may often be one of the causes of wanton aggression. The followers, especially the working class, have much less to gain and much more to lose. In her analysis of working-class men supporters of Bush, Hochschild (2004) proposed that they appreciate his hypermasculine style, since it is like their own, or the style that they would like to have: shoot first, ask questions later.

## Discussion

Of the many issues that need further exploration, one stands out: the extent to which some women accept/encourage hypermasculinity in men. In my various presentations of the idea of hypermasculinity, there is usually a woman who ruefully tells me, after the talk, that she is drawn to hypermasculine men. Perhaps there is a type of femininity that exactly fits with, and encourages hypermasculinity, women who want a strong, silent man to protect them because they anticipate being victimized.

Such women would seek hypermasculine men as husbands and encourage hypermasculinity in their male children. Systematic studies by Smith et al. (1995) and Maybach and Gold (1994) seem to support this idea. Both studies found a correlation between hyperfemininity and attraction to macho men. Like the other studies of hyperfemininity that I have seen, these don't actually define what the term means. If future studies are able to clearly define hyperfemininity, they might help explain why modern societies continue to have high proportions of men who are hypermasculine, or at least show some of its characteristics.

Except for the Maybach and Gold and Smith et al. studies, I have found only hints in this direction in the literature on masculinity. Reardon (1985) went only so far as to suggest that the pattern of women submitting to male domination contributes to the warfare system (19). Jackson's (1990) study of violent men states that they usually saw their mothers as passive victims (88), but the author didn't try to ascertain the accuracy of their view.

My hypothesis is that there is a common emotional/relational configuration for women that would be the (partial) opposite and therefore complement of hypermasculinity. In the emotion realm, *hyperfeminine* women would suppress anger, on the one hand, and act out fear of being victims, on the other. In terms of relationships, these women would be *engulfed* with others, giving up crucial parts of self in order to be loyal. Norwood's (1985) study of women who tolerated abuse of self and/or their children by their husband provides an example.

The nationally syndicated columnist Michelle Malkin's idea that she is a "security mom" seems to provide an example of the acting out of fear.

She says that being afraid since 9/11 is not the same thing as living in fear (Grewal, 2006). But the examples she gives from her daily life suggests that indeed she does live in fear: monitoring all the other passengers on trains and buses, and when driving, paying attention to all vehicles like large trucks and tankers that might harbor a bomb. Her columns are not perfect examples of this model of hyperfemininity, however, since she seems to be enraged at all liberals.

These two hypergenders would be mutually reinforcing, creating a social institution of gender that would support warfare. Being only a surmise, to be taken seriously, it would have to have to be supported by actual studies. One direction would be to study gender differences in preferences, and responses to, certain types of films. The "action" film, revenge by men acting out anger through aggression and violence, seems to be the favorite of hypermasculine men. The corresponding favorite for hyperfeminine women, if my hypothesis is correct, would involve the acting out of fear, as in films that portray victimization of women by intruder(s) in the home, and other threats of violence against defenseless victims. These films are not as plentiful as action films except in certain venues (such as the Lifetime TV Channel).

My treatment of hyperfemininity in terms of its emotional/relational components contrasts with virtually all other studies of this topic. None of the studies consider emotions, and very few relationships. As with most other studies in the social/behavioral sciences, focus is on cognition and behavior. For example, Mahalik et al. (2005) report the following components in their scale on the degree of femininity: Nice in Relationships, Thinness, Modesty, Domestic, Care for Children, Romantic Relationship, Sexual Fidelity, and Invest in Appearance. These are all highly visible, cognitive, and behavioral, rather than the mostly hidden emotions that I consider to cause these thoughts and behaviors.

## Conclusion

The theory of violence outlined in this chapter suggests that massive violence can be understood in terms of the same kinds of cultural processes that give rise to hypermasculinity. Furthermore, hypermasculinity may be in part produced by hyperfemininity, a reciprocal process. The unbelievable energy involved in massive violence might be explained by a model of feedback loops of alienation and emotion within and between individuals and groups. Perhaps the next step in constructing such a theory would be illustrating and testing the idea of a hyperfemininity that would complement and encourage hypermasculinity, using both the part/whole and web of concepts approaches.

# References

Adler, Alfred. 1956. *The Individual Psychology of Alfred Adler.* New York: Basic Books.

Collins, Randall. 1990. "Violent Conflict and Social Organization: Some Theoretical Implications of the Sociology of War." *Amsterdams Sociologisch Tijdschrift* 16: 63–87.

———. 2008. *Violence: A Micro-sociological Theory.* Princeton, N.J.: Princeton Univ. Press.

Elias, N. 1972. *What Is Sociology?* London: Hutchison.

———. 1978. *The History of Manners.* New York: Pantheon.

———. 1982. *Power and Civility.* New York: Pantheon.

Farrell, Warren. 1993. *The Myth of Male Power.* New York: Simon and Schuster.

Feshbach, S. 1971. "The Dynamics and Morality of Violence and Aggression." *American Psychologist* 26: 281–292.

Geen, R. G. 1968. "Effects of Frustration, Attack, and Prior Training in Aggressiveness upon Aggressive Behavior." *Journal of Personality and Social Psychology* 9: 316–321.

Goffman, Erving. 1967. "Where the Action Is." In *Interaction Ritual.* New York: Anchor, 149–270.

Grewal, Inderpal. 2006. "Security Moms in Early 21st Century USA." Unpublished manuscript. Univ. of California, Irvine.

Hochschild, Arlie. 2004. "Let Them Eat War." *European Journal of Psychotherapy, Counseling & Health* 6(3), December: 1–10.

Jackson, D. 1990. *Unmasking Masculinity: A Critical Autobiography.* London: Unwin-Hyman.

Kohut, H. E. 1971. "Thoughts on Narcissism and Narcissistic Rage." In *The Search for the Self.* New York: International Univ. Press.

Krystal, Henry. 1988. *Integration and Self-healing: Affect, Trauma, Alexithymia.* Hillsdale, N.J.: Analytic Press

Levine, Judith. 2003. *My Enemy, My Love: Man-hating and Ambivalence in Women's Lives.* Berkeley: Thunder's Mouth Press.

Lewis, Helen. 1971. *Shame and Guilt in Neurosis.* New York: International Universities Press.

Mahalik, James, E. B. Morray, A. Coonerty-Femiano, L. H. Ludlow, S. M. Slattery, and Andrew Smiler. 2005. "Development of the Conformity to Feminine Norms Inventory." *Sex Roles* 52: 7–8, 417–435

Marx, Karl. 1844[1975]. *Early Writings.* New York: Vintage Books

Maybach, Kristine, and Gold, Steven. 1994. "Hyper-femininity and Attraction to Macho and Non-macho Men." *Journal of Sex Research* 31(2): 91–98

Nandy, Ashis. 1983. *The Intimate Enemy: Loss and Recovery of Self Under Colonialism.* Part 1: "The Psychology of Colonialism." Delhi: Oxford.

Nathanson, Paul, and Katherine K. Young. 2006. *Legalizing Misandry: From Public Shame to Systemic Discrimination Against Men.* Montreal: McGill-Queen's Univ. Press.

Newman, Kathryn. 2004. *Rampage.* New York: Basic Books.

Norwood, Robin. 1985. *Women Who Love Too Much.* New York: Pocket Books.

Patai, Daphne. 1993. *Professing Feminism: Cautionary Tales from the Strange World of Women's Studies.* Lanham, Md.: Lexington Books.

Phillips, Bernard. 2001. *Beyond Sociology's Tower of Babel: Reconstructing the Scientific Method.* New York: Aldine de Gruyter.

Phillips, Bernard, and Louis C. Johnston. 2007. *The Invisible Crisis of Contemporary Society: Reconstructing Sociology's Fundamental Assumptions.* Boulder, Colo.: Paradigm Publishers.

Reardon, Betty. *Sexism and the Warfare System.* New York: Teachers' College, Columbia.

Santa Barbara News-Press. 2005. "Shooting at Red Lake, MN." March 25, 2005.

Scheff, Thomas J. 1994. "Hitler's Appeal to the Germans." In *Bloody Revenge.* Boulder, Colo.: Westview, chapter 5, (reissued in 1999 by iUniverse).

——. 1997. *Emotions, the Social Bond, and Human Reality: Part/Whole Analysis.* Cambridge: Cambridge Univ. Press

——. 2003. "Male Emotions and Violence: A Case Study," *Human Relations,* 56: 727.

——. 2006. *Goffman Unbound: Toward a New Paradigm in Social Science.* Boulder, Colo.: Paradigm Publishers.

Smith, Eleanor, Donn Byrne and Paul Fielding. 1995. "Interpersonal Attraction as a Function of Extreme Gender Role Adherence," *Personal Relationships* 2(2): 161-172.

Sommers, Christina H. 2001. *The War Against Boys: How Misguided Feminism Is Harming Our Young Men.* New York: Simon & Schuster

Taylor, Graeme J., R. Bagby, and J. Parker. 1997. *Disorders Of Affect Regulation: Alexithymia In Medical And Psychiatric Illness.* New York: Cambridge Univ. Press.

Taylor, Shelley, et al. 2000. "Biobehavioral Responses to Stress in Females: Tend and Befriend, Not Fight or Flight." *Psychological Review.* 107: 411-429.

Tucker, R. C. 1978. *The Marx-Engels Reader.* New York: W. W. Norton

Volkan, Vamik. 2004. *Blind Trust: Large Groups and Their Leaders in Times of Crisis and Terror.* Charlottesville, Va.: Pitchstone.

Watzlawick, P., Beavin J. H., and Jackson, D. (1967). *The Pragmatics of Human Communication.* New York: Norton.

CHAPTER 9

# Institutionalized Elder Abuse

## Bureaucratic Ritualization and Transformation of Physical Neglect in Nursing Homes

*Jason S. Ulsperger*
*and J. David Knottnerus*

In *Beyond Sociology's Tower of Babel,* Bernard Phillips (2001) describes the foundation of the Web and Part/Whole Approach using the concept of bureaucracy to explain problems with sociology and the scientific method. His description is not only important in illustrating faults in research methods and the hyperspecialization of sociology, but also in highlighting problems of bureaucracy. Max Weber (1921/1968) predicted organizational growth years ago. He anticipated the rise of organizations characterized by impersonal interaction, written rules, and clearly defined hierarchy. He indicated that soon social life would be impossible without bureaucracy. However, as Phillips (2001) indicates with his assessment of the profession of sociology, bureaucratization is now a fundamental problem.

Acknowledging the importance of a broad approach to the scientific method and the Web and Part/Whole Approach discussed in this book's introduction, this chapter proposes that bureaucratic rituals are an important part of social life for nursing home employees. Using forty autobiographies, biographies, and research monographs to examine everyday life in nursing homes, this chapter reviews various symbolic themes expressed through work rituals. The themes involve general concepts related to the fundamental problem of bureaucracy. Employing structural ritualization theory, the chapter suggests that certain ritualized practices that express bureaucratic themes influence the behaviors of nursing home employees and contribute to the unintended maltreatment of residents. In turn, this chapter focuses on several research questions. How did bureaucracy come to have an influence on nursing homes? Does bureaucracy influence for-profit and nonprofit nursing homes in different ways? How do aspects of bureaucracy lead to the poor treatment and more specifically the physical neglect of residents? Can we consider alternative patterns of interaction that have the ability to counter bureaucracy and lower resident neglect?

## The Bureaucratization of U.S. Nursing Homes

According to the Web and Part/Whole Approach, it is important to consider circumstances leading to the development of a problem. To understand how bureaucracy facilitates physical neglect in both for-profit and nonprofit nursing homes, it is relevant to reflect on multiple factors. This includes historical aspects of nursing homes, legal developments, and organizational variation.

The modern nursing home industry has roots in early colonial life. In colonial times, public policy followed the tradition of English poor laws leaving the care of dependent elderly people in the hands of community governments (Hawes and Phillips, 1986). For the aged, this meant one of the only forms of public support was from poor farms, which also provided care for the poor, sick, mentally ill, and lawbreakers (Vladeck, 1980). In 1935, the government established the Social Security Act. Elderly eligible for Old Age Assistance (OAA) received no more than $30 per month. The use of this money led to an increase in what we now know as nursing homes (Hawes and Phillips, 1986).

Many welcomed the use of organizations specifically caring for the dependent old. However, some were discontent with conditions. Stories of physical and financial abuse leaked to the public. Policymakers seemed to ignore them. At the same time, lobby groups, such as the American

Nursing Home Administration, gained power fighting for government funding increases and regulations favoring their facilities. National expenditures for elder care increased. Estimates indicate they were nearly $33 million in 1940, and $187 million by 1950. By 1965, they were $1.3 billion (Giacalone, 2001). In the early stages of nursing home growth, the federal government was only paying 10 percent of expenses. By the 1960s, they paid 22 percent (Hawes and Phillips, 1986).

In the 1960s, the Kerr-Mills Act replaced OAA with Medical Assistance for the Aged (MAA). It allowed states to control the criteria for government assistance. It soon provided support for over half of nursing-home residents. The establishment of MAA was important, but the 1965 amendments to the Social Security Act continue to be the most relevant policies for nursing-home funding. They fostered Medicare and Medicaid, which started to fund an array of nursing-home expenditures (Lidz, Fischer, and Arnold, 1992). Through the 1970s, people became increasingly concerned with quality of care, particularly in for-profit facilities. Individuals and corporate entities own for-profit nursing homes, as opposed to nonprofit government and religious-sponsored facilities. The main objective of the former is revenue generation. Research indicates for-profit facilities focus more on administrative services, give less personal attention to residents, receive more complaints, have fewer staff members per patient, and spend less per resident (see Holmberg and Anderson, 1968; Winn, 1974; Brooks and Hoffman, 1978; Koetting, 1980; Elwell, 1984; Hawes and Phillips, 1986; Jenkins and Braithwaite, 1993; Ulsperger and Ulsperger, 2001).

In the mid to late 1980s, the cost of care in nursing homes reached an unprecedented level. Both for-profit and nonprofit homes had trouble keeping pace. The average annual expenditure on one resident went from $5,100 in 1970, to $23,300 in 1985. By 1990, the average was $30,000. Small facilities closed because they could not logistically meet new requirements. The bureaucratic demands also created a need for specialization. With requirements for activities, food, rehabilitation, the preservation of records, and worker certification, facilities needed specific departments. Nursing-home care became more complicated and the bureaucratic logic in nursing homes was in full swing (Giacalone, 2001).

## Structural Ritualization Theory and the Web and Part/Whole Approach

*Structural ritualization theory* (SRT) focuses on the fundamental role rituals play in everyday social life and the structuring of social events. They help provide symbolic meaning to our actions, give direction to human behavior, and create a sense of stability. According to the theory, ritualization involves interaction sequences that occur in multiple contexts including secular, sacred, formal, and informal settings (Knottnerus, 1997). According to the theory, *ritualized symbolic practices* (RSPs) are an important dimension of social behavior. The theory emphasizes the processes by which RSPs in larger social environments influence embedded groups. The theory argues that four factors are essential to ritualization and the structural reproduction process. They include *repetitiveness, salience, homologousness,* and *resources.*

Repetitiveness involves the "relative frequency with which a RSP is performed" (Knottnerus, 1997: 262). The idea here is that the repetition of RSPs varies. Great differences may exist in the degree to which RSPs occur in different social settings or domains of interaction. For example, in one area within an organization such as a cafeteria, actors may never engage in a specific RSP. In another, such as a boss's office, people may repeatedly engage in it. Salience involves the "degree to which a RSP is perceived to be central to an act, action sequence, or bundle of inter-related acts" (Knottnerus, 1997: 262). This involves the prominence of a RSP, which too can vary. In other words, actors' perceptions of ritualized practices can differ in the extent to which they stand out. Homologous-ness implies a "degree of perceived similarity among different RSPs" (Knottnerus, 1997: 263). It is possible that different RSPs exist in a social setting. However, they may or may not be similar in meaning and form. The more they are alike, the more likely they strengthen each other. This enhances the impact of RSPs. Finally, resources are "materials needed to engage in RSPs which are available to actors" (Knottnerus, 1997: 264). The greater the availability of resources, the more likely an individual will participate in a RSP. Resources include nonhuman materials such as money, time, clothes or uniforms, and physical items (e.g., musical instruments, furniture, buildings). They also include human traits such as intellectual capacity, interaction skills, physical strength, and cognitive/perceptual abilities. *Rank* is another important concept in the theory. It involves "the relative standing of a RSP in terms of its dominance" or importance (Knottnerus, 1997: 266). According to the theory, rank is a function of repetitiveness, salience, homologousness, and resources. A RSP ranks high if it is repeated often, is quite visible, is similar to other RSPs, and people have resources to take part in it. When a RSP in a wider social environment has high rank, it is more likely it will appear in an embedded group.

SRT parallels many aspects of a broad approach to the scientific method augmented by the Web and Part/Whole Approach. The Web and Part/Whole Approach recommends scholars refocus on Mills's (1959) idea of the sociological imagination and Gouldner's (1970) thoughts on reflexive sociology. The sociological focus on grand theory and abstracted empiricism fails to generate significant questions about society. Moreover, many sociologists fail to view their own beliefs in the way they view the beliefs of others. In turn, the Web and Part/Whole Approach considers both basic assumptions that shape methods as well as theoretical consequences. Specifically, the approach calls for defining and linking a specific problem to other fundamental problems, moving up language's ladder of abstraction by using high-level ideas for understanding, moving down language's ladder of abstraction in obtaining facts, and integrating knowledge from specialized fields (Kincaid, 1996; Scheff, 1997; Phillips, 2001; Phillips, Kincaid, and Scheff, 2002; Scheff, 2006; Phillips and Johnston, 2007). With defining and linking fundamental social problems, researchers have used SRT to examine an array of sociological topics in different historical periods and milieus. This includes the development of aggression in ancient civilizations (Knottnerus and Berry, 2002), hierarchical distinctions on slave plantations (Knottnerus, 1999), social identity for immigrants (Guan and Knottnerus, 2006), and corporate crime (Knottnerus, Ulsperger, Cummins, and Osteen, 2006).

In terms of moving up the conceptual ladder of abstraction, SRT systematically focuses on specific aspects of ritual behavior—repetitiveness, salience, homologousness, and resources. This allows researchers to use a clearly defined theory of rituals. It also provides researchers the ability to move down the ladder of abstraction, simplify complex interaction, collect concrete measures, and draw basic conclusions. Furthermore, SRT allows researchers to move up and down the ladder of abstraction by examining how social structure produces everyday rituals and how everyday rituals reinforce social structure. Finally, both SRT and the Web and Part/Whole Approach emphasize the need for theory integration and cooperative efforts aimed at theory development and synthesis, which also implies openness to using various research methods.

Addressing bureaucracy, this chapter examines everyday taken-for-granted work rituals that facilitate the maltreatment of residents in for-profit and nonprofit nursing homes. The rank of RSPs of bureaucracy and physical neglect are assessed using measures of repetitiveness and salience. Guided by the Web and Part/Whole Approach, it also provides practical suggestions that could facilitate alternative RSPs that could replace or offset existing RSPs involving physical maltreatment in long-term care.

## Methodology

This work employs a literary ethnography, which is a six-stage process of text analysis. Researchers use literary documents, often autobiographical in nature, to explore common themes. Similar to the typical content analysis, the steps include: identifying a scope of sources, reading and interpreting the documents, identifying textual themes, classifying textual themes, developing a set of analytic constructs, and rereading documents for contextual confirmation. These steps focus on thick descriptions that generate themes representing a portrait of actors' experiences (Van de Poel-Knottnerus and Knottnerus, 1994).

## The Literary Ethnography and the Web and Part/Whole Approach

Literary ethnographies reflect aspects of the Web and Part/Whole Approach. They help identify problems but also further conceptualize issues contributing to the problem with intense reading of personal documents. They help researchers move up and down the ladder of abstraction. Applying textual themes to analytic constructs allows researchers to target abstract concepts (such as bureaucracy), read first-hand accounts, and see how abstract concepts are applicable to concrete situations (such as instances of neglect). Once those applications are established, a literary ethnography allows researchers to test particular ideas, reevaluate them, and move back up the ladder of abstraction through the contextual confirmation process.

## Analyzing Rituals of Bureaucracy

In this study, we used forty autobiographies, biographies, and research monographs to analyze the bureaucratic rituals of employees in nursing homes (see the Appendix, which comes just before the references at the end of this chapter). These sources of data are from 1963 to 2000: the time when the federal government first introduced nursing home regulations. Twenty sources focused on for-profit homes while the rest focused on nonprofit facilities.

Reading revealed several textual themes. We grouped the readings according to these themes, then applied them to constructs of bureaucracy. Following Weber's (1921/1968) work, we defined bureaucracy as "any aspect of the social environment and its processes that involve the notation of staff separation and hierarchy, rules, documentation, and efficiency." These provided subdivisions (see table 9.1). Staff separation and hierarchy involved ritualized distinctions between levels of employees. Rules involved official regulations about the way to do something. Documentation concerned references to recording aspects of nursing home life in written form. Efficiency involved demands to behave quickly and effectively. An open category of "other" was also used to identify emerging themes. To gauge variation of bureaucratic RSPs in for-profit and nonprofit sources, we used SRT to analyze "rank" using repetitiveness and salience factors.

**Table 9.1 Frequencies for Bureaucratic Rituals**

| Subdivision | Number (% within subdivision) | | Overall % |
|---|---|---|---|
| Staff Separation and Hierarchy | 716 | (100.0) | 34.5 |
| For-Profit | 297 | ( 41.5) | |
| Nonprofit | 419 | ( 58.5) | |
| Rules | 522 | (100.0) | 25.1 |
| For-Profit | 202 | ( 38.7) | |
| Nonprofit | 320 | ( 61.3) | |
| Documentation | 490 | (100.0) | 23.6 |
| For-Profit | 243 | ( 49.6) | |
| Nonprofit | 247 | ( 50.4) | |
| Efficiency | 241 | (100.0) | 11.6 |
| For-Profit | 116 | ( 48.1) | |
| Nonprofit | 125 | ( 51.9) | |
| Other | 107 | (100.0) | 5.2 |
| For-Profit | 38 | ( 35.5) | |
| Nonprofit | 69 | ( 64.5) | |
| Total | 2,076 | | 100.0 |

## Analyzing Rituals of Physical Neglect

To categorize specific rituals of physical neglect, we included any act lead-ing to medical dereliction, personal negligence, environmental negligence, or bodily harm (see table 9.2). Medical dereliction involved the failure to deliver medicine and services to residents or the questionable use of drugs to control a resident's behavior. Personal negligence concerned staff failing to provide adequate upkeep of residents, such as clothing and personal hygiene needs. Environmental negligence included staff ritualistically not maintaining regions such as living areas, recreational rooms, kitchens, and grounds of the facility. Bodily harm involved actual physical abuse of resi-dents by staff, including the overuse of physical restraints to control resi-dents. Here, an additional "other" category emerged through our rereading and contextual confirmation. Our analysis of rituals of physical neglect also utilized SRT to analyze "rank" using repetitiveness and salience.

## Reflexivity Issues

In line with the Web and Part/Whole Approach's emphasis on reflexivity, it is important to note that both researchers have first-hand experience with nursing homes. This involves family members who lived in them, years of volunteer service, and limited employment. There is little doubt exposure to everyday life in nursing homes helped shape our concerns

**Table 9.2 Frequencies for Physical Neglect Rituals**

| Subdivision | Number (% within subdivision) | | Overall % |
|---|---|---|---|
| Medical Dereliction | 119 | (100.0) | 22.0 |
| For-Profit | 78 | ( 65.5) | |
| Nonprofit | 41 | ( 34.5) | |
| Personal Negligence | 111 | (100.0) | 20.5 |
| For-Profit | 76 | ( 68.5) | |
| Nonprofit | 35 | ( 31.5) | |
| Environmental Negligence | 99 | (100.0) | 18.3 |
| For-Profit | 74 | ( 74.7) | |
| Nonprofit | 25 | ( 25.3) | |
| Bodily Harm | 97 | (100.0) | 17.9 |
| For-Profit | 70 | ( 72.2) | |
| Nonprofit | 27 | ( 27.8) | |
| Other | 115 | (100.0) | 21.3 |
| For-Profit | 83 | ( 72.2) | |
| Nonprofit | 32 | ( 27.8) | |
| Total | 541 | | 100.0 |

and approach to this project. These experiences helped us reflect upon, and authenticate aspects of the project.

# Findings: Rituals of Bureaucracy and Physical Neglect

## Bureaucratization

There are 2,076 references to bureaucracy in this research. Table 9.1 shows 716 (34.5 percent) references to RSPs of staff separation and hierarchy. Of those, 297 (41.5 percent) appear in for-profit sources with 419 (58.5 percent) in nonprofit sources. RSPs of staff separation and hierarchy are salient in for-profit and nonprofit sources. Discussions usually involve work duties. For instance, in one for-profit facility, residents look forward to coffee served by the activity director. The source notes that sometimes residents confined to their rooms want aides to bring it to them. Aides often resist believing bringing coffee to residents is exclusively the activity director's responsibility (Kayser-Jones, 1981). In another for-profit source, strict lines exist between workers. Administrators have luxurious air-conditioned and heated offices. Diamond explains when he worked in a nursing home he would see administrators get off the elevator coming to the floor and make a "sudden leap from 70 degrees to over 90" (1992: 49). Shield describes,

"Several implicit hierarchies—medical, administrative, nursing, and social service—operate within the bureaucracy" (1988: 93).

Rule RSP references appear 522 (25.1 percent) times in the sources. In one source, Foner suggests nursing homes are under a "tyranny" of rules and regulations (1995: 231). This is true for both for-profit and nonprofit sources. More references in nonprofit sources exist in this area. In for-profit facilities, 202 (38.7 percent) references appear with 320 (61.3 percent) in nonprofit sources. With the salience of rituals of rules in for-profit facilities, Fontana points out the idea of "rules above compassion" dominates (1978: 130). Formal rules regulate what many would consider routine. Sources point to ritualistic rules for everything from feeding to personal care. Laws even require staff to help residents bathe. One resident told Howsden (1981), "I feel so strangled here. So many rules and regulations that don't make any sense" (1981: 144). Rules appear salient in nonprofit descriptions as well. Foner (1994: 68) states:

> [R]esentments ran especially high because, in an effort to upgrade the facility, the new administrator was tightening enforcement of existing rules and adding new ones. A seemingly endless onslaught of new rules affected even the smallest details of work life. One day aides could wear jewelry to work; the next, after a memo went out, only watches, engagement and wedding rings, and small earrings were allowed.

In this study, facilities also emphasize informal rules. In one for-profit home, an aide comments on another employee violating an informal rule. The violator scalded a senile resident with bath water. Implying the scalding was intentional, the aide says the person should have known that "crazy patients are not punished for cursing aides" (Stannard, 1973: 338).

Documentation rituals appear 490 (23.6 percent) times, having similar patterns in for-profit and nonprofit sources. In for-profit sources, 243 (49.6 percent) references appear with 247 (50.4 percent) in nonprofit sources. Documentation rituals are salient in for-profit and nonprofit sources. One for-profit administrator comments "there is so much of it there is little time left to do anything else" (Farmer, 1996: 20). Our findings suggest these rituals shape the way nurses think, speak, and provide care. Diamond (1992: 160) states:

> Staff continually cursed at being overwhelmed with paperwork. Denny once waved his hand at the whole row of binders containing these records. "Oh, they're just a formality," he said. They were a formality with force—made of forms, and forming the contours of the job, both in doing the prescribed work and in certifying that it had been done. Sometimes they formed the way we spoke.... A nursing assistant once

approached a charge nurse [and asked about a crying resident]. "Oh," said the nurse, immersed in the medications checklist, "Don't worry about it, it's nothing physical, just emotional."

As Howsden notes, "written documentation provides a medical rationale" for dealing with patients (1981: 89). The RSP of writing things down shapes the way staff members view residents. Diamond explains that a nurse made it clear to him that documentation is a primary objective. Expressing his displeasure with the facility's focus on writing so much down, the nurse once pointed to a sign posted in the nursing home reading "If It's Not Charted, It Didn't Happen" (1992: 131). Regardless, documentation rituals shape actions in nonprofit religious facilities as well. One account from Gubrium (1975: 144) explains:

> Top staff expects floor staff to chart clientele systematically.... Charting is fairly well routinized on the floors.... Whenever a patient or resident has an accident such as falling or fainting, an incident report is written. One of the floor nurses may be asked to complete the report if she is considered to be well acquainted with the person involved and the circumstances under which the accident occurred. The report contains a variety of questions.
>
> In addition to name and room number, the person filling out the report is asked for the location of the incident, an account of any property involved, the names of witnesses, a description of the incident, and the patient's or resident's condition before it occurred.

Efficiency rituals appear 241 (11.6 percent) times. There are 116 (48.1 percent) in the for-profit sources and 125 (51.9 percent) in the nonprofit. This research indicates the emphasis on efficiency is similar in both for-profit and nonprofit settings. In terms of salience, for-profit and nonprofit facilities emphasize efficiency rituals. Large amounts of staff stress exist due to the "pressure of time" (Diamond, 1992: 79). With one for-profit facility, Fontana (1978: 130) notes:

> There was usually a minimal number of aides on the ward, and in order to meet administrative demands the aides would accomplish their daily assignments as quickly as possible.... The patient was scrubbed, washed, turned over, rinsed—and the aides were ready for the next patient. Feeding the patients followed the same course. In the rushed meal hour, food was shoved down open mouths or splattered on closed mouths as the aides carried on without missing a beat. The aides broke the rules concerning good care, but it mattered little to them since the goal of efficiency was seemingly more important.

Similar accounts exist for nonprofit facilities. A good worker is not a worker who cares for residents, but one who executes tasks quickly. Foner (1994: 60) states:

> Ms. James was typically the first nursing aide in the day room at lunchtime getting residents ready to eat. She was a fast worker. She finished her "bed and body" work early and was punctilious about getting her paper work done neatly and on time.... Ms. James' attitude toward dressing, bathing, and feeding patients was much the same as her attitude toward her other chores. She was determined to get them all done quickly, whether patients liked it or not. Residents in her view had no choice but to take prescribed medicines, eat so they would not lose weight or be forced to go on tube feeding, or "do a BM" so they would not get impacted. She had no tolerance for patients' resistance, which slowed her down.... In fact, Ms. James was proud that she could get patients to eat and "do a BM" so they would not get impacted. I overheard her explain, indeed justify, her approach to one of the therapists: "Schmidt eats for me, but if anyone hears me they're gonna get me for patient abuse...."

As mentioned, this analysis was open to emerging themes not discovered in the early phases of the research. In the category of other, a common theme emerged concerning ritualistic meetings. Since this theme emerged during the analysis, our data in this subdivision do not cover all references to RSPs as other categories do. Ritualized meetings involve staff members and/or family assembling. As table 9.1 shows, from the time we started counting them, the sources reference meetings 107 times (5.2 percent). In for-profit sources, 38 (35.5 percent) references exist with 69 (64.5 percent) in nonprofit sources. One type of gathering discussed as important in for-profit and nonprofit sources is an in-service meeting. These are required meetings for lower-level employees that focus on continuing education. Ironically, these formal sessions sometimes take place during hours when employees should be directing their attention to residents. Foner (1994: 72–73) describes the disruption they create:

> During my research, aides had to attend an average of three or four in-service sessions a month, each lasting about half an hour. Five of the "in-services" given annually—on fire safety, needs of the elderly, patients' rights, body mechanics and infection control are mandated.... One aide told me that in-services were the most difficult aspect of her job. "When you have too many meetings in a day, they take you from your direct work and take your time away from the patient and slow you up." In fact, conscientious and caring aides were often the most

vocal in their resentment of in-services, for they wanted to spend their time doing a good job for their residents.

## Physical Neglect

We found 541 ritual acts of abuse involving physical neglect. Table 9.2 shows 119 (22 percent) references to medical dereliction. In for-profit sources, 78 (65.5 percent) references appear with 41 (34.5 percent) in nonprofit sources. For-profit sources reveal salience of these RSPs. For instance, they indicate that nurses working for facilities sometimes fail to provide medical care. Kayser-Jones (1981: 77) notes: "at Pacific Manor the lack of medical care and concern for medical needs was frequently a subject for discussion both with patients and the nursing staff. Inattention to patients' needs at Pacific Manor causes anxiety, stress, and fear among patients."

The lack of medical attention in for-profit facilities revolves around monetary issues. Diamond reports that the administrator in the facility he worked at was not spending money on medical needs while aides often brought supplies from home. One of the better aides complained once, "Damn.... I forgot to bring those Epsom salts. Now Violet is not going to be able to soak her foot" (Diamond, 1992: 151). Regardless of this altruism, employees sometimes engage in overmedication rituals. As mentioned before, they will overmedicate residents that cause disruptions to bureaucratic work demands. Fontana (1978) points out that workers will label resident behavior deviant even when medications to control them cause the initial problem. This RSP is not limited to for-profit facilities. Gubrium (1975: 148), in relation to a nonprofit facility, states:

> Early in the day shift, it is not unusual for various aides on the floor to pass the nurses' station and ask, "Did Max get his shot today?" or "I hope you remembered to give Emma her Thorazine. I have a lot of work to do, you know." When the nurses forget to sedate such patients, concerned aides repeatedly remind them of it early in their shifts. Nurses usually oblige them if they claim to be busy, "just to get her [an aide] off my back so we can all get our work done." When they do not, aides may threaten to do nothing until their request is granted.... As one floor nurse stated to several aides just before leaving for her break, "Well, I guess I can take my break now. Everyone's sedated."

Gubrium (1975: 148–49) also explains that the power to label residents as deviant lies in the hands of staff members, who often abuse this power:

Patients and residents do not necessarily enter the Manor with physician's orders for tranquilizers. However, when aides define them as "troublemakers," they get tranquilizers shortly after. Tranquilizers are mostly prescribed "PRN," which means that they may be administered as needed at the discretion of the floor nurses. In practice, however, the discretion involved is that of the aide, who asks for, or reminds a floor nurse of "her need" for a sedative.

Personal negligence rituals appear 111 (20.5 percent) times. In for-profit sources, 76 (68.5 percent) appear with 35 (31.5 percent) in nonprofit sources. Compared to medical dereliction, personal negligence seems to have lower salience. Nevertheless, in for-profit sources, accounts clearly demonstrate how busy aides often fail to properly clean or clothe residents. It would be easy to assume that rituals of putting on dresses backwards are mistakes, not intentional personal negligence. However, this is not the case. Kayser-Jones (1981: 46) explains:

> To lack underclothes or to have clothes put on backwards is ... dehumanizing for the elderly. Robes often are put on this way, staff informed me, to decrease the amount of work involved in changing an incontinent patient and to decrease the amount of laundry. If robes are put on backwards and not tucked under, they are not soiled when patients are incontinent.

In regard to RSPs involving personal negligence, Gubrium (1975) stresses that staff members make the lack of hygienic care routine. They turn actions other people find repugnant into something normal. In this study, nonprofit sources reveal how personal negligence can even be a punishment. Shield states, "... staff retribution can result when residents are too demanding. In subtle and not so subtle ways, staff members neglect or delay doing things" (1988: 159). Personal negligence RSPs, similar to bureaucratic RSPs, speed up the process of care and foster dehumanization.

Environmental negligence rituals appear 99 (18.3 percent) times. For-profit sources contain 74 (74.7 percent) references with 25 (25.3 percent) in nonprofit sources. We found the theme of environmental negligence especially strong in for-profit sources. Gubrium (1993: 170) provides one such account from a former nursing-home surveyor turned resident:

> I think that cleanliness is a problem. I think here roaches are a problem. We are having a roach war here, okay? They are trying to kill the roaches. I myself am not a roach person. I don't like them. I used to write out nursing homes for roaches all over. And this place has probably got as good roaches as I have ever run into.... I mean, I was sitting with

Harry [another resident] last night talking and one of them walks up the back of my dresser. I do not keep loose food in my room, okay? An experienced surveyor knows this. We have got a really, truly serious, bad roach problem.

Though environmental negligence references appear less and are less intense in nonprofit sources, examples exist. Many involve staff not cleaning messes in resident rooms. In facilities, this type of physical neglect leaves residents feeling less than human. Henry (1963: 405) states that it communicates to residents that "they all have become junk" not worthy of well-kept surroundings.

Bodily harm rituals appear 97 (17.9 percent) times. In for-profit sources 70 appear (72.2 percent), while nonprofit sources have 27 (27.8 percent). We found them salient in both types of nursing homes. As previously discussed, Stannard (1973) suggests staff in for-profit facilities sometimes give scalding hot baths to residents as a form of punishment for disrupting work. Other for-profit sources suggest that staff may tie residents up with restraints when they disrupt schedules. Paterniti (2000: 106) indicates:

> Out of frustration and a perceived need to keep Scott restrained, aides frequently tied a square knot in the nylon vest restraint that secured Scott in a reclining Gerry chair. Some even remarked, "If you're a mechanic, let's see you get yourself out of this one!" On one occasion, an aide locked Scott, tied to a chair, in the janitors' closet. The aide entertained himself by keeping records of how long it took Scott to work his way out of the restraints and to the door of the closet. Ironically, additional work to this staff member's schedule, generated under his own control, seemed to present no obstacle to his work timetable.

A form of psychological terrorism, residents experience discomfort and pain when tied down. This relates to bureaucratic and profit issues. Diamond (1992: 182) notes:

> Mary Ryan, like many others, spent all day in the day room, secured to her chair with a restraining vest.... I [once asked] Beulah Feders, the LPN in charge...."Beulah, why does she have to wear that thing all the time?" Beulah accompanied her quick comeback with a chuckle. "That's so they don't have to hire any more of you."

Nonprofit sources have accounts of this ritualized behavior as well. Tisdale's conversation with a staff member describes one worker's opinion on bodily harm, "Some are kind, some are cruel ... They kick me, I kick them" (1987: 109). However, not all staff members have the same perspective on bodily harm. Shield (1988: 76) describes the attitude of one physical therapist working in a nonprofit facility:

> She is telling me about the time one of the residents came to physical therapy and had a bruise that, to the physical therapist, looked suspicious. She was sticking her neck out, she knew, by reporting it, but she decided to act. She phoned the charge nurse on the resident's floor and reported it. She also wrote it up. Though she knew she was inviting employee resentment and anger by her actions, she felt it was important to be a resident's advocate and agent for change in this way.

Such actions by physical therapists are rare in the literature. Lower-level employees sometimes normalize neglect, but physical therapists, not being floor or upper-level administrative staff, are in a unique position. Stannard (1973) explains that in nursing homes, administrative staff members, far removed from resident domains of interaction, seldom actually see neglectful and abusive behavior. They, like the lower staff, develop a culture of accounts to deal with repetitive cases of abuse. As with lower staff, this allows them to normalize maltreatment with specific vocabularies of motive (for more see Mills, 1940). Stannard's (1973) work indicates the therapist in the preceding example lacked successful socialization to the organization's culture. Her attitude shows that people use different RSPs when dealing with residents in specific locations. In that regard, Shield (1988) describes the physical therapy room as a unique social setting which exhibits a different atmosphere. When residents are there they joke, smile, laugh, and flirt with one another.

In the "other" category, we noted themes dealing with limited supplies and inappropriate architecture. Keep in mind, we started counting references to this "other" category long after the research started, and numbers for them do not include all references in the texts. Table 9.1 indicates 115 (21.3 percent) references in the other category. For-profit sources have 83 references (72.2 percent) while nonprofit sources have 32 references (27.8 percent). References to the absence of limited supplies only appear in for-profit documents. The cost-cutting mentality may explain this phenomenon. References to inappropriate architecture exist, but do not appear salient, in the for-profit or nonprofit sources. Regardless, Bennett (1980: 65–6) provides an interesting example: "A four-foot passageway at the foot of the beds is unreasonably small. It does not allow patients to go by one another without some risk ... a patient ambulating in this passageway tripped over another's foot, fell down, and fractured his hip."

Staff abuse does not always cause bodily harm. Residents do things to hurt themselves. However, the inappropriate architecture does not help as O'Brien (1989: 216) notes:

Many Bethany Manor residents described both falls and the fear of falling. Mrs. Cavanaugh, a five-year resident, reminisced, "I have had 14 falls since I have been here. The first day I was here I went downstairs to breakfast in the main dining room and I used the walker. After breakfast I came back to the elevator, and before I could get on, the door closed on me and knocked me down in the elevator."

While inappropriate architecture cannot be considered a RSP, it creates a situation where simple tasks like getting out of bed or going to another floor of the building are dangerous. We believe such conditions also send a symbolic message to residents that their physical needs are not important.

## Summary

The sources in this study reveal multiple kinds of bureaucratic RSPs. Most commentary concerns staff separation and hierarchy, with more references appearing in nonprofit sources. We believe staff separation rituals have a social-psychological effect on workers. Workers tend to perform duties if it is specifically their responsibility. Different organizational units develop their own norms. For example, employees at lower levels sometimes accept neglect and abuse as a punishment if their work routine is disrupted. New aides who socialize with other aides learn to neutralize abuse (for more on this process, see Sutherland, 1940; Sykes and Matza, 1957). Top staff may see neglect or abuse as deviant, or may avoid it because it does not occur in their domains of interaction.

In this research, many references to rule rituals exist, more from nonprofit sources. RSPs of rules are salient in both for-profit and nonprofit settings. Formal rules dominate. However, informal ritualized rules also exist. Various sources suggest that some abuse rituals depend on rules related to resident senility. Fewer references are made to rituals of documentation and efficiency. Nevertheless, similarities exist in for-profit and nonprofit sources in terms of repetitiveness and salience. With documentation, work rituals involving paperwork even influence church-operated facilities. We believe documentation of most, if not all, aspects of the job ritualistically turns residents into objects of work. Personal acts turn into impersonal quantitative measurements, making maltreatment more likely. The emphasis on efficiency does not help. Regardless of ownership type, a prominent goal of nursing homes is for workers to complete their duties as rapidly as possible. In addition to these points, ritualistic meetings unintentionally lead to poor care. Modern organizations think they have to *act* like organizations. Meetings are a part of this (see Meyer and Rowan, 1991). As this research shows, this ceremonial legitimation of organizations has negative, unintended consequences for nursing home residents.

With RSPs of physical neglect, more references exist in for-profit sources. They are highly salient in most of the subdivisions in both for-profit and nonprofit texts. In terms of medical dereliction rituals, employees ritualistically fail to provide adequate care in certain situations. Some facilities simply do not purchase medical products, while aides bring what they need to care for residents from home. For-profit and nonprofit staff members ritualistically overuse medications and tie residents down to control the impediment of their efficiency, all the while labeling residents deviant to justify such actions.

Considering personal negligence, busy aides sometimes fail to clean residents properly, intentionally failing to dress them correctly to speed up work. Aides in nonprofit facilities sometimes ritualistically neglect the personal care of residents to punish them for being demanding. In terms of environmental negligence, accounts in sources describe how the ritualistic failure to adequately clean rooms sends a symbolic message to residents that they are not worthy of good care. With bodily harm rituals, references to explicit physical abuse exist in all documents. They show employees sometimes justify the physical abuse of residents with eye for an eye, revenge justifications, claiming residents abuse them so they deserve it. Aides and nurses sometimes give scalding hot baths, unnecessarily restrain, and even lock up residents to control or punish them. Specifically in relation to for-profit sources, restraint use is an effective means of cost control. Sources indicate employee feelings that a small staff can easily handle many residents—if they are tied down.

## Policy Recommendations: Transforming Maltreatment and Physical Neglect

In relation to a broad approach to the scientific method and the Web and Part/Whole's emphasis on the practical application of research, ritualized practices can involve innovative processes, which lead to novel social structures. *Transformative structural ritualization* is concerned with how new ritualized behaviors may emerge in social settings (Knottnerus, 1997). We believe nursing home employees can encourage and activate new rituals to lessen the impact of bureaucratic rituals and neglect by attempting the following:

### Recognize and Downplay Bureaucracy

Facilities should take steps toward open discussions about bureaucratic constraints. Executive directors could conduct an initial meeting to orient staff to bureaucratic concepts; then carry out a needs assessment to identify bureaucratic problems and ritualized behaviors that could be reduced within state and federal guidelines.

## Limit Specific-Job/Specific-Task Mentality

Directors of facilities should emphasize to all staff that if a resident is in need with a minor problem any employee should help. Moreover, if a worker does not have the correct training to help with a serious issue, he or she should make it a priority to find someone who does.

## Integrate Meetings

If certain meetings are short or issues they deal with are not of immediate importance, consolidate meetings and in-service training sessions. Also, do not schedule in-services during times when resident care should be occurring.

## Simulation Exercises

Have all staff members go through simulation exercises involving short stints as "mock residents." To sensitize staff, require all employees to be tied down to a bed, fed, and inadequately dressed.

## Revise Wage Standards

Increase pay for low-level staff. Also, provide extra funds when staff members perform in a way that discourages physical neglect.

## Clothing Design

To create a middle ground between dress and efficiency, it might be possible to design dignified clothing conducive to the bureaucratic necessity of working quickly.

## Increase Upper-Level Staff and Resident Interaction

To lower objectification, facilities should create measures for top staff to communicate with residents. Make it a requirement that they spend time during the workday visiting with residents.

## Preventive Architectural Design

Too often, nursing homes resemble hospitals or are designed with a bureaucratic or medical rationale in mind. Designers could start considering how the layout of a facility negatively influences resident wellbeing and then consider the relevance of design on the ritualized behaviors of employees.

# Appendix

## Literary Sources

| Title | Author | Year |
|---|---|---|
| "Rosemont" | J. Henry | 1963 |
| "The Tower Nursing Home" | J. Henry | 1963 |
| "Muni San" | J. Henry | 1963 |
| "Old Folks and Dirty Work" | C. Stannard | 1973 |
| *Living and Dying at Murray Manor* | J. Gubrium | 1975 |
| "The Internal Order of a Home for the Jewish Elderly" | Watson/Maxwell | 1977 |
| *The Last Frontier* | A. Fontana | 1977 |
| "Ripping off the Elderly" | A. Fontana | 1978 |
| *Limbo* | C. Laird | 1979 |
| *Nursing Home Life* | C. Bennett | 1980 |
| *Old, Alone, and Neglected* | J. Kayser-Jones | 1981 |
| "Nursing Home Housekeepers" | J. Henderson | 1981 |
| *Work and the Helpless Self* | J. Howsden | 1981 |
| "The Reluctant Consumer" | M. Vesperi | 1983 |
| "Goffman Revisited: Relatives v. Administrators" | M. Richard | 1986 |
| *It's OK Mom* | J. Retsinas | 1986 |
| *Harvest Moon* | S. Tisdale | 1987 |
| *Uneasy Endings* | R. Shield | 1988 |
| "Social Networks, Social Support, and Elderly Institutions" | B. Powers | 1988 |
| "Self-Perceived Health of Elderly Institutionalized People" | B. Powers | 1988 |
| *Anatomy of a Nursing Home* | M. O'Brien | 1989 |
| *Borders of Time* | Crandall/Crandall | 1990 |
| *The Ends of Time* | J. Savishinsky | 1991 |
| *The Erosion of Autonomy in Long-term Care* | Lidz/Fischer/Arnold | 1992 |
| *Making Gray Gold* | T. Diamond | 1992 |
| *Speaking of Life* | J. Gubrium | 1993 |
| *The Caregiving Dilemma* | N. Foner | 1994 |
| "In and Out of Bounds" | J. Savishinsky | 1995 |
| "Ethics in the Nursing Home" | R. Shield | 1995 |
| "The Head Nurse as a Key Informant" | McLean/Perkinson | 1995 |
| "Relatives as Trouble" | N. Foner | 1995 |
| "From the Inside Out" | B. Powers | 1995 |
| "The Culture of Care in a Nursing Home" | J. Henderson | 1995 |
| "The Hidden Injuries of Bureaucracy" | N. Foner | 1995 |
| "Life at Lake Home" | C. Wellin | 1996 |
| *A Nursing Home and Its Organizational Climate* | B. Farmer | 1996 |
| *Television in the Nursing Home: A Case Study* | W. Hajjar | 1998 |
| *Maudie: A Positive Nursing Home Experience* | R. Metz | 1999 |
| "The Micropolitics of Identity in Adverse Circumstance" | D. Paterniti | 2000 |
| "Emotional Labor as Cultural Performance" | J. Sass | 2000 |

# References

Bennett, Clifford. 1980. *Nursing Home Life: What It Is and What It Could Be.* New York: Tiresias Press.

Brooks, Charles H., and John A. Hoffman. 1978. "Type of Ownership and Medicaid Use of Nursing-care Beds." *Journal of Community Health* 3: 236-244.

Diamond, Timothy. 1992. *Making Gray Gold: Narratives of Nursing Home Care.* Chicago: Univ. of Chicago Press.

Elwell, Frank. 1984. "The Effects of Ownership on Institutional Services." *Gerontologist* 24: 77-83.

Farmer, Bonnie Cashin. 1996. *A Nursing Home and Its Organizational Climate: An Ethnography.* Westport, Conn.: Auburn House.

Foner, Nancy. 1994. *The Caregiving Dilemma: Work in an American Nursing Home.* Univ. of California Press.

———. 1995. "The Hidden Injuries of Bureaucracy: Work in an American Nursing Home." *Human Organization* 54: 229-237.

Fontana, Andrea. 1978. "Ripping off the Elderly: Inside the Nursing Home." In *Crime at the Top: Deviance in Business and the Professions,* ed. John M. Johnson and Jack D. Douglas. Philadelphia: J. B. Lippincott, 125-132.

Giacalone, Joseph. 2001. *The U.S. Nursing Home Industry.* Armonk, N.Y.: M. E. Sharpe.

Gouldner, Alvin W. 1970. *The Coming Crisis of Western Sociology.* New York: Basic Books.

Guan, Jian, and J. David Knottnerus. 2006. "Chinatown Under Siege: Community Protest and Structural Ritualization Theory." *Humboldt Journal of Social Relations* 30: 5-52.

Gubrium, Jaber F. 1975. *Living and Dying at Murray Manor.* New York: St. Martin's Press.

———. 1993. *Speaking of Life: Horizons of Meaning for Nursing Home Residents.* New York: Aldine de Gruyter.

Hawes, Catherine, and Charles D. Phillips. 1986. "The Changing Structure of the Nursing Home Industry and the Impact of Ownership on Quality, Cost, and Access." In *For-Profit Enterprise in Health Care,* ed. Bradford H. Gray. Washington, D.C.: National Academy Press, 492-541.

Henry, Jules. 1963. *Culture Against Man.* New York: Random House.

Holmberg, R. Hopkins, and Nancy N. Anderson. 1968. "Implications of Ownership for Nursing Home Care." *Medical Care* 6: 300-307.

Howsden, Jackie L. 1981. *Work and the Helpless Self: The Social Organization of the Nursing Home.* Lanham, Md.: Univ. Press of America.

Jenkins, Anne, and John Braithwaite. 1993. "Profits, Pressure and Corporate Lawbreaking." *Crime, Law and Social Change* 20: 221-232.

Kayser-Jones, Jeanie. 1981. *Old, Alone, and Neglected: Care of the Aged in Scotland and the U.S.* Berkeley: Univ. of California Press.

Kincaid, Harold. 1996. *Philosophical Foundations of the Social Sciences: Analyzing Controversies in Social Research.* Cambridge: Cambridge Univ. Press.

Knottnerus, J. David. 1997. "The Theory of Structural Ritualization." In *Advances in Group Processes* 14, eds. Barry Markovsky, Michael J. Lovaglia, and Lisa Troyer. Greenwich, Conn.: JAI Press, 257-279.

————. 1999. "Status Structures and Ritualized Relations in the Slave Plantation System." In *Plantation Society and Race Relations,* ed. Thomas J. Durant Jr. and J. David Knottnerus. Westport, Conn.: Praeger, 139–147.

Knottnerus, J. David, and Phyllis E. Berry. 2002. "Spartan Society: Structural Ritualization in an Ancient Social System." *Humboldt Journal of Social Relations* 27: 1–41.

Knottnerus, J. David, Jason S. Ulsperger, Summer Cummins, and Elaina Osteen. 2006. "Exposing Enron: Media Representations of Ritualized Deviance in Corporate Culture." *Crime, Media, Culture* 2: 177–195.

Koetting, Michael. 1980. *Nursing Home Organization and Efficiency: Profit Versus Non-Profit.* Lexington, Mass.: Lexington Books.

Lidz, Charles, Lynn Fischer, and Robert M. Arnold. 1992. *The Erosion of Autonomy in Long-Term Care.* New York: Oxford Univ. Press.

Meyer, John W., and Brian Rowan. 1991. "Institutionalized Organizations: Formal Structure as Myth and Ceremony." In *The New Institutionalism in Organizational Analysis,* ed. Walter W. Powell and Paul J. DiMaggio. Chicago: Univ. of Chicago Press, 41–62.

Mills, C. Wright. 1940. "Situated Actions and Vocabularies of Motive." *American Sociological Review* 5: 904–913.

————. 1959. *The Sociological Imagination.* New York: Oxford Univ. Press.

O'Brien, Mary E. 1989. *Anatomy of a Nursing Home: A New View of Residential Life.* Owings Mills, Md.: National Health Publishing.

Paterniti, Debora. A. 2000. "The Micropolitics of Identity in Adverse Circumstance: A Study of Identity Making in a Total Institution." *Journal of Contemporary Ethnography* 29: 93–119.

Phillips, Bernard. 2001. *Beyond Sociology's Tower of Babel: Reconstructing the Scientific Method.* Hawthorne, N.Y.: Aldine De Gruyter.

Phillips, Bernard, and Louis C. Johnston. 2007. *The Invisible Crisis of Contemporary Society: Reconstructing Sociology's Fundamental Assumptions.* Boulder, Colo.: Paradigm Publishers.

Phillips, Bernard, Harold Kincaid, and Thomas J. Scheff. 2002. *Toward a Sociological Imagination: Bridging Specialized Fields.* Lanham, Md.: Univ. Press of America.

Scheff, Thomas J. 1997. *Emotions, the Social Bond, and Human Reality: Part/ Whole Analysis.* Cambridge: Cambridge Univ. Press.

————. 2006. *Goffman Unbound! A New Paradigm for Social Science.* Boulder, Colo.: Paradigm Publishers.

Shield, Renee R. 1988. *Uneasy Endings: Daily Life in an American Nursing Home.* Ithaca: Cornell Univ. Press.

Stannard, Charles. 1973. "Old Folks and Dirty Work: The Social Conditions for Patient Abuse in a Nursing Home." *Social Problems* 20: 329–342.

Sutherland, Edwin. 1940. *White Collar Crime.* New Haven, Conn.: Yale Univ. Press.

Sykes, Gresham, and David Matza. 1957. "Techniques of Neutralization: A Theory of Delinquency." *American Journal of Sociology* 22: 664–670.

Tisdale, Sallie. 1987. *Harvest Moon: Portrait of a Nursing Home.* New York: Henry Holt.

Ulsperger, Jason S., and Kristen Kloss Ulsperger. 2001. "Profit, Ownership, and the Corporation: Deviance in American Elder Care." *Free Inquiry in Creative Sociology* 29: 5-9.

Van de Poel-Knottnerus, Frederique, and J. David Knottnerus. 1994. "Social Life Through Literature: A Suggested Strategy for Conducting a Literary Ethnography." *Sociological Focus* 27: 67-80.

Vladeck, Bruce C. 1980. *Unloving Care: The Nursing Home Tragedy.* New York: Basic Books.

Weber, Max. [1921]1968. *Economy and Society.* 3 vols. Totowa, N. J.: Bedminster Press.

Winn, Sharon. 1974. "Analysis of Selected Characteristics of a Matched Sample of Non-profit and Proprietary Nursing Homes in the State of Washington." *Medical Care* 12: 221-228.

CHAPTER 10

# Discipline and Publish

## Public Sociology in an Age of Professionalization

*Arlene Stein*

IN 1895, IN THE FIRST ISSUE of the *American Journal of Sociology,* founding editor Albion Small described the goal of the journal as follows:

> [This journal will] attempt to translate sociology into the language of ordinary life.... It is not ... essential to the scientific or even the technical character of thought that it be made up of abstractly formulated principles. On the contrary the aim of science should be to show the meaning of familiar things, not to construct ... a kingdom for itself in which, if familiar things are admitted, they are obscured under an impenetrable disguise of artificial expression." (Quoted in Buxton and Small, 1992: 376)

Only six decades later, Talcott Parsons, perhaps the most influential sociologist of his generation, promoted a very different conception of the field. In a 1959 address to the American Sociological Association, he declared that as a scientific discipline sociology "is clearly primarily dedicated to the advancement and transmission of empirical knowledge" and only "secondarily to the communication of such knowledge to nonmembers." By this time, the movement toward disciplinarity, professionalism, and scientism was rapidly under way, transforming sociology journals into highly specialized publications catering almost exclusively to professional social scientists—a trend that continues to this day.

Of course sociology is not alone. Speaking of general trends in American intellectual life, Russell Jacoby charges that academia killed the public intellectual (1987), Richard Rorty chastises the "introverted hyperprofessionalism" of the modern academic (1998: 111), Richard Posner (2002) suggests that the modern intellectual buys "intellectual power at the expense of scope," and Martha Nussbaum (quoted in Posner, 2002: 323) laments that "too often our insularity is evident in the way we write."

As the story goes, once upon a time, there were intellectuals who felt a responsibility to engage with the public about the great issues of the day. But that world is no longer. Today's intellectual careerists care more about advancing their professional interests than advancing independent thought, more about investigating narrowly defined problems than with thinking broadly and engaging with nonacademic publics. With the academicization of the American left in the early 1970s, argues Jacoby, we see a decline in the quality of publicly oriented critical writing. Instead, there is an increasing introvertedness: tendencies to use obfuscatory language, to employ ever-narrowing bands of specialized opinion, and address concerns that are mainly disciplinary in origin—the "private" as opposed to the public intellectual. Consequently, the majority of the American public experiences criticism as increasingly irrelevant.

Jacoby's ideal-type "public intellectual" is a "writer and thinker who addresses a general and educated audience" (1987: 5). He/she—though typically a "he"—publishes essays in general-interest periodicals, is independent and unaffiliated, and is a generalist. Jacoby excludes intellectuals whose work is "too technical or difficult." He may be correct that it is more difficult to be a critical public intellectual who is able to make a livelihood by writing books and publishing in journals and magazines in the United States. (This is far less the case for conservative intellectuals, who have a better funded and more widely institutionalized array of think tanks and publications to choose from.) Yet the narrative of public intellectual decline may romanticize the "independent" intellectual (typically white and male) and views "academic" and "public" intellectuals as mutually exclusive categories.

But intellectuals are a diverse group. They can be grassroots community intellectuals, who articulate collective identities and help to forge a sense of group loyalty; professional intellectuals employed by universities and think tanks; knowledge and media workers of various kinds, as well as uninstitutionalized writers, thinkers, and artists. "Public intellectuals," then, are intellectuals who transcend the academy and communicate beyond university audiences at least some of the time.

C. Wright Mills embraced this broader conception of the publicly engaged intellectual, one in which academics could more comfortably fit. Academics, he suggested, could be public intellectuals if they so desired, though professionalization, he believed, was making that goal more difficult to achieve (Mills, 1959). Mills lambasted the rise of "abstracted empiricism" and "grand theory," which, he believed, fragmented sociological knowledge and removed it from important public debates (1959). He wrote about being at a party of sociology graduate students at Columbia, who were working on their PhDs. "After they'd introduced themselves, I'd ask: What are you working on?" It would always be something like "The Impact of Work-Play Relationships among Lower Income Families on the South Side of the Block on 112th St between Amsterdam and Broadway." And then I would ask: Why?" (Mills and Mills, 2001: 12). Professionalization, Mills believed, was the culprit. By modeling itself on the physical sciences in order to establish itself as a legitimate area of study, sociology, he believed, was losing its critical edge.

In the following, I explore how professionalization shapes the ways sociologists do and don't address the public. Sociological professionalism, which values rigor over range, and disciplinary rather than publicly accessible forms of knowledge, emerges gradually over the course of the twentieth century, accelerating in the period after World War II. It leads to a fragmentation of sociological research into disparate, specialized areas of investigation and loss of an integrated sociological imagination that is both broad and deep. While professionalization alone cannot explain the decline of public sociology, it goes a long way toward accounting for why few sociologists see engagement with audiences beyond academia as important and worthy of their attention, and why fewer still are able to publish work that is publicly accessible and engaging. I end with some suggestions on how to reinvigorate public sociology, drawing upon the insights of Mills, and those who have been inspired by his vision.

## From Range to Rigor

Through professionalization, producers of special services seek to constitute and control a market for their expertise (Sarfatti Larson, 1977). Professionalization encourages the view that to become a sociologist and reap the benefits of membership in that group, one must be socialized into a profession that possesses particular norms, understandings, and rules for "doing" sociological work (Reinharz, 1979: 378). It requires some central regulatory body to exercise power and control over entry into the profession to ensure the standard of performance of individual members, enforce a code of conduct, carefully manage knowledge in relation to the expertise that constitutes the basis of the profession's activities, and control the process of selecting and training new entrants. The professionalization of sociology, beginning in the late nineteenth century and accelerating during the post–World War II period, led to the codification of knowledge, the establishment of professional associations, and the development of disciplinarity.

Schorske (1998) describes a "new rigorism" in the social sciences generally—a shift from "the nineteenth century primacy of a loose, historical conception of meaning-making to the privileging of a scientific one." In the 1930s and '40s, he suggests, instructors shared "a public intellectual's kind of vocation—to show us in a rudimentary way how their disciplines could identify and address economic and social problems. They had an interest in institutional description and social criticism, which they saw as constitutive of, rather than ancillary or irrelevant to, their disciplines" (314).

During the postwar period, many academic disciplines, sociology among them, became more democratic and open to previously disenfranchised groups, and at the same time increasingly committed to a scientific model that demanded more highly codified professional rules. Professional gatekeeping institutions, including the American Sociological Association, regional sociological associations, academic journals, and federal funders such as the National Science Foundation, were increasingly called upon to evaluate sociological work. For his own part, Talcott Parsons sought to outline a general theory of social action which would endow the social sciences with the status of physical sciences and establish sociology's special claims to expertise, a consensus on sociology's goals, and thereby further the project of professionalization.

By the 1950s we see the beginning of a passage "from range to rigor, from a loose engagement with a multifaceted reality historically perceived to the creation of sharp analytic tools that could promise certainty where description and speculative explanation had prevailed before" (Schorske, 1998: 315). This "new rigorism" in the social sciences marked a shift from "the nineteenth century primacy of a loose, historical conception of meaning-making to the privileging of a scientific one." A central innovation was the process of peer review, which protected the academic freedom of scholars, privileging audiences of peers, and encouraging an emphasis upon method. The unintended but long-term effect of this reorientation of research was a certain distancing of academic work from society at large (Bender and Schorske, 1998: 29).

Professionalization went hand in hand with the rise of what Smelser (1992: 53) calls "midwestern positivism"—an emphasis on quantitative analysis of empirical "facts," a stress on induction as the main avenue to scientific truths, and an aspiration to some kind of natural-science model. A greater premium was placed on "scientific credibility," the capacity of claims makers to enroll supporters behind their claims, to legitimate their arguments as authoritative knowledge, and to present themselves as the sort of people who can give voice to science. Credibility, therefore, can be considered a system of authority in Weberian terms, combining aspects of power, dependence, legitimation, trust, and persuasion (Weber, 1978, 212–54; Epstein, 1995).

As Bender and Schorske (1998) suggests "the disciplines were redefined over the course of the half century following the war: from the means to an end they increasingly became an end in themselves, the possession of scholars who constituted them" (22). Growing commitment to the profession, and to the idea of scientific expertise, meant diminished commitment to the public beyond the university, as exemplified by shifts in the discourse of sociology toward specialization and fragmentation into subspecialties, and toward what Agger (2000) calls the "science aura" of journal writing.

In the *American Sociological Review* in the 1940s and '50s, the writing was essayistic, dialogical, and filled with the author's presence. By the 1970s, however, the *ASR* came to resemble natural science journals in terms of style—with growing attention placed on literature reviews, charts and tables, and methodologically driven articles. This and other top journals of sociology came to publish what Kuhn (1962/1970) called "normal science," which involves small increments in knowledge.

As sociology became more professionalized, and more committed to a positivist model that discouraged interdisciplinarity and policed professional boundaries, it became more complex, leading to a proliferation of subfields lacking a central "core" or identity (Crane and Small, 1992). The rapid growth of the discipline during the postwar era meant that it became impossible for any one person or persons to master the whole field. A growing proliferation of a wide array of different subspecialties is reflected in the proliferation of sections of the American Sociological Association—of which there are forty-three today, encompassing such subfields as "Theory," "Sex and Gender," and "Alcohol and Drugs." When new fields and subfields develop, they quickly breed their own technical languages. The consequence of this is that many people experience their professional identities in relation to their participation in subfields rather than in the discipline as a whole (Crane and Small, 1992; Calhoun, 1992: 185). Sociology, once seen as offering a "general understanding of society," has come to focus instead on a series of smaller, relatively disconnected problems.

Specialization oriented sociologists toward disciplinarity: increasingly, they came to imagine their public as other sociologists, and they wrote for fellow specialists on narrow topics, using jargon familiar mainly to them. Because many (if not most) sociologists came to see themselves as cumulating knowledge primarily for and within a universe of sociological experts, they were less likely to situate their work in relation to a larger world, drawing upon literature outside of their discipline, or outside of academia.

Today, the field of sociology is larger and in many respects more decentralized than even twenty years ago, but hierarchies of prestige and power are inherent in the rankings of academic journals and graduate departments, which reinforce this model. Particularly when competition for employment and promotion is fierce, greater rewards accrue to those who adopt professional identities that conform closely to hegemonic understandings of the discipline. Enforcement of the dominant positivist paradigm occurs through the delineation of boundaries between "sociology" and "not sociology"—in other words, through the promotion of disciplinarity and specialization and denigration of interdisciplinarity and less specialized knowledge. Students and faculty internalize these understandings, and receive rewards for adhering to them. Professionalization made possible the sociology we know today, and the serious, rigorous, analysis of social issues. It established important disciplinary institutions that support and nurture sociological work. At the same time, it privileged the "scientific expert," who is committed to engaging with professional rather than nonprofessional publics.

## The Rise and Fall of Popular Sociology?

The brief history I've sketched suggests that structural pressures toward professionalization favor positivist approaches that place less value on engagement with nonacademic publics. "Scientific experts" tend to see their primary audience as other experts with whom they communicate primarily in the pages of academic journals. They attribute less value to publishing work in unofficial venues, such as general-interest periodicals, and sometimes even look down upon such efforts. Here, critics like Jacoby, Rorty, and others are right: professionalization leads to introversion and the production of intellectuals who have little incentive to translate their work to broader publics.

While the public intellectual's death has been exaggerated, certain *types* of public intellectuals are clearly more likely to get their work heard than others. In the field of sociology, the "scientific expert" is much more likely to gain a forum and an audience than the "social critic." Quantitative sociologists who study microlevel issues and processes are in favor, particularly if they package their work in upbeat sound bites; in contrast, theoretical, interpretive sociologists who write books and ask "big questions" are less likely to be heard from. The concentration and commercialization of the media, dominated by the bottom line and operating within certain conceptions of truth and "objectivity," favors the sociological sound bite, offering limited opportunities for more critical, interpretive, or complex analysis. The changing economics of the publishing industry has made it more and more difficult for academic intellectuals to publish trade books that engage with nonacademic publics.

Evidence suggests, for example, that few sociologists publish op-eds for such national media as the *New York Times* (Jacobs and Townsley, 2004), or best-selling books (Gans, 1989; Ritzer, 1998). Sociological interventions in the media take place in an increasingly entertainment-oriented environment organized to maximize financial returns. This is particularly true of television, where, as Bourdieu (1998) tells us, in order to be heard, academics must play the part of celebrity-experts, participating in staged "games" to entertain audiences. In the United States, sociologists are more likely to interact with print media, which are likely to utilize academic experts if they are capable of offering concise sound bites, presenting digestable "facts" for mass-public consumption. The more one can break up knowledge into discrete, consumable "factoids," the more likely one is to get coverage.

The concentration and commercialization of the media, dominated by the bottom line and operating with certain conceptions of truth and "objectivity," favors the sociological sound bite or factoid. We find the sociological expert pronouncing upon the cause of a particular social problem, such as: "As gun crime escalates, a top sociologist sees a link between rap music and violence" (*N.Y. Times* "Education Supplement," Jan. 31, 2003), or a University of Michigan study that suggests that "older people who were helpful to others reduced their risk of dying by nearly sixty percent" (*JET*, Dec. 16, 2002). There is also the news report on a recently released sociological survey or poll: "Forty percent of Belarus population is computer literate" or "Total Number of Unmarried Couples Surges." Journalists rarely look to sociologists for critical, interpretive, or complex analyses of social issues.

Those who go public frequently encounter difficulties if they express more complex, critical views. Stacey (2004), in a reflection upon the way she was used by the media as an expert on families, concluded that "even when progressive sociologists gain access to public pulpits and deliver sociological sermons from a critical perspective the very act of participating risks reinforcing structures of thought and value antithetical to a critical sociological stance and to issues of social justice" (132). By serving as media experts, Schwartz (1998) suggests, sociologists "have been merely hitching on to a juggernaut that uses them up in drive-by quotations on random topics." If sociologists wish to make a real contribution, she suggests, they must "frame the debate, by creating and interpreting the data more polemically, earlier in the game ... or we become mere sound bites in someone else's more ambitious effort to create meaning and policy" (439). But how to do so?

Historically, it takes book-length works to really frame a debate in new ways. Books have the potential to spark public conversations, shaping the way that people understand themselves and their world; at times, works of sociology have exerted this kind of influence.[1] In the 1950s and '60s, for example, the work of Robert Lynd, C. Wright Mills, and David Riesman was widely read. Writing about the popular influence of Riesman's *The Lonely Crowd*, the best-selling work of sociology, Gitlin (2000) suggests: "For years, the book made 'inner-direction' and 'other direction' household terms.... It was read by student radicals in the making ... as a harbinger of alienation leading to affluent revolt" (35). In the 1970s and '80s, books by Robert Bellah et al. (1985), Lillian Rubin (1977), and others traversed academic and popular audiences.

Herbert Gans (1989), examining the characteristics of best-selling works of sociology, suggests that they have some things in common: they are jargon free, written in a language that "at least educated readers can understand"; they are often interdisciplinary, attracting readers from other disciplines; they try to understand American society as a whole; and they tend to be empirical research reports, particularly ethnographies. Three-quarters of the best selling works of American sociology were published by trade rather than university presses, which are typically better equipped to sell a book to nonacademic publics, having larger marketing budgets, more extensive distribution networks, and more clout with book reviewers at important national media outlets.

Over the past few decades, book-length sociological works appealing simultaneously to academic and lay publics have declined in influence. Although more and more works of sociology and related fields are being published today than ever before, few books sell more than a few thousand copies; of the fifty-three sociological works that have sold over 50,000 copies since 1940, only two were published after 1990. Writing in 1997, Gans predicted that by 2007, under pressure to produce higher-profit margins, few commercial publishers would be publishing works of sociology. There are numerous indicators that this shift may be occurring.[2] Although more than 50,000 new books are published each year in the United States, the consolidation of the publishing industry has meant that business considerations increasingly guide publishing decisions.

At the end of World War II, most publishing houses still belonged to the people who started them, who knew that some types of books were bound to lose money, and who saw their goal as stimulating debate and raising general levels of literacy. As late as the Vietnam War, Bantam and other mass-market publishers offered collections of political essays and criticism written for the broader public—including C. Wright Mills's *Listen Yankee*, on the Cuban revolution. Editors and intellectuals traveled in similar circles, and powerful editors at top presses could turn obscure academics into public intellectuals with an audience beyond the Academy (Coser et al, 1982; Kadushin, 1974; McLaughlin, 1998).

Publishing houses are increasingly part of international corporate conglomerates. Viacom is the parent of Simon & Schuster, Bertelsmann owns Random House and Knopf, for example. Today, five conglomerates control eighty percent of book sales; the top twenty publishers comprise 93 percent of sales; the top ten, 75 percent of sales. The consequence is that "There is pressure not just for hits, but for every title—or at least every imprint—to pay its way." Since the bottom line increasingly dictates what books are to be published, entertainment or "hard information" rather than books offering new ideas are favored. Books without a clearly defined potential audience are unlikely to be published.

While a focus on the changing political economy of publishing is important, it does not tell the whole story. While "popular sociology" may have declined, sociological kinds of books are more popular than ever. People are interested in what makes societies tick. They find gender inequality, social trends and "epidemics," and the problems facing schools interesting and intriguing topics. Consider the popularity of books such as Barbara Ehrenreich's *Nickel and Dimed,* or Malcolm Gladwell's *The Tipping Point,* which draw upon sociological work, and make sociological arguments, but are pitched to a broad audience. Why aren't more sociologists publishing such books?

Sociologists, one editor complained, "are too likely to use the passive voice, obscure jargon or an overly self-reflexive mode of writing"—all of which spell death to the goal of reaching a broader public.[3] Indeed, according to Gans (1989), the best selling works of sociology tend to be jargon free, written in a language that "at least educated readers can understand," and they are often interdisciplinary. And they try to understand American society in a holistic way rather than focus on a discrete, narrowly defined question. But this type of holistic, jargon-free sociological work is at odds with the kinds of work that graduate students are trained to do today.

Comparing the citation patterns for the *AJS* during the late 1940s and '50s to today, Calhoun (1992) found frequent references to popular magazines, general intellectual periodicals, and journals from the humanities during the earlier period—and very few today. "Nearly every introductory sociology textbook on the market," writes Calhoun (138) "carries a paragraph (or several) claiming to distinguish sociology rather sharply from other social sciences. We discourage interdisciplinary work by graduate students and young faculty" (185). The professionalization of sociology, and the valuation of scientific rigor over communication with nonacademic publics means that graduate students in sociology are trained to write for academic publications, not for the general public.

Indeed, when scientific rigor becomes a primary marker of good scholarship, the worst insult one can lodge against a work of scholarship is that it's "journalistic" or "popular"—signifying that it is lacking in rigor. Harvard sociologist Orlando Patterson (2002) suggested that the best-selling work of sociology, Riesman's *The Lonely Crowd,* based on what he calls a "more or less random sample," could not have been published today by a sociologist seeking to further his/her career, where the peer review process enforces methodological rigor and discourages authors from making sweeping claims that they cannot substantiate exhaustively. But it's precisely those sweeping claims—about changes in American character and culture—that were so provocative, and that made the book so popular, and influential.

The rise of rigorism has sacrificed range, and an understanding of sociology as a holistic discipline dedicated to intellectual breadth as well as depth. But people do hunger for an understanding of their lives and the world they live in. The failure of sociologists to write books that are both sophisticated and accessible has left the field ripe for popularization by those outside the discipline. A recent ad in *The New Yorker* for a book by a business writer named James Surowiecki is telling on this score. The book, *The Wisdom of Crowds: Why the Many Are Smarter than the Few and How Collective Wisdom Shapes Business, Economics, Societies, and Nations,* is written by a business journalist and published by Doubleday. An ad boldly touts the book as "something surprising and new: a sociological tract as gripping as a good novel."

When sociologists communicate with the public via the media, they are typically presented as experts, as professional monopolists of expertise, knowledgeable about a discrete, narrowly defined subject area. Limited in their capacity to shape the terms of discussion, they fall short of C. Wright Mills's dream that sociology might encourage a "sociological imagination" that illuminates the connection between "personal troubles" and "public issues." The consequence, according to George Ritzer (1998) is that "sociology is largely invisible to the general reading public"—or at least sociology written by sociologists. While sociology is certainly not alone in this respect, the discipline's relatively low public profile is particularly odd in view of its unique status as a field that tries to systematically examine the dynamics of contemporary societies, and to understand society in a holistic or general way. But it doesn't have to be this way.

## Toward a More Public Sociology

Fifty years ago, Mills implored sociologists to exercise their "sociological imagination," and connect "personal problems" and "social issues." He called for a bigger, bolder sociology, one that would take on the big problems of the day, in a fashion that would help people living in an increasingly complex world make sense of their lives. Today, a number of leading sociologists agree, in large part, with Mills's assessment (Burawoy, 2002a, 2002b; Gans, 1989; Gitlin, 2000; Patterson, 2002). They want more sociologists to become "public intellectuals."

What are the prospects for reinvigorating a tradition of public sociological work? Burawoy (2002a, 2002b) imagines a renewed "public sociology" that would encourage individuals to reframe the issues at hand, think critically about them, and in doing so enlarge the democratic public sphere. Rather than imagine public intellectuals and professional sociologists as necessarily at odds with one another, he believes that professional sociology could help generate public sociological work, and describes four different types of relationships between sociological knowledge and its audiences.

*Professional sociology* is concerned with accumulation of knowledge, organized by and for sociologists in various research programs. It produces instrumental, largely positivistic knowledge for academic audiences, disseminated through professional journals. *Policy sociology* applies that knowledge to problems defined by agencies, corporations, organizations. *Critical sociology* engages sociologists in a critical evaluation of what they are doing rooted in sociology's abiding values (equality, social justice, etc). *Public sociology* promotes public discussion and debate about those values. It produces reflexive types of knowledge that engage publics in discussion of values and issues that confront society. Rather than sacrificing rigor for range, the public sociologist makes use of analytic clarity to speak to both academic and nonacademic audiences, addressing and enlarging the democratic public sphere.

By shifting the focus from "public intellectuals" to "public sociology," this schema suggests that many individuals wear multiple hats, that the professional and public sociologist are not mutually exclusive categories. While overprofessionalization may provide disincentives for public sociology, professionalization makes public sociology possible, providing the salaries, institutional support, and knowledge base for public sociology. Without these professional networks, public sociology is simply "popular sociology," lacking a firm foundation in ongoing intellectual debates and an institutional base. Professional sociology's "scientific expert," in other words, exists in relation to and in tension with public sociology's "social critic." Too much professionalization spells death for public sociology, but too little may undermine the institutional basis of (relatively) free intellectual inquiry.

Many sociologists yearn to address larger audiences, but lack an understanding of what it takes to do that, or the connections and credibility to pull it off. Publishers are less likely to take risks on books that won't sell, and sociologists are also less equipped to write books that combine intellectual depth with popular appeal that could sell. In an effort to establish credibility, sociologists define themselves as "not-journalists," and write ever more rigorous articles and books, equating "public sociology" with "pop" (read: thin, speculative) sociology.

To stimulate public sociological work, a number of steps are in order, including establishing institutional spaces that might nurture such work. Academic professionalization and media concentration has segmented sociologists and journalists into separate worlds. The public intellectual spaces of old—journals of opinion, coffeehouses, and free-floating social worlds—in which "undisciplined" ideas were nurtured—are fewer and fewer. Such worlds, while they cannot be resurrected, could be partially reconstructed, in the form of "salons" for intellectuals and intellectually minded journalists, or publications in which academics and journalists interact. Many of these spaces will, no doubt, be virtual.

Thanks to the Internet, the opportunities for conveying one's ideas outside of the corporate-controlled media universe are more numerous than ever before. An op-ed published in a newspaper can be reprinted and posted on a number of web sites almost instantaneously. Electronic discussion lists on any number of imaginable topics tap into ideas and reproduce them rapidly for huge, fragmented, indeterminate publics. These platforms offer intellectuals unprecedented reach and influence (Rice, 2007). They also set everyone up as a potential "expert," potentially diminishing professional intellectuals' claim to privileged expertise—making the process of adjudicating among different claims and establishing credibility among different experts even more important. In this brave new world of information flows, there is new uncertainty and also great democratic potential (Said, 2001).

That new forms of media will compete with book-length works of sociology, challenging the dominance of trade publishers as vehicles of critical sociological ideas, doesn't mean that good writing will cease to be important. Speaking about the "craft" of sociological writing, Mills advised budding sociologists: "Before you are through with any piece of work," Mills wrote, "orient it to the central and continuing task of understanding the structure and the drift, the shaping and meanings, of your own period ... [Work conducted in this spirit] has a chance to make a difference in the quality of human life" (Mills and Mills, 2001: 111). A firmer understanding of the "craft of writing" (Mills, 1959) would go a long way toward expanding the audiences that take sociological work seriously. Currently, few if any graduate departments of sociology teach the craft of sociological writing in ways that go beyond "bureaucratic science." But good sociological writing is a craft, and also an art form, and should be taken more seriously.

And finally, to become better communicators with the public, we sociologists must enlarge our sociological imagination, and go beyond the current vision of a "bureaucratic science (Phillips, 2001) that analyzes discrete problems having little connection to one another. During the past few decades, a number of critiques of sociological positivism have focused on the ways professional sociology sacrifices range for rigor. In the 1970s, for example, feminists posed alternatives to sociological positivism (Laslett and Thorne, 1997; Smith, 1990) offering a vision of sociology as bridge between the personal and the political, an understanding of how everyday life is shaped by structural inequalities, and a reflexive orientation—reminiscent of Mills's understanding of sociology. Mills argued that sociology could provide a bridge between "biography" and "history," offering the individual a way of understanding his/her place in history and social structure. It could help him/her to understand how "personal problems" are often rooted in "social issues." It could empower the individual to see her/his life as part of a larger whole. Yet sociology itself has become a casualty of that narrowing of vision.

In order to broaden the sociological imagination, some suggest that we need to do a better job of linking abstract theoretical concepts with concrete evidence, integrating discrete bodies of knowledge into a coherent whole. Certainly, this expanded vision could go a long way toward countering premature specialization and the fragmentation of knowledge (Scheff, 2007). Toward this end, Phillips (2001) offers what he calls a "Web and Part/Whole Approach," a reconceptualization of the mission of sociology that offers researchers a way to connect their individual projects with a broader conceptualization of the field, integrating social knowledge and linking it with work outside the discipline. Helping sociologists understand their work in a more holistic way could go a long way toward empowering them to be credible public analysts of the complex social issues that shape our world. This doesn't mean that we should all become public sociologists, but it does suggest that such efforts could renew and reinvigorate the discipline and deepen public intellectual engagement in general.

## Notes

Arlene Stein may be contacted at the Department of Sociology, Rutgers University, New Brunswick, NJ. E-mail: arlenes@rci.rutgers.edu. Mailing address: 111 Second St. South Orange, NJ 07079.
1. Curiously, one of the rare opportunities to encounter extended discussions of sociological ideas in the media is in the obituaries of notable sociologists. We learn, for example, in an obituary for William H. Whyte, who wrote the sociological classic *The Organization Man,* that Whyte challenged and refuted claims of entrepreneurial vigor and daring in business by describing an ongoing bureaucratization of white-collar environments—board rooms, offices, laboratories (*New York Times,* January 13, 1999). David Riesman's obituary explains his analysis of "other-directed" and "inner-directed" personality types, and its relationship to his analysis of American character and culture (*New York Times,* May 11, 2002). And noting the passing of Robert Merton in February,

2003, a number of leading newspapers in the United States and the United Kingdom offered a summary of his intellectual contributions. Is the best sociologist a dead sociologist?

2. Sociologists' own assessments of important and influential works are often at odds with public perceptions of their value, as a comparison between Gans's "Sociological Bestsellers" (1997) and Clawson's Sociology's Most Influential Books (1998) suggests.

3. Interview with author.

# References

Abbott, Andrew. 1999. *Department and Discipline*. Chicago: Univ. of Chicago Press.

Agger, Ben, 2000. *Public Sociology*. Boulder: Rowman and Littlefield.

Bauman, Zygmunt. 1987. *Legislators and Interpreters*. Cambridge: Polity.

Becker, Howard S. 1990. "The Most Critical Issue Facing the ASA," *American Sociologist* 21 (Winter 1990), no. 4.

Bellah, Robert, Richard Madsen, William Sullivan, Ann Swidler, and Steven Tipton, 1985. *Habits of the Heart: Individualism and Commitment in American Life*. Berkeley: Univ. of California Press.

Bender, Thomas, and Carl Schorske, eds. 1998. *American Academic Culture in Transformation*. Princeton: Princeton Univ. Press.

Bloom, Allan. 1987. *The Closing of the American Mind* (New York: Simon and Schuster).

Bourdieu, Pierre. 1998. *On Television*. New York: New Press.

Burawoy, Michael. 2002a. "Gans and Beyond: Notes on an Inclusive Public Sociology," unpublished ms.

———. 2002b, "Models of Public Sociology," *ASA Footnotes*, December 2002: 6.

Buxton, William, and Stephen P. Turner, 1992. "From Education to Expertise: Sociology as a Profession." In *Sociology and Its Publics*, ed. Terence C. Halliday and Morris Janowitz. Chicago: Univ. of Chicago Press.

Calhoun, Craig. 1992. "Sociology, Other Disciplines, and the Project of a General Understanding of Social Life," in *Sociology and Its Publics*, ed. Halliday and Janowitz. Berkeley: Univ. of California Press.

Clawson, Dan. 1998. *Required Reading: Sociology's Most Influential Books*. Amherst: Univ. of Massachusetts Press.

Coser, Lewis, et al., 1982. *Books: The Culture and Commerce of Publishing*. New York: Basic Books.

Crane, Diana, and Henry Small. 1992. "American Sociology Since the Seventies: The Emerging Identity Crisis in the Discipline," in *Sociology and its Publics*, ed. Terence C. Halliday and Morris Janowitz. Chicago: Univ. of Chicago Press.

Epstein, Steven. 1995. "The Construction of Lay Expertise: AIDS Activism and the Forging of Credibility." *Science, Technology & Human Values* 20 (4): 409–439.

Foucault, Michel. 1997. "Polemics, Politics and Problematization: An Interview," *Essential Works of Foucault*, ed. P. Rabinow. New York: New Press.

Gans, Herbert J. 1989. "Sociology in America: The Discipline and the Public" *American Sociological Review.*

Gans, Herbert J. 1997. "Best Sellers by Sociologists: An Exploratory Study," *Contemporary Sociology* 26: 2.

Gitlin, Todd. 2000. "How Our Crowd Got Lonely," *New York Times Book Review,* January 9, 2000: 35.

Habermas, Jürgen, 1974. "The Public Sphere: An Encyclopedia Article," *New German Critique* No. 4.

Halliday, Terence, 1992. "Sociology's Fragile Professionalism." In *Sociology and its Publics,* ed. Terence C. Halliday and Morris Janowitz. Chicago: Univ. of Chicago Press.

Jacobs, Ronald, and Eleanor Townsley, 2004. "Media Intellectuals and Public Sociology: The Case of Op-Eds in the *New York Times.*" Paper presented at American Sociological Association meetings, San Francisco, August 2004.

Jacoby, Russell, 1987. *The Last Intellectuals: American Culture in the Age of Academe.* New York: Basic Books.

Kadushin, Charles. 1974. *The American Intellectual Elite.* Boston: Little Brown.

Kuhn, Thomas. [1962]1970. *The Structure of Scientific Revolutions.* Chicago: Univ. of Chicago.

Laslett, Barbara, and Barrie Thorne. 1997. *Feminist Sociology: Life Histories of a Movement.* New Brunswick: Rutgers.

McLaughlin, Neil. 1998. "How to Become a Forgotten Intellectual: Intellectual Movements and the Rise and Fall of Erich Fromm." *Sociological Forum* 13(2) (June 1998): 215–246.

Mills, Katherine, and P. Mills, eds. 2001. *C. Wright Mills: Letters and Autobiographical Writings.* Berkeley: Univ. of California Press.

Mills, C. Wright. 1959. *The Sociological Imagination.* London: Oxford.

Patterson, Orlando. 2002. "The Last Sociologist." *New York Times,* May 19, 2002.

Phillips, Bernard. 2001. "Beyond Sociology's Tower of Babel: Reconstructing the Scientific Method." http://www.sociological-imagination.org/tower_of_babel.htm.

Posner, Richard, 2002. *Public Intellectuals: A Study of Decline.* Cambridge, Mass.: Harvard Univ. Press.

Reinharz, Shulamit. 1979. *On Becoming a Social Scientist.* New Brunswick: Transaction.

Rice, LaVon. 2007. "Portrait of the Sociologist as Blogger." *American Sociological Association Footnotes,* February: 4.

Riesman, David et al. 1950. *The Lonely Crowd.* New York: Doubleday.

Ritzer, George. 1998. "Writing to be Read: Changing the Culture and Reward Structure of American Sociology." *Contemporary Sociology* 27, no. 5.

Rorty, Richard. 1998. *Achieving Our Country.* Cambridge, Mass.: Harvard University Press.

Rubin, Lillian. 1977. *Worlds of Pain: Life in the Working-Class Family.* New York: Perseus Books.

Rudel, Thomas, and Judith Gerson. 1999. "Postmodernism, Institutional Change, and Academic Workers: A Sociology of Knowledge." *Social Science Quarterly* 80(2).

Said, Edward, 2001. "The Public Role of Writers and Intellectuals." *The Nation* (September 17, 2001): 24.

Sarfatti Larson, Magali. 1997. *The Rise of Professionalism*. Berkeley: Univ. of California Press.

Schorske, Carl E. 1998. "The New Rigorism in the Human Sciences, 1940–1960." In Thomas Bender and Carl Schorske, eds. *American Academic Culture in Transformation*. Princeton: Princeton Univ. Press.

Schiffrin, Andrew, 2000. *The Business of Books*. New York: Verso.

Schwartz, Pepper, 1998. "Stage Fright or Death Wish: Sociology in the Mass Media," *Contemporary Sociology* 27(5).

Scheff, Thomas J. 2007. *Goffman Unbound*. Boulder: Paradigm Publishers.

Smelser, Neil. 1992. "External Influences on Sociology." In *Sociology and Its Publics*. Ed. Terence C. Halliday and Morris Janowitz. Chicago: Univ. of Chicago Press.

Smith, Dorothy. 1990. *The Conceptual Practices of Power*. Boston: Northeastern Univ. Press.

Stacey, Judith. 2004. "Marital Suitors Court Social Science Spinsters: The Unwittingly Conservative Effects of Public Sociology," *Social Problems* Vol. 51: 131–145.

Weber, Max. 1978. *Economy and Society: An Outline of Interpretive Sociology*, ed. Guenther Roth. Berkeley: Univ. of California Press.

# CHAPTER 11

# Public Opinion and Social Movements

## A Sociological Analysis

*Louis Kontos*

SOCIAL-MOVEMENT ORGANIZATIONS NORMALLY TRY to influence public opinion and to convert passive public support into active participation. This involves framing issues as "problems" within compelling narratives—that is, narratives that embody a sense of urgency or crises and that provide pragmatic solutions. Such narratives are invariably ideological in nature, in that they draw on collective concepts, themes, imagery, and myths that represent the common sense of any given culture, and that inform generalized expectations and judgments. In which case the question arises as to how any movements can change the cultural framework within which they operate. The question is relevant to any sociology that posits the need for social change and that understands itself as having a stake in the outcome of progressive movements—as with the sociology expounded in this volume under the headings "Web and Part/Whole Approach."

As the sociological study of social movements evolves into a hyperspecialized discipline, it also appears more objective and scientific—its "data" appear to fit naturally within various theoretical categories, as if the sociologist is merely allowing the data to speak for themselves and as if the data speak naturally in the language of one theory or another. It is conspicuous in this regard that social movements "in general" were conceptualized within mainstream sociology until the late 1960s as disorganized, spontaneous, and unpredictable—which is to say, as instances of "collective behavior," alongside cults, fads, and riots—and now generally appear in the sociological literature as orderly, quasi-institutional or bureaucratic, and entirely predictable. Hence, an earlier, impressionistic, one-sided *sociological* reality has been effectively replaced by another, empirically grounded, equally one-sided sociological reality—obscuring the *social* reality of movements as complex, multidimensional phenomena. Also obscured in the process is the difference between questions of "why" and "how" in connection with the topic of social movement participation—whereby the discovery that participation takes form under certain conditions and in response to specific organizational strategies and narratives, and the like appears as an explanation of motive. The ideal-typical participant, in this case, is one with transparent needs and interests that translate directly into motives for participation, motives that can be made transparent to observers who are then able to generalize, quantify, and construct elaborate typologies. Thus analysts increasingly rely on surveys that resemble public-opinion polls; that contain clear-cut definitions of issues and that pose questions to respondents like how they feel about them, with what degree of intensity, whether they plan to act, under what hypothetical conditions they might engage in various hypothetical acts, and so on (cf. Klandermans and Oegema, 1997). Several underlying assumptions are problematic in this scenario, including that respondents share the necessary concepts and background assumptions with analysts, that they are willing to state controversial positions truthfully to those same anonymous analysts, and that "preferences," "choices," "motives" or "reasons" are discernable causal mechanisms within any course of action.

There is also now great reliance on secondary sources and narratives of events, which provide a basis for comparison and quantification—in that it becomes possible to identify organizational strategies, propaganda, and other social-movement phenomena. Newspapers are most accommodating since they provide contemporaneous accounts and written text that can be content-analyzed for ideological bias and distortion. However, such data—newspaper accounts of public events, social issues, and movements—are "sporadically collected" and their criteria of selection and categorization are often "vague and subject to changes over time" (Koopmans, 1999: 92). Objectivity is lacking, then, throughout analyses that are credulous toward News—including as a source from which to discern the frequency, intensity, or form of events. As one observer puts it, there is no way to tell with any certainty "whether we are analyzing patterns of historical events or patterns of news reporting" (Franzosi, 1987: 6).

In contrast, "collective-behavior" theorists in the 1950s and '60s were drawn to News with a more limited but ambitious purpose, namely to discern the perception created for targeted audiences about the ways in which other people are like or unlike themselves, whether they are insiders or outsiders, and moreover, whether movement goals are balanced, pragmatic, fair-minded, and so on. As Turner (1969) argued, in order for outside groups (third parties) to see a particular disruptive event as an instance of legitimate protest, "an optimal combination of threat and appeal" is needed (821). That is to say, outsiders must attribute reason to the participants based on an understanding of conditions or problems to which they (participants) are supposedly responding appropriately. Participants, then, must not appear to be "using" those events for personal advantage, or "enjoying" themselves at the expense of others who are the object of protest, or appear unwilling to offer conciliatory gestures or engage in conciliation. In most cases, Turner notes, representatives of the group that is the object of criticism need hardly do anything more, with regard to third parties, than appear to oblige the demand for conciliation by introducing impersonal bargaining procedures which, as events recur, work against seeing them as legitimate—as real protest. By the same token, it is possible for groups that are the object of criticism to reestablish their public image through acts of reciprocity—or generosity, kindness, social awareness, and the like—and for critics to counter the image of illegitimacy with symbolic language and through the transformation of protest into institutional politics.

Where movements offset stigma by limiting extrainstitutional activities—direct action—contexts and situations become recursive, offsetting the possibility of anything new or different. Such movements (or aspects or stages of movements) have indeed been effective in recent history. Their growth has altered the dynamics of political dissent and opposition, in that struggles within bureaucratic environments take place primarily among professionals who work behind the scenes and away from public scrutiny and interference and, by definition, exclude those without money, expertise, and time. They do not bring ordinary people together in circumstances of deep consequence, as was the case, for instance, with the labor movement throughout the early 20th century in American society, the civil rights movement of the 1960s, among others; nor do they challenge the status quo in any fundamental way. Consequently, the means prejudice the ends. Wage increases have nothing to do with the goal of ending the exploitation of the many by the few—whereas they have not even kept up with inflation since the 1970s. Gains in civil rights, as we now know, can coexist with institutional discrimination and exclusionary networks of power and privilege. Institutionalized movements that support such "progressive" agendas may in fact continue to expand and multiply without struggle or controversy within (notwithstanding) a long wave of counterrevolution—on the condition that their goals are tightly circumscribed and tactics associated with them are self-repetitive, thus predictable.

Inversely, social movements and whatever public events and propaganda become associated with them appear "new" or different for any number of reasons. For instance, they may be novel, as was the case with the use of "puppet theater" in recent protests against the World Trade Organization, particularly the mass demonstration that came to be known as the Battle of Seattle; or they may embody ideas and objectives that cannot be reconciled within public morality, as is now the case with aspects of the antiwar movement, animal liberationists, certain religions that are deemed cults, etc. Even "traditional" movements appear new when their place in mainstream public discourse is precarious—seemingly coming out of nowhere for whatever inexplicably nefarious reasons the corporate media impute to them. Thereby, socialist groups are more controversial than labor unions, even when they appear to struggle for the same objectives, since the rhetoric of these groups puts into question the institutional framework and political economy within which the majority of workers do not identify with the label "working class" and want nothing more than to gain rather than lose further ground. The fact that unions and other organizations that ostensibly seek to advance limited goals that are widely considered "just" are dismissively called "socialist," is a stark testimony to the effectiveness of propaganda in contemporary society; in that, in becoming ubiquitous, it assumes the quality of what Durkheim called "social fact"—a force outside the individual that shapes desires and expectations, that establishes the parameters of acceptable thought and behavior.

In response, there is a growing concern within leftist circles with finding a "common conceptual language" around which arguments on behalf of universal programs and the democratization of social institutions are possibly accepted by outsiders—the majority—as rational and consistent with public morality and "American tradition." By the same token, the traditional emphasis of New Deal liberals shifts dramatically from education and ideology critique to more and better propaganda— as if all relevant truth is known by a select few, and such truth cannot be stated plainly to the frightened and bewildered masses. Doing effective propaganda for progressive causes, in this sense, means that social commentary and narratives regarding social problems must be moral rather than political, with veiled or explicit appeals to self-interest that emulate the appeals of the right. For example, arguments on behalf of greater funding for schools are now routinely laced with projections of rising crimes—i.e., warning that if nothing is done to ensure that other people's children are minimally educated, "our" children are put at risk. Arguments on behalf of universal health care normally come with warnings about health hazards—for example, sick people making the rest of us sick.

## Political and Normative Ideology in Social Research

The question of how movement organizers might best appeal to "ordinary" and "working-class" people is engaged in a widely cited study by Gamson (1996). It is fashioned as an attempt to determine what prevents these folks from adopting "critical frames" of issues that "support" progressive causes and organizations. Specifically, it seeks to determine the role of the following sources of influence: "media discourse," "personal experience," and "popular wisdom." In this study the majority of respondents appear remarkably uninformed and indeed reactionary toward practically every issue put before them.

In addition, although only "working-class" people were included, none referred to themselves in that way, preferring instead the labels "middle class" and "working people." This self-labeling could be construed as ideological, or as reflexive avoidance of the stigma associated with "working class" in contemporary bourgeois society, or something else entirely. For Gamson the problem is that most working-class people really see themselves as middle-class, while, deep down, they are ambivalent about their goals and ways of life—as if being working-class amounts to failure and as if identification with other members of the working class amounts to resignation. It is perhaps better in this scenario to embrace the American Dream, even if it can't be lived, than to admit the American Nightmare. It is definitely easier, since one does not have to explain or justify strenuous or futile efforts to maintain the appearance of a middle-class lifestyle—evidence of appropriate commitments and attitudes provide all the justification that is needed; whereas incredulity requires justification. To be sure, there is normally ambivalence regarding brutal facts of life, such as the lack of fulfilling work and the day-to-day degradation experienced in trying to make a living. It is evidenced not only in focus groups but also in public-opinion surveys and experimental situations; in that people often contradict themselves when the same questions about social issues are "framed" differently, or when they are presented with counterarguments. (Alternatively, it might be the case that most people don't have any real opinions about most issues they are asked to comment upon, that "public opinion" is mostly an artifact of research.)

For Gamson the "discovery" of ambivalence provides reason to doubt the existence of ideological support for the rightward turn of the American political establishment over the last few decades. In this view, widespread ambivalence with regard to social and political issues is the next best thing to an informed and mobilized public, since it holds a "resonance" with "critical frames" of social and political issues.

The argument is elaborated through a series of discoveries. For instance, he discovers that most respondents are willing to stand corrected in the course of conversation regarding a broad range of issues they know little about—especially distal issues, like foreign policy. But we are not told why or how this willingness indicates ambivalence, as opposed to, say, politeness or an attempt to identify with the researcher, or whatever else; nor why political ambivalence, assuming this very thing, should be interpreted as limited to liberal and conservative alternatives. Rather, it is simply assumed that people normally experience ambivalence regarding political issues, and further, that they are troubled by it; lacking the information and concepts through which it may be resolved. It also affirms the researcher's role as strategist par excellence.

This mode of reasoning—sociological pragmatism—reappears in a number of Gamson-inspired studies, most notably in Sasson's (1995) study of "neighborhood-watch" groups, involving group organizers who agreed to host discussions with members of their group. Analysts asked questions designed to elicit conversation around the "dimensions and sources of the crime problem," with follow-up questions designed to represent three distinct frames of reference: "social breakdown," "faulty system," and "blocked opportunity." Respondents were subsequently asked whether they agreed or disagreed with those statements. Sasson found that media discourse, as opposed to popular wisdom and personal experience, is most often used as a "resource" to support the frame "blocked opportunity," and that experience is referred to most often in support of the frames "system inefficiency" and "social breakdown." He, like Gamson, surmises that if activists are interested in developing public support for their causes, they must frame their arguments in terms of theories that they, themselves, invariably, reject. The central rhetorical mistake among activists, in this view, is making critical claims that are not framed in appropriate ideological terms—no matter how well founded the claims—such as "the claim that poverty causes crime," which is "natural on the political left" but "strikes many people as itself *immoral*" (170). In order to gain support for such objectives as greater fairness and equality, then, in this view, the left must better emulate the arguments of the right, even while contesting the assumptions and factual claims about "social problems" that buttress those arguments. This logic revolves around the assumption that most people share at least some of the least controversial objectives of "the left" but not consistently and without having resolved the contradiction within and between notions of equality, merit, competition, and the like.

It is further assumed in this respect that leftist ideologies and the social and historical alternatives they represent lack resonance, and thereby credibility, as sources of definition; but in a more pragmatic mode, as solutions to problems already defined "conventionally" and "experientially," they may become credible. This strategy has questionable merits politically—at least with regard to institutional politics with which it is solely concerned. But it makes sociology irrelevant and nonsensical; reinforcing, with analytical rigor, the very concepts and stereotypes that mainstream, apolitical sociology has thus far routinely debunked as a matter of routine—in order to reveal social facts, to support its claim of being an objective or superior form of knowledge about the social and, most importantly, to demonstrate a need for itself. There are several faulty premises in the kind of reasoning exemplified by framing theorists like Gamson and Sasson, including: that people are primarily oriented toward "representations" rather than expectations, that conflicting frames and claims around social and political issues constitute, for such people, dilemmas that they would like to resolve any way they can, including through self-reflection, lacking the necessary information and concepts with which to do so. What is missing, by the same token, is a recognition of the fact that observers are occasioning (or provoking) ambivalence around *their* constructs and toward sources of judgment *concomitant with the goals of research*—for instance, to see how aware people are, to see what types of beliefs they hold, or to see how well they can learn.

Furthermore, this mode of theorizing obscures the distinction between natural and artificial settings and, more importantly here, between active participation, which requires special motivation—or "inspiration" (cf. Snow and Benford, 1988)—and the type of support normally granted by "third parties," namely voting, contributing money, or simply withdrawing opposition. In the "pragmatic" posturing of framing theorists, such differences become irrelevant. Thus, what appears important about "progressive" movements is, not the possibility of generating new contexts and situations that support new ways of life, but that movement goals gain legitimacy in the eyes of indifferent or skeptical third parties. In which case, as Buechler (1993) puts it, movements appear concerned with "the public good." But such legitimacy does not inspire either active participation or sustained commitment. Rather, as Williams (1995) says: "If a movement manages to create a 'definitive' (meaning 'effective') claim to the public good, bystander publics can only oppose the movement at the risk of a charge of 'self-interest'" (140). And therein lies an interesting dilemma, since the ability to mobilize people by stigmatizing opposition in "causes" that are widely understood to be "just" is predicated on contradictory ideas, beliefs, or "norms." The contradiction between self-interest and the public good is normally reconciled through heteronymous concepts, including a conception of the public as comprised of nomads and opportunists. Moreover, in contemporary bourgeois society, the charge of "self-interest" is hardly comparable to that of being too far to the left and thereby out of touch with reality, being deviant, or unpatriotic, for example.

Ideological indoctrination in modern bourgeois societies is an increasingly difficult and fragile accomplishment, since the dynamics of political economy sweep up traditional ways of life and bring historical alternatives into view. Therefore, normative ideology requires constant reinforcement through "propaganda and agitation" (Gramsci, 1971). The problem, in this respect, is that its ideological concepts appear increasingly detached from social reality, therefore vacuous, including the concept of a "free market" in which hard work and ingenuity are supposedly rewarded and the opposite leads to failure. Moreover, arguments that serve to naturalize the status quo inevitably resort to the twin logic of scarcity and necessity, in which a lack of resources is the reason, not only for class warfare by whatever name, but also for indifference to society's most vulnerable members—its children, the elderly, and the handicapped. This argument is indeed a hard sell. It became unconvincing, as Keynes (1925/1972) wrote, during World War I, when a massive expenditure of public wealth and resources instantly materialized. The same can now be said about current military adventures, including the invasion and occupation of Iraq—where, presto, massive sums of money are suddenly found, found again, and again. Conversely, credulity to ideological arguments is not necessary in order for the propaganda surrounding them to be effective, assuming its ubiquity and association with structures of power, including the mainstream media, that routinely silence dissent and demonize outsiders (Noelle-Newman, 1993).

## The Web Approach

These are the problems that confront the "web approach" in its commitment to the idea of a politically engaged sociology in the vein of C. Wright Mills—who not only inspired generations of students to undertake a rigorous study of society and to apply what they learn in ways that make a difference to the lives of ordinary people, but who was not averse to political controversy. Phillips admires in Mills his ardent belief that a "sociological imagination" can migrate outside of sociology, becoming a mode of critical self-consciousness. How exactly that is to happen, Mills does not say. Phillips makes the opposite point: under current conditions, given the direction of the field, it cannot possibly happen. He makes much of the fact that sociology has become increasingly fragmented and formalized, such that sociologists working within particular subfields are seemingly obligated to use a specialized, technical language that, at best, illuminates only some particular aspect of the phenomena at hand, and does not attempt to come to terms with their complexity. Such attempts would require, at least, a broader and more flexible use of technical vocabulary in sociology.

The central metaphor in Phillips is that of the "web," used in various contexts to underline the fact that disparate concepts from disparate modes of discourse or theorizing are routinely not incorporated into sociological explanations even where they might enhance those explanations—disciplinary and subdisciplinary boundaries inhibit understanding and effective communication. The web, in this sense, is comprised of concepts, ideas, allegories, and the like. The metaphor of a "web" is also used in this work to underscore the complexity of sociological phenomena. Indeed, complexity itself cannot be grasped through any concept—nor is complexity a concept. To say that any phenomena are complex for this or that reason is to say nothing. Instead, the discovery of a "web of relations" through which sociological phenomena take form requires an appropriate conceptual language through which inquiry relates parts with wholes, particularity with universality, micro with macro, and so on. The question then becomes how is this done. What determines appropriate levels of abstraction? What determines the selection of parts, wholes, and relations among them as being in some sense essential or sociologically significant rather than merely epiphenomenal? Are there any objective or "scientific" criteria—any criterial auspices through consensus—from which to discern the validity of accomplished syntheses of concepts, ideas, facts, objects, situations, and events that constitute a "web"?

Mills had no illusions with regard to the capacities and limits of sociology. He did not construe the field as either actually or potentially "scientific" or "pragmatic" in any straightforward sense—notwithstanding the fact that he believed sociology could provide concepts and insights through which ordinary people could better understand themselves and their social environment. The idea of "relevance" in the work of Mills takes the form of a "critical" statement about contemporary affairs in sociology and society—in that mainstream sociology is deemed irrelevant to politically aware and engaged publics, which groups are deemed few are far between—rather than a simple admonition against any particular social or political group, or merely practical advice for schoolteachers or policy makers. (Not coincidently, Mills's work was taken up in a big way by the counterculture of the 1960s, which he didn't live to see.) Furthermore, the central claim of his seminal work, *The Sociological Imagination,* that we, or anybody, need to differentiate between "personal problems" and "social issues," and concomitantly that we need to integrate "personal biography" and "social history" begs the question. If such differentiation and integration is not normally done, arguably it is not because people are stupid—or misinformed, or lacking particular sociological concepts and insights. It is not done because such thinking puts one at odds with reason and authority within any institutional setting—within the institutional matrix of society—and because any way of thinking outside of official common sense makes people vulnerable to charges of heresy, being unrealistic, extremist, unreasonable, etc. Mills's second notable claim in the same text is rarely engaged in a serious way—and it is not engaged in this volume to my knowledge. That is, Mills argued that "social issues" (the same stuff we now call "social problems") are not soluble within a capitalist political economy. Rather, "antagonisms and contradictions" inhere in a status quo, which is antithetical to any and every conception of a "good society," and which reveal high stakes for sociology—in that the need to take sides confronts it at every turn. This—in effect, Marxist language—has a peculiar place in Mills. He does not expound upon it, except to underline the obvious, namely that what sociologists call "social problems" are not seen as a problem at all—in any sense of the word—by large segments of the public. The wealthy, as a class, certainly know better than to treat unemployment as a problem—unless of course it exceeds levels that cause severe inflation, provokes social unrest, etc. Nor are they particularly concerned about "the environment" or whatever else might be construed as being consistent with their own "long-term interests," since competition is a day-to-day affair. Government regulation ostensibly creates a level playing field for internal capitalist rivalries, curtailing the race to the bottom, but the established political parties have long ago abandoned any real engagement with civil society—now, under the strict control of corporate puppet masters and interest groups, they have little more to offer the electorate than protection from crime and terrorism. This long wave of counterrevolution must at least be called what it is by any sociology worth its name.

On the question of language, there is much in the web approach that I find worthwhile and I look forward to developments of this aspect in future work along the lines of this volume. Let's take up a couple of points herein dealing with language. First, Phillips (in this and other volumes) has made much of the fact that sociological vocabulary has become too highly specialized and therefore *nonrelational,* in fact, oftentimes irrelevant within sociology itself, everywhere outside the realm of particular subfields. In addition, he makes much of the fact that levels of abstraction are often inappropriate to the subject matter of sociology—that is, since sociological phenomena are complex and multidimensional, not discreetly contained such that observers can somehow capture their essence, as if with a bird's-eye view. Any "social problem" may be construed as the product of larger social forces that can only be named and analyzed at high levels of abstraction—for example, Phillips draws heavily on Merton's analysis of a growing "gap" between goals and means in American society, which then supposedly causes anomie—the strain that people feel when they are not able to fulfill their aspirations—the response to which is supposedly various forms of stereotypical deviance (economic crime, drug use, etc.—not suicide, as Durkheim believed when he developed the concept of "anomie"). The theory suffers from what Sutherland

(1947) said about "general" theories, namely that when they appear to be able to explain everything, they are actually explaining nothing at all. On another, lower level of abstraction, Phillips posits such concepts as interaction, intra- and intergroup expectations and association (drawing, for example, on Thomas Scheff's work on "shame"). To be sure, the social world makes no sense without an understanding of the ways in which social action is oriented to expectations, near and far. As Parsons (1971) aptly noted, the nature of the relation between action and expectation is never one-way, never simply contingent; rather there is always "double contingency," since "ego" makes decisions in relation to "alter" who does the same.

But, speaking of Parsons, it must be asked how the meaning of any concepts may be determined outside of use. Mills's famous "translation" of Parsons's work (already in English) set a bad example, as passage after passage of Parsons was translated into a few sentences. Certainly it is possible to translate the whole of Mills's work, if one were so inclined, into a few paragraphs, maybe less. What is gained? Parsons, lest we forget, was not writing for a broad audience. His audience was professional sociology, scholars in the humanities, university students, and other overeducated people with an interest in a "system"-oriented account of society and its problems. Mills, who wrote for a crossover audience, succeeded wildly in his goal. I encourage Phillips to persevere in the same direction.

Finally, the idea that properly educated people—people with the sociological imagination—can make better political decisions as well as hold their representatives accountable is hard to deny. It is also obvious enough that people oftentimes don't support progressive movements because they have been misinformed about issues, problems, or events—since reactionary propaganda is now ubiquitous and the corporate media have lost even the veneer of objectivity. (But do they really need to understand much about the workings of society in order to support political candidates that advocate a decent standard of living for ordinary people, or who oppose draconian criminal justice policies?). But with regard to movements themselves, the important sociological fact, as Blumer (1997) points out, is that movements are embodied in the group, as opposed to the audience, the crowd, or the mass of people. Groups form their own cultures that shape specific attitudes, opinions, and expectations—and that establish contexts that give rise to specific modes of interaction and association. Accordingly, while it is important for progressive movements that their beliefs, grievances, or claims are accepted by outside audiences, the more critical task is to form a public. It is significant, then, that "as a social movement develops, it takes on the character of a society. It acquires organization and form, a body of customs and traditions, established leadership, an enduring division of labor, social rules, and social values—in short, a culture, a social organization, and a new scheme of life" (Blumer,

1997: 81). Some new schemes indeed could use sociological recognition and support.

## Conclusion

Assumptions about the value of pragmatism versus idealism are never scientific but rather are ideologically based. Even where incremental reform toward social justice or democratization of the institutions of society is the goal, it is necessary to consider the fact that prior successes in this direction came about only where there was the need to stave off larger "threats." For example, the New Deal staved off the "communist menace." The "war on poverty" staved off a wide range of radical demands of a politicized student counterculture allied with civil-rights groups. Even so-called identity movements contain the seeds of a larger threat to the status quo; whereas the controlled dynamics of contemporary progressive movements, generally, entail severe limitations on collective thought and action, such that social and historical ideals appear always "unrealistic" and dangerously "naïve." Sociology gains nothing—it becomes redundant—when it affirms this "progress" over idealism. Finally, whether even minimal meaningful consensus can ever be achieved in this disorganized field, and whether any "critical" sociological concepts or insights will ever prove relevant to large audiences, beyond the occasional work (like the work of Mills, and the more dense, abstract, work of Riesman, whose *Lonely Crowd* has outsold everything else written by a professional sociologist, or Marcuse, whose *One Dimensional Man* inspired a whole generation of student activists), remains to be seen.

## References

Alexander, Jeffrey. 1987. "The Centrality of the Classics." In *Social Theory Today,* eds. Anthony Giddens and Jonathan Turner. Stanford, Calif.: Stanford Univ. Press.

Benford, Robert, D., and Scott A. Hunt. 1992. "Dramaturgy and Social Movements: The Social Construction and Communication of Power." *Sociological Inquiry* 62, no. 1: 36-55.

Blumer, Herbert. 1997. "Elementary Collective Groupings." In *Social Movements: Perspectives and Issues,* eds. Steven M. Buechler and F. Kurt Cylke Jr. Mountain View, Calif.: Mayfield, 72-90.

Buechler, Steven, M. 1993. "Beyond Resource Mobilization? Emerging Trends in Social Movement Theory." *The Sociological Quarterly* 34: 217-235.

Chong, Dennis. 1991. *Collective Action and Civil Rights Movement.* Chicago, Univ. of Chicago Press.

Collins, Randall. 1975. *Conflict Sociology.* St. Louis, Mo.: Academic Press.

Dionne, E. J. 1997. *They Only Look Dead: Why Progressives Will Dominate the Next Political Era*. New York: Touchstone.

Foucault, Michel. 1978. *The History of Sexuality*, Vol. 1. New York: Vintage Books.

Franzosi, Roberto. 1987. "The Press as a Source of Socio-Historical Data: Issues in the Methodology of Data Collection from Newspapers." *Historical Methods* 20.

Gamson, William A. 1990. *The Strategy of Social Protest*. Belmont, Calif.: Wadsworth.

———. 1996. *Talking Politics*. New York: Cambridge Univ. Press.

Garfinkel, Harold. 1967. *Studies in Ethnomethodology*. Cambridge, Mass.: Polity Press.

Gould, Kenneth A., David N. Pellow, and Allan Schnaiberg. 2008. *The Treadmill of Production: Injustice, Unsustainability in the Global Economy*. Boulder, Colo.: Paradigm.

Gramsci, Antonio. 1971. *Selections from the Prison Notebooks*. New York: International.

Habermas, Jürgen. 1988. *On the Logic of the Social Sciences*. Cambridge, Mass.: MIT Press.

Jacoby, Russell. 1987. *The Last Intellectuals*. New York: Noonday Press.

Keynes, John Maynard. [1925]1972. *Essays in Persuasion*, Vol. 9. New York: St. Martin's Press.

Kincaid, Harold. *Philosophical Foundations of the Social Sciences*. New York: Cambridge Univ. Press, 1996.

Klandermans, Bert, and Dirk Oegema, 1997. "Potentials, Networks, Motivations, and Barriers: Steps Toward Participation in Social Movements." In *Social Movements: Perspectives and Issues,* ed. Steven M. Buechler and F. Kurt Cylke Jr. Mountain View, Calif.: Mayfield, 342–359.

Koopmans, Ruud. 1999. "The Use of Protest Event Data in Comparative Research: Cross-National Comparability, Sampling Methods and Robustness." In *Acts of Dissent: New Developments in the Study of Protest,* ed. Dieter Rucht, Ruud Koopmans, and Friedhelm Neidhardt. Lanham, Md.: Rowman and Littlefield, 90–110.

Kuhn, Thomas S. 1992. *The Trouble with the Historical Philosophy of Science*. Cambridge, Mass.: Dept. of the History of Science, Harvard Univ.

Latour, Bruno. 1987. *Science in Action*. Cambridge, Mass.: Harvard Univ. Press,

Lukacs, Georg. 1971. *History and Class Consciousness*. Cambridge, Mass.: MIT Press.

McAdam, Doug. 1997. "Culture and Social Movements." In *Social Movements: Perspectives and Issues,* ed. Steven M. Buechler and F. Kurt Cylke Jr. Mountain View, Calif.: Mayfield, 473–487.

McCarthy, John D., and Mayer N. Zald. 1977. "Resource Mobilization and Social Movements: A Partial Theory," *American Journal of Sociology*. 82: 1212–1241.

Merton, Robert. 1957. *Social Theory and Social Structure*. Ontario, Canada: The Free Press.

Muller, Edward, N. 1979. *Aggressive Political Participation*. Princeton, N.J.: Princeton Univ. Press.

Noelle-Neumann. 1993. *The Spiral of Silence: Public Opinion—Our Social Skin.* Chicago: Univ. of Chicago Press.

Parsons, Talcott. [1937] 1968. *The Structure of Social Action*, Vol. 2. Florence, Mass.: Free Press.

———. 1971. *The System of Modern Societies.* Englewood Cliffs, N.J.: Prentice-Hall.

Phillips, Bernard. 2001. *Beyond Sociology's Tower of Babel: Reconstructing the Scientific Method.* New York: Aldine de Gruyter.

———, ed. 2007. *Understanding Terrorism: Building on* The Sociological Imagination. Boulder, Colo.: Paradigm Publishers.

———. 2009. *Armageddon or Evolution? The Scientific Method and Escalating World Problems.* Boulder, Colo.: Paradigm Publishers.

Phillips, Bernard, and Louis C. Johnston. 2007. *The Invisible Crisis of Contemporary Society: Reconstructing Sociology's Fundamental Assumptions.* Boulder, Colo.: Paradigm Publishers.

Phillips, Bernard, Harold Kincaid, and Thomas J. Scheff, eds. 2002. *Toward a Sociological Imagination: Bridging Specialized Fields.* Lanham, Md.: Univ. Press of America.

Rorty, Richard. "Science as Solidarity." In *The Rhetoric of the Human Sciences,* ed. John Nelson. Madison: Univ. of Wisconsin Press, 1987.

Sasson, Theodore. 1995. *Crime Talk: How Citizens Construct a Social Problem.* Hawthorne, N.Y.: Aldine de Gruyter.

Scheff, Thomas J. 1990. *Microsociology: Discourse, Emotion, and Social Structure.* Chicago: Univ. of Chicago Press.

———. 1994. *Bloody Revenge: Emotions, Nationalism, and War.* Boulder, Colo.: Westview.

———. 1997. *Emotions, the Social Bond, and Human Reality: Part/Whole Analysis.* Cambridge: Cambridge Univ. Press.

———. 2006. *Goffman Unbound! A New Paradigm for Social Science.* Boulder, Colo.: Paradigm.

Schutz, Alfred. 1967. *The Phenomenology of the Social World.* Evanston, Ill.: Northwestern Univ. Press.

Senechal de la Roche, Roberta. 2004. "Toward a Scientific Theory of Terrorism," *Sociological Theory* 22 (March 2004): 1-4.

Smelser, Neil, J. 1963. *Theory of Collective Behavior.* New York: Free Press.

Snow, David, and Robert Benford. 1988. "Ideology, Frame Resonance, and Participation Mobilization." *International Social Movement Research,* 1: 197-217.

———. 1992. "Master Frames and Cycles of Protest." In *Frontiers in Social Movement Theory,* ed. A. Morris and C. Mueller. New Haven, Conn.: Yale Univ. Press, 133-55.

Stebbins, Robert. *Between Work and Leisure: The Common Ground of Two Separate Worlds.* New Brunswick, N.J.: Transaction Publications, 2004.

Sutherland, Edwin, H. 1947. *Criminology.* 4th ed. New York: J. B. Lippincott.

Tarrow, Sidney. 1996. "States and Opportunities: The Political Structuring of Social Movements." In *Comparative Perspectives on Social Movements.* Ed. D. McAdam, J. D. McCarthy, and M. N. Zald. New York: Cambridge Univ. Press, 41-61

Tilly, Charles. 1995. "To Explain Political Processes," *American Journal of Sociology* 100: 1594–1610.

Turner, Ralph, H. 1969. "The Public Perception of Protest," *American Sociological Review* 34, no. 6: 815–831.

Turner, Stephen Park, and Jonathan H. Turner. 1990. *The Impossible Science: An Institutional Analysis of American Sociology.* Newbury Park, Calif.: Sage.

Van Delinder, Jean. *Struggles before Brown: Early Civil Rights Protests and Their Significance Today.* Boulder, Colo.: Paradigm, 2007.

Williams, R. H. 1995. "Constructing the Public Good: Social Movements and Cultural Resources." *Social Problems* 42: 124–144.

# PART III

# Conclusions

In this final part of the volume we take up ideas that can help us all learn to use the scientific method in everyday life: "deep dialogue," "deep democracy," and "the East-West strategy." In Chapter 12 our focus is on deep dialogue, which has to do with our ordinary conversations. Can we learn to have the kinds of conversations that shed light on our own basic assumptions? Can we come to face up to the problems or contradictions within those assumptions, assumptions that bear on nothing less than our worldview or metaphysical stance? Can those conversations help us to develop alternative assumptions that promise to help us solve those problems? We also touch very briefly on the idea of deep democracy. For we can learn to develop the kind of metaphysical stance that points us away from stratified and bureaucratic assumptions and toward democratic or evolutionary ones that can guide us not just in the voting booth but also in all of our relationships, whether in the family, at school, at work, or in houses of worship.

In Chapter 13 we will center on the East-West strategy for problem-solving in everyday life. This idea was introduced initially in the last chapter of *Armageddon or Evolution* (Phillips, 2008).

The East-West strategy I've put forward is to lower one's aspirations in the short run so as to narrow the aspirations-fulfillment gap and as a result, shift away from negative reinforcements and toward positive reinforcements, thus following a Buddhist orientation. Given that narrowed gap, the individual can then learn, in the long run, to continue to raise both aspirations and their fulfillment, following a Western orientation.

This strategy involves procedures for using a broad approach to the scientific method to help us confront everyday problems, for that method can help us to narrow our aspirations-fulfillment gap (Eastern orientation) as well as raise both aspirations and our ability to fulfill them (Western orientation). It is a strategy that includes our behavior in social relationships, such as our conversations within the family, the school, at work, in houses of worship or with those in politics. It also includes the full range of our behavior outside of those relationships, such as when we are alone.

## Reference

Phillips, Bernard. 2009. *Armageddon or Evolution? The Scientific Method and Escalating World Problems.* Boulder, Colo.: Paradigm Publishers.

# CHAPTER 12

# Deep Dialogue and Deep Democracy

*Bernard Phillips and Louis Kontos*

## Introduction by Phillips

THE TOPIC OF SOCIAL MOVEMENTS is of particular importance for an understanding of fundamental social problems, for both bear directly on the phenomena of social and cultural change. In this chapter, I and Louis Kontos—whose chapter on public opinion and social movements precedes this one—illustrate the idea of "deep dialogue." Kontos's chapter 11 initiates the dialogue. And in this chapter the two of us go back and forth: I comment on chapter 11, he responds to my comments, and I then respond to his response to my comments. Of course, this is by no means the same as what we all experience in our everyday conversations, since we have the opportunity to think long and hard about what to write, and that gives us chances to bring forward systematically whatever knowledge we have acquired that bears on our comments. Nevertheless, our exchange in this chapter at least suggests a way to move in the direction of achieving deep dialogues within our everyday conversations and, as a result, move toward egalitarian relationships in all areas of life that point toward deep democracy.

To introduce the nature of deep dialogue by contrast with our ordinary conversations or professional communication, we contrast "iron-man" dialogue with "straw-man" dialogue. Within "iron man" dialogue—a term that I used in my classes at Boston University—we listen so closely to a partner in conversation that we learn to extend the thrust of his or her ideas, even if only to provide an additional illustration, thus carrying them even further than he or she originally conveyed. By so doing, we make it easier to learn from them, seeing how they differ from our own hidden assumptions, metaphysical stance, or worldview. We then attempt to either change those assumptions or reinforce them, depending on what we have learned from the exchange, and we then communicate the result of our analysis. This approach is quite the opposite of setting up another's argument as a "straw man," where we stereotype it negatively and weaken it so that we can easily refute it and thus have no need to examine our own assumptions and question them. Playing iron man illustrates the idea of deep dialogue which, I believe, is rare either in the academic world or in our personal lives. Straw man, by contrast, is our general pattern of discourse, where we remain unable to genuinely listen to another's ideas when they contradict some of our own hidden assumptions.

This approach to deep dialogue suggests the reflexive approach that Mills and especially Gouldner called for, since one can learn to use dialogue as a basis for uncovering one's own hidden assumptions. Unless this is accomplished, one remains a victim of those assumptions, protecting them at all costs instead of learning the nature of one's own internal forces and how they shape our behavior. A reflexive orientation will point the Western individual toward more of an inward-outward orientation—fundamental to an evolutionary or interactive worldview—since the Western bureaucratic or stratified worldview points outward. And given the spread of the Western technological revolution throughout the world, that outward orientation is to be found among Easterners as well as Westerners, granting that Westerners generally share that orientation to a greater extent. Yet given the general prevalence of a bureaucratic or stratified worldview—as illustrated by the prevalence of bureaucratic organizations throughout contemporary society—taking Mills's or Gouldner's advice is most difficult.

## Commentary on Chapter 11 by Phillips

Kontos in his "Public Opinion and Social Movements" succeeds in alerting me to my own limited emphasis on concrete aspects of social problems. For example, he refers to "brutal facts of life, such as the lack of fulfilling work and the day-to-day degradation experienced in trying to make a living," by contrast with my own more abstract or general presentations on, say, the aspirations-fulfillment gap and my concerns with metaphysics and very broad concepts like social stratification and cultural values. The problem here is not mine alone but extends throughout the academic world. And it extends not merely to pronouncements by social scientists within the mass media but also to the social scientist's ability to listen to and learn from nonprofessional people who use ordinary or vernacular language.

I might also cite Kontos's deep emotional commitment to confronting fundamental problems throughout the social sciences, and within the literature on social movements in particular. For example, Kontos is most critical of the efforts of leftist social movements themselves, for he believes that they "do not bring ordinary people together in circumstances of deep consequence, as was the case with the labor movement throughout the early 20th century in American society, or with the civil rights movement of the 1960s. Further, he believes that leftist social movements do not "challenge the status quo in any fundamental way." Here, Kontos reinforces the importance of what I have attempted to do all my life: learn to express my emotions more fully. We have seen the impact of such commitment in the case of C. Wright Mills. Without it, the swinging pendulum of the scientific method becomes blocked from moving very far to the left, where awareness of and commitment to a problem are developed. Yet emotional commitment to confronting fundamental problems may point in a bureaucratic or stratified direction and, thus, requires an intellectual orientation that points toward democratic values.

What I have also learned from Kontos is a more pragmatic approach to my efforts to mount a social movement throughout the social sciences. My own orientation has focused on achieving change by communicating procedures for using the scientific method in everyday life. But I've not given sufficient attention to partial efforts to move in this direction. Yet, given the present world situation, partial efforts are crucial. For example, Arlene Stein's chapter 10 makes some progress toward alerting readers to the importance of getting out in the trenches rather than remaining comfortable within their ivy tower. And the chapters on the situation of the working class (chapter 6), the U.S. government's actions in Puerto Rico (chapter 7), and elder abuse (chapter 9) all alert not only academicians but also political leaders and the general public to problems in society that should be addressed. Thus, they all make partial contributions to confronting social problems. It is essential that political leaders learn to put out fires throughout the world while we await the possibilities of fundamental changes in contemporary society. And those leaders along with people in general require such partial measures that move us in effective directions.

Yet another insight conveyed by Kontos has to do with my efforts to organize a social movement within the social sciences for confronting their failures along with escalating problems throughout society:

But with regard to movements themselves, the important sociological fact, as Blumer (1997) points out, is that they are embodied in the group, as opposed to the audience, the crowd, and the mass ... It is significant, then, that "as a social movement develops, it takes on the character of a society. It acquires organization and form, a body of customs and traditions, established leadership, an enduring division of labor, social rules and social values—in short, a culture, a social organization, and a new scheme of life." (81)

Up to now my communications with others in the Sociological Imagination Group have been limited to e-mail letters throughout the year—largely to the group as a whole—plus a short conference once a year. What Blumer and Kontos imply is that this is insufficient for the generation of a social movement. I had been treating the Sociological Imagination Group as an audience more than as a group requiring a great deal of personal interaction.

Following "iron man" and "deep dialogue," I might now point up what I see as limitations to Kontos's analysis. Overall, I see him as usefully criticizing problems within sociology as well as social movements, yet failing to move constructively toward specific procedures for solving those problems. A key example, in my view, is his failure to give credit to the achievements of other sociologists and suggest directions for building on those achievements, rather than focusing almost exclusively on their limitations. The result is a failure to build bridges connecting achievements throughout the discipline and, consequently, a continuation of the lack of much cumulative development within sociology and the other social sciences. But this failure is not Kontos's failure alone, as it is evidenced throughout the social sciences. And the result, unfortunately, is the lack of any substantial influence by the social science community as a whole on political leaders and social movements.

Mills also was guilty of this same hubris, for he did not develop much of a following while he was alive. Although he is presently widely revered, that reverence generally is metaphorical and does not yield a clear direction for action to change the ways of doing business throughout the social sciences. Mills illustrated this when he bragged to me and others in his class at Columbia—all the while smiling impishly—about how he treated Eisenhower, who was then president of Columbia. When Eisenhower walked into his classroom unannounced one day and took a seat in the back row, Mills immediately launched into a contrived lecture on how the class would continue to work with him as a cell for launching a violent revolution in the United States. Eisenhower finally walked out and Mills never heard from him, yet Mills had destroyed an opportunity to work with Eisenhower toward common objectives.

Another failure that Kontos illustrates is his lack of any systematic usage of the core concepts of sociology and, instead, his use of vernacular language to mount his argument. From my own perspective, this is a most serious matter if indeed social scientists wish to develop a fully scientific approach to human behavior. An alternative orientation is suggested by a broad approach to the scientific method that emphasizes the importance of moving to high levels of linguistic abstraction. This is an orientation that Mills favored in *The Sociological Imagination* in his emphasis on shuttling up and down language's levels of abstraction. What is at stake here is nothing less than an ability to build on the literature of the social sciences, which is fundamental to the nature of the scientific method.

Another criticism of Kontos's analysis—and here again this is a criticism that can be leveled very widely at the social science community as a whole—is an implicit failure to follow the key dictum of Charles Peirce, the founder of the philosophy of pragmatism: "Do not block the way of inquiry." Kontos fails us in not indicating the kinds of research that we need to carry much further our understanding of public opinion and social movements. Perhaps he believes that we already have enough understanding of these phenomena, and that the time has come to act and not to gain more understanding. Yet it is indeed possible to act on what we already know and also to work toward deepening that knowledge, and Kontos could be giving us guidance on how to deepen that knowledge. Once again, my analysis of Kontos's chapter illustrates my analysis of the general situation within the social sciences, where no more than lip service is given to the need for "further research."

Finally, I come to Kontos's failure to move far up language's ladder of abstraction to the ethereal level of metaphysics. Although he does in fact level criticism at the methodology employed by some sociologists, he fails to tackle in any systematic way the general methodological approach adopted throughout the social sciences. And it is exactly that approach, in my own view, that has yielded our lack of substantial cumulative development and ability to understand—much less solve—our mammoth and escalating social problems. If Kontos feels free to claim that I do not say how "a 'sociological imagination' can migrate outside of sociology, becoming a mode of critical self-consciousness," why does he not address my published work on the metaphysical stance widely shared both inside of and outside of the academic world? For it is that stance—with its lack of reflexivity—that is the major bulwark against the achievement of that critical self-consciousness. I do not claim here that I have found procedures for developing such critical self-consciousness throughout society, but I do claim that I have made progress in this direction. And I do claim that, once again, Kontos fails to recognize, constructively, the contributions of others and build on them.

## Response to Phillips's Commentary by Kontos

I would like to thank Phillips for discussing my chapter on "Public Opinion and Social Movements" and for giving me the opportunity to address his commentary.

### Sociology as Science

In the introduction to this volume and elsewhere (particularly *Beyond Sociology's Tower of Babel*, 2001), Phillips depicts sociology as a scientific discipline, replete with "a general method and epistemology" and "cumulative knowledge." Several trends in the discipline appear to him as inimical to the further development of this "science"—among them, the fragmentation of the field, the routine failure of sociologists to build on the work of other sociologists, a general proclivity among sociologists to use vernacular terms in place of "technical" and "abstract" sociological concepts, and the lack of "bridges" between sociology, other disciplines, and outside publics. (My chapter seems to exemplify each of these trends and tendencies.) In addition, Phillips believes that a "science" of society is now urgently needed, given the nature and extent of current "social problems."

I see matters somewhat differently. Sociology is no more of a science, in my view, than psychoanalysis or any other mode of discourse that lacks professional consensus around topics that have been exhaustively researched and about which much has been written. Nor do I see anything resembling "a general epistemology" in the field. The closest approximation of that ideal was structural functionalism during the 1950s, when it appeared practically synonymous with sociology itself, and when quantitative methods were neatly attached to it—routinely demonstrating various "effects" of "units" of social action on particular social systems (Turner and Turner, 1990). Now the field supposedly has three "paradigms," among which functionalism appears to be the least popular. But it's hard not to notice that there are substantial, unresolved debates within each of these "paradigms," and further, that each one is immune to anomalies and contradictions—therefore not really a paradigm but simply a mode of theorizing. Indeed, there is not a single sociological phenomenon that cannot be "explained" by a sophisticated functionalist. Nor is there a single event or problem that cannot be translated into an instance of "conflict" or that cannot be seen as a microcosm of some kind through the lens of whatever version of "symbolic interactionism."

The unifying thread in contemporary sociology, with its forty-six official subfields, is not "general epistemology," in my view, but instead its increased formalization coupled with a longstanding tendency to emulate a scientific style of writing and positive, fact-stating mode of discourse.

It does this through colorless language, endless citation, translation of observations and interpretations into "discoveries"—as if the sociologist is constantly surprised—and, most importantly, the trope of irony. Irony became an elemental feature of sociology with Parsons's (1968) interpretation (and canonization) of Weber, for whom history takes place "behind the backs" of individuals. For Parsons, the consequences of any sustained course (unit) of action are, not only always partially or mostly inadvertent, but always consequential to a larger entity, a type of system, about which sociology always already knows much about—its stock of knowledge appears, by the same token, "cumulative" and therefore a basis for what Parsons and Weber before him called "general social theory." No such thing can now be claimed in sociology. Disagreements among sociologists over substantial matters are too great. Yet, there is a common conceptual vocabulary, as Phillips points out.

The "core" concepts of sociology remain functionalist (Alexander, 1987), despite the waning fortunes of functionalist theory and the fact that most contemporary sociologists explicitly reject the work of Parsons in its entirety, along with that of his disciples (though Merton remains exempt)—which is to say, they reject Parsons by way of arguments derived from one or two of his most notable critics, particularly Mills. (Who now reads Parsons?) This vocabulary is problematic. The seemingly "technical" language of functionalism—role, system, part, strain, and so on—turns out to be no such thing. It is merely metaphorical and colloquial (Collins, 1975). Even the term "stratification," which Phillips uses throughout his recent work, which is derived from functionalism (from Parsons via Weber), invariably does the work it was originally meant to do, namely drawing focus to the institutional, predictable side of life; in the process obscuring the fact that "society" is reproduced in ways that no one can predict, through collective struggles—battles lost and won—and that "social problems" are never discreetly contained and never merely the product of (bad) social planning, greater complexity, or whatever else relieves the sociologist of the obligation to take sides in cases where there is much at stake for "society." (This obligation, it should be noted, is perfectly consistent with notions of objectivity and neutrality where the former is understood as an issue of method and the latter a matter of rejecting party politics and governmental influence and demands upon research, which is how Weber understood "neutrality.")

Rarely within mainstream sociology—and conspicuous by its absence—is there anything resembling what Schutz (1967) called "a failure to connect" between "our" concepts and phenomena at hand—such that we would have to reevaluate any concepts or theory. Whatever is new, different, or strange about any phenomena is canceled out, time and again, with what amounts to a theoretical sleight of hand—by demonstrating, through selective observation, that what appears new (even a new social problem, contradiction, or crisis) is really not, but merely a version or instance of something else, something we already know much about; something which evokes an ideal-type; a closed system of variables; a string of conceptual and empirical references that support a few, competing, explanations among which we are seemingly free to choose.

At the same time, the "core" concepts of sociology prove rather elastic in the course of dialogue, debate, explanation, interpretation, etc. The concept of "anomie," for instance, means something altogether different in Durkheim's explanation of modernity with its loosening of social bonds and greater complexity, interdependence, individuation, and existential dilemmas, than it does in the work of Merton (1957), who equates "anomie" with strain and then again with normlessness, resulting from a single cause—in his technical language: a gap—to which there are only five modal responses (including conformity [?!] and excluding suicide). It hardly seems that we need to involve sociology, any version of it, in order to realize that American society is too materialistic and that large numbers of people want things that they can't afford, that they feel constantly judged by virtue of not having them ("symbols of success"), that they are more likely to bend rules under these circumstances than they would in traditional societies. Rather, it takes sociology to cause confusion by categorizing drug users "in general" as retreatists, and by putting "rebels" in a typology that includes crooks (innovators) and people who go along to get along (ritualists). Yet, Merton's "Anomie and Social Structure" (1949: 125-149) remains the single-most cited paper in the history of the field—and, oddly enough, occupies a central place in the "web approach." Merton, it seems to me, stands for just about everything the Sociological Imagination Group opposes. His paper is not only reductionistic but also flippant and dismissive toward "psychology" (particularly Freud); initiating a trend that seemed to begin with Durkheim (against the "reduction" of sociological phenomena to individual, intrapersonal variables), but, in retrospect not, since practically every sociologist prior to Merton was versed (or, at least, expected to be versed) in the language of psychology, philosophy, politics, and economics. What makes Merton's work a sociological masterpiece? Answer: It perfectly embodies the common sense of bourgeois society (even more so than it did in 1937, when the paper was published). Dialogue is made easy around such work. Since it explains everything and nothing, and since it offers both ideology and ideology critique—something for everybody.

## The Question of Influence

What makes any academic work "influential" beyond academia? Any sociologist can point to specific works in sociology that have influenced policy makers, activists, movement organizers, and other kinds of people in some big way. But influence is (or should be) a problematic notion for sociology. It equates more directly with ideology and propaganda than it does with enlightenment or self-awareness. In this regard, Phillips's emphasis on teaching and learning seems contradictory, particularly when he says things like "It is essential that political leaders learn to put out fires throughout the world while we await the possibilities of fundamental changes in contemporary society." Progressive policy initiatives materialize, as a rule with notable exceptions, not when establishment politicians advance their learning but when social movements are strong enough to pose an actual threat to the corporate structure or the political establishment, such that concessions have to be made. The crux of the problem is made explicit in the second part of Phillips's sentence "while we await the possibilities of fundamental changes," in that fundamental changes require progressive movements that are now mostly on the defensive, mostly trying to preserve gains of the past, rather than advance radical or revolutionary agendas. How, exactly, would any sociology be able to "influence" anybody to support progressive movements or social policies?

Phillips takes up this question in a modeled endeavor, which is made explicit in his commentary on my chapter, around a significant accomplishment by Mills and Riesman, namely reaching a broad audience outside of academia. (How this might happen, is unclear to me.) Mills did it not with his book (coauthored with Hans Gerth) on Weber, but with more polemical and "socially relevant" books like *The Power Elite*. And, as I noted in my chapter, his popularity grew leaps and bounds after his death, when a youthful counterculture actively sought out this type of work. Similarly, the fact that Riesman's book *The Lonely Crowd* found a place in "popular" culture tells us something not only about the nature and quality of Riesman's work, but also about changes in American popular culture. Phillips, in his commentary, evokes yet another problem, namely that the popularity of any work with particular audiences does not necessarily involve "dialogue" (see his concept of "Iron Man"). The idea of constant and reciprocal learning in sustained dialogues between sociologists and others, outsiders, is a worthy goal—to be sure. But without interlocutors there is no dialogue—only monologue. Jacoby (1967) recounts the entire history of sociology around this problem, and points out that many first- and second-generation sociologists were either journalists prior to joining academia, or published their work regularly in periodicals and other popular venues. They published therein and their books were widely read because they had the good fortune of being surrounded by "aware" and "attentive" publics, and because the publishing industry and corporate media were less scandalous in relation to organized power than what is now the case, not because they chose popularity over scholarship. It's hard to imagine a popular audience for such work in contemporary society, much less a "dialogue."

## Sociology as a Critical Discipline

What do people (anybody) need to learn from sociology? Is it fair to say that "ordinary people" are so completely "socialized" and ideologically indoctrinated or susceptible to propaganda that they are blinded as to their interests—that they are "dopes," as Garfinkel (1967) tells us sociology normally sees them? Indeed, this view supports the self-representation of sociology as a scientific form of knowledge and voice of reason. The concept of social relevance is unproblematic when the people who are supposed to learn from sociology—policy makers, movement organizers, and ordinary people—come to appear misguided, lacking sociological knowledge or imagination. It becomes problematic when they appear to be pursuing interests and objectives the best way they know how, and when those interests prove incompatible among social groups and economic classes. Oftentimes, as Habermas (1988) put it, the problem is not that people fail to understand each other, but that they understand each other too well. By the same token, sociology cannot be all things to all people. Selections are necessarily made, for example, regarding what to observe, what is relevant about what is observed (and what is irrelevant, therefore omitted), how observations are "translated" into data, what concept categories are used to explain them. It is refreshing when those selections are explicit—as is the case with Phillips's recent work (the web approach); where assessments of current social problems also embody a sense of urgency. His concern with the conceptual vocabulary of sociology—in particular regarding levels of abstraction and differences between vernacular and technical terms—warrants greater exploration and discussion. My response to this concern, here, admittedly, does only partial justice.

## Response to Kontos's Response by Phillips

I applaud the clarity and forcefulness of Kontos's response. In a very brief space Kontos has nevertheless succeeded in carrying further five points he made in his chapter that have added substantially to my own insights. Those points are: (1) concern with the concrete aspects of social problems and not just general problems like the aspirations-fulfillment gap; (2) depth of emotional commitment to praxis; (3) immersion within specialized literatures, illustrated by the literature on social movements; (4) pragmatic approach to progress on social problems; and (5) advice on how to develop an effective social movement.

One criticism that I want to make in this rejoinder is Kontos's failure to address the point in my commentary on the centrality of metaphysical assumptions like a bureaucratic worldview, which I believe are absolutely crucial for explaining the general failure of social scientists to confront effectively what Mills called "personal troubles" and "public issues." As a result of that avoidance, he fails to address a fundamental point of my commentary, and we largely pass one another like ships in the night. It is the social scientist's worldview or metaphysical stance that is central for understanding social science's failures. All six of the key books of the Sociological Imagination Group—including this one—emphasize this point.

Given my own deep criticisms of contemporary social science, I can well understand Kontos's statement that "Sociology is no more of a science ... than psychoanalysis or any other mode of discourse that lacks professional consensus around topics that have been exhaustively researched and about which much has been written." However, I would claim that sociology is a partial science that it is being held back or trumped by the bureaucratic worldview that we all share to varying degrees. Yet should we, as a result, give up on the possibility of a science of sociology? Shouldn't we take into account the incredible complexity of human behavior, and the fact that we are not even two centuries old while the physical sciences extend over close to five centuries? Shouldn't we also understand that society has never funded social-science research in any way comparable to physical and biological science, thus increasing the one-sided nature of the academic and research worlds? And let us not forget that social scientists are working with phenomena that are largely invisible, making for substantial difficulties. Yet even social scientists generally remain largely unaware of these barriers to the success of their own efforts.

Granting all of these problems, in my own view the most fundamental problem pervading the social sciences—in addition to a bureaucratic worldview—is a lack of understanding of the severe limitations of the research methods that they employ. This lack is linked to their worldview, for that metaphysical stance promotes those limitations. For example, the lack of awareness of the enormous complexity of human behavior has influenced the development of many highly specialized subfields within sociology with little communication among them. This is a most serious matter, since human complexity demands research that encompasses the knowledge from a very wide range of specialized fields, versus oversimplified approaches wedded to highly specialized fields. Another problem, one that is nearly universal, is the failure of social scientists to pay attention to their own impact on every phase of the research process. We know, for example, how much the behavior of interviewers as well as the wording of questions influences the answers of respondents, yet it is a very rare study that attempts to assess that impact. "Investigator effects" introduce a great deal of complexity into the research situation, yet researchers within the many specialized fields remain largely unaware of such complexity as they continue with their simplistic procedures.

I believe that Kontos's statements in this exchange reveal a lack of reflexivity. For, despite my arguments about the importance of one's metaphysical stance in my commentary and in the key books cited above, he makes no explicit effort to reveal his own metaphysical assumptions. The result of all of this oversimplification is a failure to live up to scientific ideals. The problem is not, then, the impossibility of a science of sociology but rather a failure to follow through on the ideals of the scientific method. In other words, it is a failure to develop and employ a scientific method broad enough to encompass the complexity of human behavior.

Kontos states that he does not see "anything resembling 'a general epistemology' in the field" of sociology. Yet I would claim that there is indeed a unifying thread throughout sociology, one that is widely shared throughout society and that works against scientific discourse: the bureaucratic metaphysical stance or worldview. Further, I would claim that this worldview has shaped the development of an oversimplified approach to the scientific method throughout the social sciences. And I would further claim that Kontos himself is a victim of that worldview—as are the rest of us to varying degrees—as illustrated by his paper as well as his response to my commentary. If indeed I am correct in my assessment, then he should proceed to look to his own failings along with his focus on the failings of others.

Kontos's implication is that I am a functionalist. I am proud to admit to using important ideas from Merton, but Kontos cannot have read my Babel book—let alone any of the others I've written that are cited above—without seeing the importance for my work of figures such as Marx, Simmel, Mills, Gouldner, Goffman, Scheff and many others who are certainly not functionalists. More specifically, although Parsons freely uses the term "stratification," the idea of social stratification was largely introduced into sociology by Marx, who was no more of a functionalist than Kontos or myself. He also suggests that my focus is on "the institutional and predictable side of life," ignoring occurrences that "no one can predict." I completely agree with Kontos that a focus on prediction is not at all appropriate for the social sciences at this time in their development. Rather, I believe that our focus should be on enlarging our understanding one step at a time, and that will lead over time to improvements in our ability to make predictions. Yet to claim that "no one can predict" a given phenomenon—if he means that no one would ever be able to predict that phenomenon—rejects human possibilities and is completely opposed to the spirit of scientific inquiry. For that would imply that Kontos opposes Peirce's central dictum: "Do not block the way of inquiry."

Kontos claims that "Sociology is no more of a science, in my view, than psychoanalysis or any other mode of discourse that lacks professional consensus around topics that have been exhaustively researched and about which much has been written." Are we to ignore completely what we social scientists have learned over our entire history about the nature of institutions, about the influence of patterns of stratification and bureaucracy, and—more generally—about the power of social structures to shape our lives? Are we to abandon all of that knowledge and now focus on reinventing the wheel? Because our present efforts to understand phenomena have as yet proved to be quite limited—in my view largely because of our metaphysical and epistemological assumptions—should we now give up on what we have learned and start afresh? Should we throw out the baby along with the bath? Thomas Kuhn's *The Structure of Scientific Revolutions* (1962) found a great deal wrong with scientific procedures. Yet some postmodernists have seized on that critique as a basis for rejecting the scientific method itself.

Overall, I believe that Kontos reveals a narrow approach to the nature of the scientific method, the same method that has proved to be so powerful—granting the ills as well as the benefits that it has yielded—throughout the five-century history of the physical and biological sciences. For that method builds on the incredible power of language, enabling us to move far up its ladder of abstraction to basic concepts like "force," "mass," and "acceleration" in physics. As for the "metaphorical and colloquial" aspects of many sociological concepts, generally they are indeed somewhat vague. Yet by linking them together in systematic ways—as illustrated by the six key books cited in chapter 1 by members of the Sociological Imagination Group—we can reduce that vagueness. Further, metaphors are certainly not to be dismissed, for to do so is to cut oneself off—narrowly—from the enormous potential of the humanities to help us social scientists communicate effectively to others and ourselves. This approach to metaphors, figures, or images is central to the enormous power of language that Mills so ably tapped, an approach examined analytically in some detail in *Babel* and in other key books cited above.

"Deep dialogue" might even prove to be a useful metaphor for the evolution of the universe itself. For it illustrates a rapid form of interaction that actually succeeds in changing—to an increasing degree—the parties to that interaction. From this perspective, the interaction among the elements of the physical universe over many billions of years—which yielded ever larger molecules with an increasing ability to develop life—was an extremely slow pattern of interaction. Yet the nature of our universe nevertheless made this possible, for no entity can be completely isolated from such interaction within the known universe. As for biological evolution, that involves more rapid interaction, for organisms require this—just as plants require rapid interaction with the sun, the atmosphere, and the soil—in order to survive. With respect to human history—given our bureaucratic worldview along with language—language has given us the basis for far more rapid interaction along with change in all of our structures. Yet that worldview has been sufficiently narrow and hierarchical to threaten our continuing evolution. From this perspective, "deep dialogue" opens up the possibility for our continuing evolution, with our learning to learn from our interactions with others, and also our learning to use the scientific method in our everyday lives. Thus, deep dialogue can help us to perceive all structures—physical, biological, social, and personality—as meaningful in relation to the evolution of the universe from one moment to the next.

Such an evolutionary perspective can in turn help us to move toward "deep democracy." For example, in situations that are stratified, such an evolutionary perspective can help those with a bigger slice of the pie of power or wealth to see the possibility of enlarging their own slice while still helping those below them to enlarge theirs. As the saying goes, a rising tide lifts all boats. In this way, we can move toward an evolutionary worldview and also move toward deep democracy.

## References

Alexander, Jeffrey. 1987. "The Centrality of the Classics." In *Social Theory Today,* eds. Anthony Giddens and Jonathan Turner. Stanford, Calif.: Stanford Univ. Press.

Blumer, Herbert. 1997. "Elementary Collective Groupings." In *Social Movements: Perspectives and Issues,* ed. Steven M. Buechler and F. Kurt Cylke Jr. Mountain View, Calif.: Mayfield, 72–90.

Collins, Randall. 1975. *Conflict Sociology.* St. Louis, Mo.: Academic Press.

Garfinkel, Harold. 1967. *Studies in Ethnomethodology.* Cambridge, Mass.: Polity Press.

Habermas, Jürgen. 1988. *On the Logic of the Social Sciences.* Tr. Shierry Weber Nicholsen and Jerry A. Stark. Cambridge, Mass.: MIT Press.

Jacoby, Russell. 1987. *The Last Intellectuals.* New York: Noonday Press.

Kuhn, Thomas S. *The Structure of Scientific Revolutions.* Chicago: Univ. of Chicago Press, 1962.

Merton, Robert. 1949. *Social Theory and Social Structure.* Ontario, Canada: The Free Press.

Parsons, Talcott, [1937]1968. The Structure of Social Action. Vol. 2. Florence, Mass.: Free Press.

Phillips, Bernard. 2001. *Beyond Sociology's Tower of Babel: Reconstructing the Scientific Method.* New York: Aldine de Gruyter.

Schutz, Alfred. 1967. *The Phenomenology of the Social World.* Evanston, Ill.: Northwestern Univ. Press.

Turner, Stephen Park, and Jonathan H. Turner. 1990. *The Impossible Science: An Institutional Analysis of American Sociology.* Newbury Park, Calif.: Sage.

CHAPTER **13**

# The East-West Strategy

*Bernard Phillips and J. David Knottnerus*

IF DEEP DIALOGUE AND DEEP DEMOCRACY illustrate usage of the scientific method within our social relationships, then the East-West strategy illustrates usage of that method over the range of our everyday experiences from one moment to the next, including those relationships. It is a general approach to solving the moment-to-moment problems that every one of us encounters as we journey through life. It is neither an Eastern approach nor a Western approach, yet it combines key elements from both. Its Western orientation largely comes from its use of the scientific method, as sketched in part I and as utilized to a large extent in every chapter of part II. That method in turn builds on our understanding of language which—joined with the scientific method—is the human being's most powerful tool for solving problems.

It was in *Armageddon or Evolution? The Scientific Method and Escalating World Problems* (2009) that Phillips developed his initial idea of the East-West strategy, and he briefly described it in an unpublished manuscript (2008) celebrating the 50th anniversary of the publication of Mills's *The Sociological Imagination* (1959):

> Following a Buddhist Eastern orientation, we can learn to lower our aspirations in the short run so as to narrow the aspirations-fulfillment gap. This approach also follows the ideals of Confucius, who saw "the

path of duty in what is near," while "men seek for it in what is remote." Given that narrowed gap—which gives us confidence in our ability to solve problems—we can then learn, in the long run, to continue to raise both aspirations and their fulfillment, following a Western orientation. By keeping aspirations and fulfillment close together we point toward the East, and by continuing to raise both of them we point toward the West. We should note that a successful East-West strategy depends on learning to use a broad scientific method in everyday life. For it is by using an ability to gain increasing understanding of our complex human problems by means of a broad scientific method that the individual is in fact able to continually raise both aspirations and their fulfillment. (Phillips, 2008)

This initial description requires substantial elaboration if indeed we are to learn how to at least begin to use this tool to address our problems from one moment to the next. For one thing, we must go back in history to understand the basis for this aspirations-fulfillment gap, which Phillips and Louis Johnston analyzed, concluding that it is continuing to increase (Phillips and Johnston, 2007). This is largely due to the "revolution of rising expectations" accompanying the scientific and technological revolutions over the past five centuries. Sociology's emphasis on such problems as alienation, anomie, and even the possibility of suicide illustrates concern for this gap. That historical orientation must also take us to the founding of Buddhism by Gautama Siddartha Sakyamuni in the 5th century BCE. Yet we must also use this historical journey to achieve focus on the individual's emotions—metaphorically, the "heart"—as the motor that can drive the individual's "head" and "hand" in the direction of widening or narrowing that aspirations-fulfillment gap. For when that gap is narrowed, it becomes the basis not for deepening problems but rather for ideas that guide actions that can be effective in solving the problem of the moment. Thus, the narrow gap encouraged by the East can yield the emotional force that is essential for the Western progress or evolution of the individual and society.

For another thing, we must come to understand how this freeing up of emotions in both the West and the East—by contrast with the Western head-hand trip and Eastern passivity—relates to our most powerful problem-solving tool: language. It was in *The Invisible Crisis* as well as in *Armageddon or Evolution?* that "heart," "head," and "hand" were systematically linked to a wide range of concepts developed throughout the academic world that bear not only on the individual but also on society. For all structures no less than history must be taken into account if indeed we are to penetrate the complexity of human behavior, including physical, biological, social, and personality structures. And it is language's emphasis on the "head," as illustrated by our academic concepts, that can help us to accomplish this. We academics must learn to reach beyond the narrowness of our own academic background and adopt an interdisciplinary tack, just as we sociologists must learn to transcend the narrowness of the forty-six sections of the American Sociological Association. To accomplish this, we must also learn to move extremely far up language's ladder of abstraction: to the height of our invisible metaphysical assumptions that structure our bureaucratic way of life, suggested by what Mills called the "bureaucratic ethos," as well as by our understanding of the near universality of patterns of social stratification and bureaucracy. And, learning to see how the bureaucratic way of life contradicts rapidly spreading and developing democratic ideals throughout the world, we can learn to move toward an alternative metaphysical stance that promises to resolve those contradictions.

And for a third thing, we must examine this East-West strategy's relation to our learning to use the scientific method in everyday life as technologists or problem-solvers, and not just as scientists focused on understanding phenomena. It was the linguistically oriented and therapy-oriented psychologist George Kelly who claimed that "every man is, in his own particular way, a scientist ... ever seeking to predict and control the course of events with which he is involved" (1963: 4). This is the approach that was taken in chapter 12 with its focus on deep dialogue. For our own everyday conversations can give us opportunities to make progress on such problems as our inner contradictions linked closely to a bureaucratic way of life, provided that our "head" gives us a direction leading toward an alternative way of life within which those contradictions are resolved. Yet by so doing—given the breadth that would necessarily be required for such an alternative vision—we would be changing not only ourselves but also culture and patterns of social organization as well. Yet Kelly's extremely democratic and nonbureaucratic vision of "man-the-scientist" requires tremendous faith in the potential for the nonbiological evolution of every human being. It is a faith in the capacities of the individual that has been shared by very few academics, yet it has been carried forward by a number of educators (see, for example, the brief discussions of John Dewey, Paulo Freire, Ivan Illich, Carolos Bernardo Gonzalez Pecotche (Raumsol), and Mohandas Gandhi in Phillips, 2001: 44-50, 190-192; and in Phillips and Johnston, 2007: 172-177, 193-198, 223-227). Given that faith, we can all continue to develop, with no limit at all, not only our "head" but also our "heart" and "hand" as well. In this way we would be learning to see the pendulum metaphor for the scientific method—as described in chapter 1—as applying not only to the scientist's work within the academic world, but also to everyone's journey through life from one moment to the next.

## "Heart": History

Phillips's very first book within the series published in the context of the Sociological Imagination Group centered on what he saw as an increasing yet invisible gap between aspirations throughout the contemporary world and their fulfillment (2001). And that very same problem has been central to his concerns in the published or in-press books that followed (Phillips, Kincaid, and Scheff, eds., 2002; Phillips and Johnston, 2007; Phillips, ed., 2007; and Phillips, 2008). It is a widening gap that derives substantially from the "revolution of rising expectations" accompanying the scientific and technological revolutions from the 16th century onward, revolutions based on a scientific method that provided the basis for unheard of progress in solving physical and biological problems. But the fulfillment of those aspirations worked to accelerate aspirations, yielding an increasing gap, with evidence for that increase presented in Phillips's recent analysis with a colleague (Phillips and Johnston, 2007). Yet nonmaterial aspirations have also been undergoing a revolution of rising expectations, and these have been linked to the rise and development of democratic forms of government throughout the world from the 17th century onward. There once again, granting that these new forms of government fulfilled aspirations to an extent, at the same time they encouraged the further acceleration of aspirations, yielding a widening gap between them and their fulfillment.

Johnston and Phillips sought to test this hypothesis in *The Invisible Crisis*: "The gap between aspirations and their fulfillment is in fact increasing in contemporary society." Their focus was on nonmaterial no less than material aspirations. Their conclusion was as follows:

> Much like Marx's description of a contradiction between the forces and relations of production, the evidence points toward a fundamental contradiction between our cultural expectations and our patterns of social organization limiting their fulfillment. Granting all of the limitations of this study, and granting the importance of further research, this is indeed substantial evidence in support of this hypothesis. Although we can speak of an increasing aspirations-fulfillment gap in a bland way, what we moderns appear to be facing is nothing less than an invisible crisis bearing down on us much like an invisible tsunami. It is a tsunami that is racing toward every single one of the institutions of contemporary society. (Phillips and Johnston, 2007: 235)

One result of this widening aspirations-fulfillment gap is the burial of feelings. For, if our aspirations yield no fulfillment—following Durkheim—the result may well be suicide. In their study of "Springdale," a small town in New York State, Arthur Vidich and Joseph Bensman documented such burial with the aid of two procedures:

> The technique of particularization is one of the most pervasive ways of avoiding reality.... The Springdaler is able to maintain his equalitarian ideology because he avoids generalizing about class differences. The attributes of class are seen only in terms of the particular behavior of particular persons.... The realization of lack of fulfillment of aspiration and ambition might pose an unsolvable personal problem if the falsification of memory did not occur, and if the hopes and ambitions of a past decade or two remained salient in the present perspective.... As a consequence, his present self, instead of entertaining the youthful dream of a 500-acre farm, entertains the plan to buy a home freezer by the fall. (1960: 299, 303)

This "technique of particularization" and this "falsification of memory" yield nothing less than the repression of emotions, a most limiting result if we are to follow the work of Sigmund Freud, Karen Horney (Phillips and Johnston, 2007: 89-95), Thomas Scheff, and Suzanne Retzinger (Phillips, 2001: 145-155; Phillips, ed., 2007: 93-114), as well as of most of contemporary psychotherapy. We might also invoke the phenomenon of alienation, especially as developed by Marx (Phillips and Johnston, 2007: 82-86). Neither should we forget Simmel's characterization of the mental life of the metropolis as "essentially intellectualistic" by contrast with the "feelings and emotional relationships" to be found in the small town (Phillips and Johnston, 2007: 88). And we also have Nietzsche's indictment of the prejudice against "gay science" with its encouragement of the scientist to express emotions (Phillips and Johnston, 2007: 130-131). Apparently our scientific, technological, and political revolutions—with all of their achievements—have yielded a fundamental step backward as well as a step forward. We have developed a "head-hand" trip by contrast with balanced development of "head," "heart," and "hand."

Yet to see our aspirations-fulfillment gap solely in a negative way, as is the emphasis within the social science literature, is most one-sided. Robert Browning suggests its positive aspects in these two simple lines of poetry:

> Ah, but a man's reach should exceed his grasp,
> Or what's a heaven for?

We need not think of aspirations as necessarily reaching far beyond their fulfillment and even continuing to widen our aspirations-fulfillment gap. Rather, we might well think of a narrow gap, just as Browning suggests, where our aspirations succeed in motivating our fulfillment of them. And Browning's reference to heaven suggests that we might continue, in this way, to move ever further toward the fulfillment of our highest ideals. By so doing he is anticipating an East-West strategy that begins by narrowing the aspirations-fulfillment gap and then continues with the raising of both aspirations and their fulfillment with no limit whatsoever.

Yet at this point we would do well to examine more closely the Buddhist orientation to narrowing that gap, which can provide an antidote to the Western wide and widening gap that is emphasized within the literature of social science. We turn to a discussion in *Armageddon or Evolution?* for a very brief sketch of Buddhism:

> Buddhist teaching is based on the Four Noble Truths and the Eightfold Noble Path. The first Noble Truth is the universal existence of *"dukkha,"* which has to do with pain, sorrow, and suffering, but more precisely suggests the lack of complete fulfillment of all human pursuits. There is, then, always an aspirations-fulfillment gap. Nothing is ever wholly satisfying, and this is true even for the most fortunate human beings. This is the problem which Gautama addressed, much like the focus of the scientific method on a problem. The law of causality—like the assumption of modern science, and like the Hindu law of karma—is the second Noble Truth: everything that happens is caused. If we remove the cause of *dukkha,* then *dukkha* will disappear. As for the third Noble Truth, it is the renunciation of desire, 'thirst" or aspirations, the removal of passions which will inevitably be frustrated to some degree. The fourth Noble Truth specifies the Eightfold Noble Path as the concrete direction for actually removing *dukkha*: right views, right aspirations, right speech, right conduct, a right livelihood, right efforts, right thoughts and right contemplation. (Phillips, 2009 chapter 2)

Buddhist teaching thus confronts the aspirations-fulfillment gap by emphasizing the importance of lowering our aspirations, or by curbing our "attachment" or "thirst" for fulfilling aspirations that continue to increase, just as Durkheim suggested. And, as a result, the aspirations-fulfillment gap will be narrowed, yielding less *dukkha.* And this can be accomplished to the extent that the individual not only accepts and becomes committed to the Four Noble Truths but also the Eightfold Noble Path. For it is that Path which can take him or her from "head" and "heart" to "hand," leading the individual to practice the Four Noble Truths from one moment to the next in everyday life. This Buddhist approach to life's problems is a most scientific one. It invokes no supernatural entities, as is the case with religion in general. It focuses on the basic problem of life—the existence of *dukkha,* as indicated by the first Noble Truth—an orientation to defining problems that is the heart of the scientific method. It also is committed to the idea of cause and effect, the second Noble Truth. Once we understand that the cause of *dukkha* is our aspirations or thirst, we can work to remove that cause if indeed we wish to remove *dukkha*, once again following the scientific method's approach to the link between cause and effect. And the Eightfold Noble Path is much like the use of the scientific method by social technologists who go beyond simply understanding the causes of a problem—as is emphasized by scientists—and proceed to solve it.

Given our ability to range widely over key elements of Western and Eastern thought with our focus on the gap between aspirations and fulfillment, this suggests the universal nature of this focus. For this aspirations-fulfillment gap is not merely one of the basic problems that we have at this time in history. Rather, it appears to have been fundamental to the human race throughout the ages. For it invokes nothing less than key elements of the human being's values or motives and his or her practices or patterns of action. We can even understand this aspirations-fulfillment relationship from a broader perspective than its relationship to human behavior. Not only does it suggest the full range of problems that we humans face in the momentary scenes of everyday life, but it also applies to the situation of all organisms, and not just human beings. For all of us organisms are able, first, to represent our environment by means of perception in any given moment. And we all have the capacity at that point not merely to respond to our environment passively but rather to respond creatively in an effort to change our environment if it does not suit us, following the analysis of George Kelly (1963). And it is we humans more than any other organisms—with our unprecedented capacity for learning with the aid of language, and with no limit whatsoever to that learning—who can do an increasingly better job of both representing the environment and responding to it creatively so as to change it in ways that suit us. Yet we must examine just how we might proceed to make fuller use of our incredible linguistic potential, given the escalating social problems that apparently now threaten our very survival.

## "Head": Language

It is here that we must build on the analysis of language—the human being's most powerful tool, the tool that distinguishes us from all other organisms—in chapter 1. It was there that we came to see the Web and Part/Whole Approach as giving us a direction for the kind of scientific method that is able to address the incredible complexity of human behavior. The fundamental idea of that approach was to make use of the way language works for all of us: helping us to understand and to solve problems—by enabling us to represent ever more of the complexity of our environment—through our ability to move up and down language's ladder of abstraction. To move beyond our analysis in chapter 1, we turn to the work of Alvin Gouldner. By so doing, we can begin to understand just how we can follow the Buddha's injunction to lower our aspirations—initially—so as to narrow our aspirations-fulfillment gap. The Eightfold Path is useful in suggesting the range of phenomena that we must learn to address. Yet a far more powerful tool awaits us: language as guided by what we have learned about the scientific method over the last 500 years. Of course, we need not stop our development or evolution once we have narrowed the aspirations-fulfillment gap, for we can then proceed to follow a Western approach by learning to raise both aspirations and their fulfillment.

In his *The Coming Crisis of Western Sociology* (1970), Gouldner built on Socrates' belief that "The unexamined life is not worth living" with his vision of a "reflexive sociology":

> What sociologists now most require from a Reflexive Sociology, however, is not just one more specialization, not just another topic for panel meetings at professional conventions.... The historical mission of a Reflexive Sociology as I conceive it, however, would be to transform the sociologist, to penetrate deeply into his daily life and work, enriching them with new sensitivities, and to raise the sociologist's self-awareness to a new historical level.... A Reflexive Sociology is not a bundle of technical skills; it is a conception of how to live. (1970: 487, 493, 504)

If individuals are to follow the Buddha's advice and learn to lower their aspirations or reduce their "thirst," then they must begin by learning to look at themselves, following the advice of both Socrates and Gouldner. Yet there is good reason why Socrates and Gouldner came up with that advice and why we continue to look to it as most important: all of us have great difficulty in following it because it points us away from our outward-oriented bureaucratic way of life. Given the near-universal existence of bureaucratic organizations with their general requirement of conformity—even within the academic world—it should be no surprise that we have great difficulty in looking inward for more than tiny stretches of time. This was the thesis of Gurdjieff, a Russian scholar of the early twentieth century who was much influenced by Eastern thought, particularly Indian and Buddhist teachings. Ouspensky, a student of Gurdjieff, recorded his teachings as including the idea of "identification": that "we become too absorbed in things, too lost in things.... We identify with things" (Ouspensky, 1957/1971: 12).

Yet if we make use of our understanding of how language works, we sociologists—and the rest of us as well—can indeed learn to be reflexive or to examine ourselves, granting the difficulty of doing so. Indeed, this is what language enables us to do to an infinitely greater extent than what any other organism can achieve. Here we should follow our understanding from chapter 1 of the importance of Mills's idea of shuttling up and down language's ladder of abstraction, only we must move very far up until we reach the level of our metaphysical assumptions or bureaucratic worldview. For it is there that we can become conscious of the contradictions that those assumptions foster, and it is there that we can equally become aware of alternative assumptions that promise to resolve those contradictions.

We can look to philosophers like Charles Peirce, the founder of pragmatism, to alert us to the importance of metaphysics for understanding how the scientific method should work ((1898/1955: 310-314). But we can also look to Gouldner:

> Background assumptions . . . are beliefs about the world that are so general that they may, in principle, be applied to any subject matter without restriction. They are, as Stephen Pepper calls them, "world hypotheses." Being primitive presuppositions about the world and everything in it, they serve to provide the most general of orientations, which enable unfamiliar experiences to be made meaningful. . . . World hypotheses are the most pervasive and primitive beliefs about what is real. . . . World hypotheses—the cat may as well be let out of the bag—are what are sometimes called "metaphysics." (1970: 29-31)

It is these invisible assumptions that succeed in shaping our behavior, just as they shape the social scientist's behavior in the direction of bureaucratic social science and away from following scientific ideals, and just as they shape the behavior of all of us in the direction of a bureaucratic way of life. But once we succeed in moving far up language's ladder of abstraction, we can become aware of these contradictions. And that awareness can translate into motivation to do something about it, invoking our "heart" no less than our "head." Yet what can or should we do? Here again, Gouldner gives us a direction: it is the language of social science that can help us to learn what we should do:

> The pursuit of . . . understanding, however, cannot promise that men as we now find them, with their everyday language and understanding, will always be capable of further understanding and of liberating themselves. At decisive points the ordinary language and conventional understandings fail and must be transcended. It is essentially the task of the social sciences, more generally, to create new and "extraordinary" languages, to help men learn to speak them, and to mediate between the deficient understandings of ordinary language and the different and liberating perspectives of the extraordinary languages of social theory. . . . To say

social theorists are concept creators means that they are not merely in the knowledge-creating business, but also in the language-reform and language-creating business. In other words, they are from the beginning involved in creating a new culture. (Gouldner, 1972: 16)

Just as the concepts of biophysical science—such as "force," "valence," and "gene"—have enabled us to penetrate the complexity of biophysical phenomena, so can the "extraordinary" language of social science with its concepts like "culture," "social stratification," and "alienation" enable us to penetrate the complexity of human behavior. Yet Gouldner leaves us hanging at this point: What concepts are we to choose? How can we possibly overcome, say, the specialization among the forty-six sections of the American Sociological Association, let alone the specialization among sociology, psychology, anthropology, political science, economics, and history? And how can we possibly do this within a window of opportunity that is rapidly closing down on us?

## "Hand": The Scientific Method in Everyday Life

It is the scientific method coupled with language—as discussed in chapter 1—that can save the day. But this is a much broader scientific method than is currently used either in biophysical or social science, a scientific method that is up to the task of penetrating the complexity of human behavior. It is here that we must abandon the elitist orientation that we academics often have in relation to the rest of humanity, and we must assume that everyone else has the capacity to do what we can do. Whether or not we actually believe this, the ability of democracy to work effectively—given our escalating social problems—requires that people in general must be able to learn the nature of our problems and make the kinds of decisions that can confront those problems effectively. At this time we should not abandon Gouldner's advice: "to create new and 'extraordinary' languages, to help men learn to speak them, and to mediate between the deficient understandings of ordinary language and the different and liberating perspectives of the extraordinary languages of social theory." But not only must we help others learn to speak the extraordinary language of social science, we social scientists must learn to speak that language ourselves before we have any chance of teaching others to speak it. Again following Gouldner, we must learn to become reflexive so as "to transform" ourselves, and thus to raise our "self-awareness to a new historical level."

In order to move from "head" to "hand," our use of concepts cannot be a sometime thing, for structures must be altered, and structures have to do with what is repeated over and over again from one moment and one scene to the next. This is why it is so essential to move up language's ladder to the level of our invisible metaphysical assumptions. Just as in the case of looking down from a mountain, the higher we go the greater is the area that we can see. And when we reach the level of metaphysical assumptions or worldviews—illustrated by our bureaucratic culture—there remains no aspect of human behavior that we cannot see. The problem for us at that point is analogous to what Thomas Kuhn faced in his *The Structure of Scientific Revolutions* (1962). We must gain awareness of the fundamental contradictions within our worldview, and we must also become conscious of an alternative worldview that promises to resolve those contradictions, such as a democratic or interactive worldview. And our behavior, actions, or "hand" must reinforce that alternative worldview from one moment to the next so that it can remain within our consciousness and continue to motivate our ideas and actions. In that way we would be able to change genuine structures, whether personality, social, biological, or physical structures. And in that way those changes could address the range of social problems that confront us, giving us the possibility not only of changing behavior but also of changing structures like patterns of social stratification and bureaucracy.

Yet what about the nature of an alternative worldview or metaphysical stance? Such an alternative was sketched by *The Invisible Crisis of Contemporary Society* (Phillips and Johnston, 2007) and *Armageddon or Evolution?* (Phillips, 2009). And we have had further ideas of its nature in chapter 12's discussion and illustration of the idea of "deep dialogue." Those ideas suggest that individuals involved in deep dialogues—whether in a book like this one or in everyday conversations—proceed to move far up language's ladder to their fundamental metaphysical assumptions or worldview. Further, it sets up a learning procedure for the participants in such a dialogue, a procedure that extends beyond the "head" to the "heart" and the "hand" as well. To the extent that people learn to practice deep dialogue in their everyday lives, they will be moving toward a democratic worldview or metaphysical stance. For this extends democracy far beyond the political institution with its voting booth, reaching out to more and more interactions within the full range of our institutions. As indicated in chapter 12, it illustrates what might be called "deep democracy," a pattern of social organization within all of our institutions—science, education, political, economic, religious, family—that encourages the development or evolution of all the people involved. John Dewey envisaged something of this nature in his *Reconstruction in Philosophy,* a pattern of social organization for society as a whole: "Democracy has many meanings, but if it has a moral meaning, it is found in resolving that the supreme test of all political institutions and industrial arrangements shall be the contribution they make to the all-around growth of every member of society" (1920/1948:186).

Granting that what is needed are literally hundreds of concrete illustrations to convey something as general as an alternative worldview, the examples of deep dialogue and deep democracy are at least a start. Yet if we are to use Kuhn's *The Structure of Scientific Revolutions* (1962) as an analogy for understanding how cultural paradigms change and how cultural revolutions develop—and not just scientific paradigms and scientific revolutions—then we require evidence bearing on worldviews or metaphysical stances. In particular, beyond the analysis in the foregoing chapters of the contradictions within bureaucratic culture, the bureaucratic ethos and a bureaucratic way of life, do we have any additional evidence for those contradictions? And beyond the illustration of deep dialogue and the very brief discussion of deep democracy in chapter 12 and in the above paragraph, do we have any evidence that a vision of deep democracy suggests the promise of resolving those contradictions? To that extent, we can entertain the possibility that we can indeed move toward a cultural revolution involving a change in our metaphysical stance in much the same way as scientific revolutions have been achieved throughout history. But that could occur only on the assumption that we take into account the enormous difficulties involved, and also that we take into account that procedures can be developed relating to "hand," procedures that are analogous to Buddhism's Eightfold Noble Path. For it would be such procedures that would be needed to carry forward the Western aspect of an East-West strategy to continue to lift both aspirations and their fulfillment, but for all people and not just for social scientists or for some other elite.

As for further evidence of the existence of contradictions within our bureaucratic way of life coupled with at least some evidence that deep democracy, with its emphasis on egalitarian interaction, suggests the possibility of resolving those contradictions, we turn to the second hypothesis guiding *The Invisible Crisis of Contemporary Society*: "To the degree that a worldview or metaphysical stance is stratified versus interactive, there will be a large gap between aspirations and their fulfillment" (Phillips and Johnston, 2007: 234). And that book equally provided evidence for the corollary to that hypothesis: To the degree that a worldview or metaphysical stance is interactive versus stratified, there will be a small gap between aspirations and their fulfillment. Here, then, we have the possibility of evidence for both the existence of contradictions within our present worldview and for the promise of resolving those contradictions within an alternative worldview. And since those contradictions involve the aspirations-fulfillment gap, they are no minor matter. For it is that gap—following the evidence in that book as well as in the other books published within the context of the Sociological Imagination Group—that fosters a range of our fundamental social problems. Here is what *The Invisible Crisis* concluded about this hypothesis:

Concerning hypothesis (2), we might note that this hypothesis implies that an interactive worldview will be associated with a small gap between aspirations and their fulfillment. Bearing in mind the limitations of this study and the importance of further research, all of the thirty-three authors yielded substantial evidence in its favor. The basic argument is that we have a continuing revolution of rising expectations associated with our continuing scientific and technological revolutions. Yet our patterns of stratification and bureaucracy—which include patterns of social stratification—limit the fulfillment of those expectations so as to yield an increasing gap worldwide between what people want and are able to get. And it is our stratified worldview with its limited utilization of the capacities of language and limited fulfillment of scientific ideals which lies behind our growing problems. (Phillips and Johnston, 2007: 235)

This is, then, some evidence for the possibility that a new cultural paradigm, illustrated by a vision of deep dialogue and deep democracy, can indeed replace our present bureaucratic cultural paradigm. Yet what is still required for that replacement—following the Western part of the East-West strategy—are concrete procedures analogous to Buddhism's Eightfold Noble Path to lift both aspirations and their fulfillment once the aspirations-fulfillment gap has been narrowed. For our Kuhnian approach is only a portion of a Western approach to raising aspirations and their fulfillment. Also, it is only a portion of what we require to learn how to lower our aspirations so as to narrow our aspirations-fulfillment gap, following an Eastern approach. It is here that we turn once again to the analysis in chapter 1 of a scientific method strengthened by an understanding of language's incredible potentials. Those are the potentials that have been brought forward by the Web and Part/Whole Approach to the scientific method. With this combination of the two most powerful tools of the human being—language and the scientific method—it appears that we can indeed learn to follow the East-West strategy of both narrowing our aspirations-fulfillment gap and then continuing to raise both aspirations and their fulfillment with no limit whatsoever.

Is the East-West strategy—integrating the tools of language and the scientific method along with the procedures of deep dialogue and deep democracy—up to the task of helping us confront effectively the escalating problems of contemporary society? Following the nature of the scientific method, as discussed in chapter 1 and illustrated by the authors in this book, this question must be tested and supported with demonstrable evidence if it is to be accepted and if it should be accepted. This chapter and this book—coupled with our earlier books—constitute no more than a beginning toward the development of such evidence. Whether or not the

East-West strategy and our earlier work ultimately prove to be effective, some approach to confronting effectively the escalating social problems of contemporary society must be invented if we humans are to have a future. This is a humongous responsibility that falls squarely on the shoulders of social scientists. For we are in the best position to understand those problems with our knowledge of human behavior.

Mills wrote about this responsibility that we social scientists share in his *The Sociological Imagination* (1959), using these words that we quoted in our preface:

> I do not know the answer to the question of political irresponsibility in our time or to the cultural and political question of The Cheerful Robot [alienated man]. But is it not clear that no answers will be found unless these problems are at least confronted? Is it not obvious, that the ones to confront them above all others, are the social scientists of the rich societies? That many of them do not now do so is surely the greatest human default being committed by privileged men in our times. (Mills, 1959: 176)

Can we social scientists become committed to taking on the responsibility of helping everyone to confront the escalating social problems and personal troubles of our time? Can we learn to use the awesome tools of language and the scientific method to work toward integrating our knowledge in order to take on that responsibility? Can we develop a movement throughout the social sciences that will motivate us to work toward that integration of knowledge and toward a commitment to taking on that responsibility?

## References

Dewey, John. [1920]1948. *Reconstruction in Philosophy.* Boston: Beacon Press.

Gouldner, Alvin W. 1970. *The Coming Crisis of Western Sociology.* New York: Basic Books.

———. 1972. "The Politics of the Mind: Reflections on Flack's Review of *The Coming Crisis of Western Sociology,*" *Social Policy* 5 (March/April), 13–21, 54–58.

Kelly, George A. 1963. *A Theory of Personality: The Psychology of Personal Constructs,* New York: W. W. Norton.

Kuhn, Thomas S. 1962. *The Structure of Scientific Revolutions.* Chicago: Univ. of Chicago Press.

Mills, C. Wright. 1959. *The Sociological Imagination.* New York: Oxford Univ. Press.

Ouspensky, P. D. [1957]1971. *The Fourth Way: A Record of Talks and Answers to Questions Based on the Teaching of G. I. Gurdjieff.* New York: Vintage Books.

Peirce, Charles S. [1898]1955. "The Approach to Metaphysics." In Charles S. Peirce. *Philosophic Writings of Peirce.* New York: Dover Press.

Phillips, Bernard. 2001. *Beyond Sociology's Tower of Babel: Reconstructing the Scientific Method.* New York: Aldine de Gruyter.

————, ed. 2007. *Understanding Terrorism: Building on the Sociological Imagination.* Boulder, Colo.: Paradigm Publishers.

————. 2008. "The Bureaucratic Ethos and the Promise of Sociology," unpublished manuscript.

————. 2009. *Armageddon or Evolution? The Scientific Method and Escalating World Problems.* Boulder, Colo.: Paradigm Publishers.

Phillips, Bernard, and Louis C. Johnston. 2007. *The Invisible Crisis of Contemporary Society: Reconstructing Sociology's Fundamental Assumptions.* Boulder, Colo.: Paradigm Publishers.

Phillips, Bernard, Harold Kincaid, and Thomas J. Scheff (eds.). 2002. *Toward a Sociological Imagination: Bridging Specialized Fields.* Lanham, Md.: Univ. Press of America,

Vidich, Arthur, and Joseph Bensman. 1960. *Small Town in Mass Society: Class, Power, and Religion in a Rural Community.* Garden City, N.Y.: Doubleday.

# About the Editors and Contributors

**J. David Knottnerus,** professor of sociology at Oklahoma State University, has published in the areas of social theory, social psychology, and social structure/inequality and is currently working on a number of projects utilizing structural ritualization theory. Recent books include *Structure, Culture and History: Recent Issues in Social Theory* (co-edited with Sing C. Chew) and *Literary Narratives on the Nineteenth and Early Twentieth-Century French Elite Educational System: Rituals and Total Institutions* (with Frederique Van de Poel-Knottnerus). He is currently working on two new books, *Ritual as a Missing Link in Sociology: Structural Ritualization Theory and Research* and *Catastrophic Rituals of Abuse in Nursing Homes: Alternatives to Bureaucracy* (with Jason S. Ulsperger).

**Bernard Phillips** studied with C. Wright Mills at Columbia and Robin M. Williams Jr., at Cornell. He taught at the University of North Carolina, the University of Illinois, and Boston University; co-founded ASA's Section on Sociological Practice; and founded the Sociological Imagination Group. His recent books include *Beyond Sociology's Tower of Babel: Reconstructing the Scientific Method*; *The Invisible Crisis of Contemporary Society: Reconstructing Sociology's Fundamental Assumptions* (with Louis C. Johnston); the edited volume, *Understanding Terrorism: Building on the Sociological Imagination*; and *Armageddon or Evolution? The Scientific Method and Escalating World Problems*. He is currently working on a manuscript with a modest title, "How to Save the World: From a Bureaucratic to an Evolutionary Way of Life."

**J. I. (Hans) Bakker** is professor of sociology at the University of Guelph in Guelph, Ontario, Canada. He was born in the Netherlands, grew up in

Ohio and Alabama, and moved to Canada in 1971 because he received a University of Toronto Open Fellowship. He has published over forty refereed articles and edited three books (on rural development, world hunger, and the Hindu classic the Bhagavad Gita). He is the author of *Toward a Just Civilization,* a book about Mahatma Gandhi's social theory. His current research focuses on the applicability of Charles Sanders Peirce's triadic epistemology and Pragmatist semiotics to sociological theory. See his web page: www.semioticsigns.com.

**Frank W. Elwell** received a Ph.D. in sociology from the University at Albany–SUNY, master's degrees from the University at Albany–SUNY (sociology) and the State University of New York at New Paltz (political science/education), and a bachelor's degree from Eastern Michigan University (history/education). He is the author of *Macrosociology: Four Modern Theorists* (Paradigm, 2006), *A Commentary on Malthus's 1798 Essay on Population as Social Theory* (Edwin Mellen Press, 2001), *Industrializing America: Understanding Contemporary Society Through Classical Sociological Analysis* (Praeger Press, 1999), and *The Evolution of the Future* (Praeger Press, 1991). His areas of academic interest are social evolution, human ecology, and social theory.

**Douglas Hartmann** is professor of sociology and associate chair of the department at the University of Minnesota. Hartmann is the author of *Race, Culture, and the Revolt of the Black Athlete: The 1968 Olympic Protests and Their Aftermath* (University of Chicago Press, 2003) and the co-author (with Stephen Cornell) of *Ethnicity and Race: Making Identities in a Changing World* (Pine Forge, 2007). His work and comments on sociology, popular culture, race, religion, and multiculturalism have been featured in *Time* magazine, numerous newspapers around the country, and National Public Radio. Hartmann is also the co-editor (with Chris Uggen) of *Contexts,* the ASA publication intended to bring sociology to broader public visibility and influence.

**Debbie V. S. Kasper** teaches and does sociology at Sweet Briar College. While her interests are diverse, her present efforts generally fall within sociological theory and environmental sociology. Her current research is an effort to better understand the conditions underlying and long-term trends in the development of ecological habitus. Toward that end, Kasper is studying ecologically focused communities and has published her initial exploratory research, "Redefining Community in the Ecovillage," in *Human Ecology Review.*

**Louis Kontos** is adjunct associate professor of sociology at John Jay College of Criminal Justice, The City University of New York, and former associate professor of sociology at Long Island University. He is the co-editor of *Gangs and Society: Alternative Perspectives* and editor of *Encyclopedia of Gangs.* He is also the author of articles on sociological theory and research published in scholarly journals.

**Vince Montes** is assistant professor of sociology at LaGuardia Community College of City University of New York. He earned his doctorate at the New School for Social Research. His current research project involves analyzing the U.S. State and attempting to web together its elusive centralized power.

**Thomas Scheff** is professor emeritus at the University of California, Santa Barbara. He is past president of the Pacific Sociological Association, and past chair of the Emotions Section of the ASA. His publications include *Being Mentally Ill*; *Microsociology*; *Bloody Revenge*; and *Emotions, the Social Bond and Human Reality.* His latest are *Goffman Unbound! A New Paradigm for Social Science* (Boulder, Colorado: Paradigm Publishers, 2006) and *Easy Rider* (New York: iUniverse, 2007). He received an honorary doctorate from Copenhagen University in 2008.

**Arlene Stein** is an associate professor of sociology at Rutgers. She is the author of three books and the editor of two collections of essays. Among them is *The Stranger Next Door: The Story of a Small Community's Battle over Sex, Faith, and Civil Rights* (Beacon), an ethnographic study of a conservative campaign against gay/lesbian rights and its impact upon one community. She received the 2006 Simon and Gagnon Award for career contributions to the study of sexualities, given by the American Sociological Association. She is currently writing a book about Holocaust storytelling in the United States.

**Jason S. Ulsperger** is assistant professor of sociology at Arkansas Tech University. He received his Ph.D. from Oklahoma State University, where faculty honored him with the O. D. Duncan Award for his scholarship and teaching. He currently teaches courses in sociology, criminal justice, and gerontology. His research focuses on occupational rituals that promote deviant and criminal behavior in organizations. His recent publications appear in *Crime, Media, Culture: An International Journal*; *Journal of Applied Social Science*; *Sociological Spectrum*; and *Free Inquiry in Creative Sociology.*